WOMEN WITH ATTENTION
DEFICIT DISORDER

WOMEN WITH ATTENTION DEFICIT DISORDER

Embrace Your Differences
And Transform Your Life
Newly revised 10th Anniversary Edition!

by Sari Solden MS, LMFT

Introduction by
Kate Kelly and Peggy Ramundo

Forewords by
Edward T. Hallowell, M.D.
and John J. Ratey, M.D.

Underwood Books
Nevada City, California

Women with Attention Deficit Disorder
ISBN 1-887424-97-0 (second edition--revised)
Copyright © 1995, 2005 by Sari Solden

For information about professional services, presentations, consultations or to order this book on CD, or Sari's other book, *Journeys Through ADDulthood* (Walker & Co., 2002) go to www.sarisolden.com or write to Sari Solden at P.O. Box 3320, Ann Arbor, Michigan 48106

Distributed by Publisher's Group West.
Wholesale orders (800) 788-3123
Manufactured in the United States of America

10 9 8 7 6 5 4 3 2

The ideas in this book are based on the author's personal experience with ADD, and as such are not to be considered medical advice. This book is not intended as a substitute for psychotherapy or the medical treatment of Attention Deficit/Hyperactivity Disorder and the various medications described herein can only be prescribed by a physician. The reader should consult a qualified health care professional in matters relating to health and particularly with respect to any symptoms which may require diagnosis or medical attention.

Cover illustration is a detail from the painting "Hera" by Francis Picabia, 1928, Collection Gaston Kahn, Paris. Type by Just Your Type, Overland Park, KS.

Library of Congress Cataloging-in-Publication Data

Solden, Sari.
    Women with attention deficit disorder : embrace your differences and transform your life / by Sari Solden.-- Newly rev. 10th anniversary ed.
        p. cm.
    Includes bibliographical references and index.
    ISBN-13: 978-1-887424-97-4 (soft cover)
    ISBN-10: 1-887424-97-0
1. Attention-deficit disorder in adults. I. Title.

    RC394.A85S66 2005
    616.85'89--dc22

2005019888

I dedicate this book with gratitude and love to my husband, Dean, who ventures boldly each day into the eye of the hurricane, where together we find calm and peace in the center of the storm.

A Note to the Reader

I wanted to write this book . . . because it became clear to me through my work as a therapist that there are many women who have been struggling with serious unexplained and often mysterious difficulties their entire lives. These women are leading lives filled with secrecy, shame, and a quiet desperation, unable to describe their difficulties to close friends, family or even mental health professionals in a way that could lead to self- understanding. Many of these women have been going through life confused and foggy, unable to access their considerable strengths. They experience their lives as a continuous treadmill, and express feelings of being trapped, unable to make sense of their lives.

I wrote this book because I've watched these women cross a line at some point and see their lives begin to shift. I want to let other women know that I've seen women with these kinds of difficulties learn how to move ahead and begin to take back their lives.

I know that other women can also embark on this same emotional journey, learning to embrace their lives in a new and powerful way.

CONTENTS

PART II: HIDING

PART III: EMERGING

PART IV: EMBRACING

FOREWORD TO THE NEW EDITION
by Edward T. Hallowell, M.D.
(2005)

Sari Solden opened up the field of women who have ADD almost single-handedly when the first version of this book appeared a decade ago. I remember how enthusiastic I was to read it back then, and I am equally enthusiastic to read this new, updated version.

Women with ADD had an immediate impact upon the many readers who were eager to know about the particulars of female life with ADD. Sari's book filled a large void and it did so beautifully. Before *Women with ADD*, many people thought that no woman could have ADD. The many who did were misdiagnosed as depressed, anxious, or just "ditsy." I have had the pleasure of treating many women, and seeing their lives change dramatically for the better, who came to see me because they had read *Women with ADD*.

What I love about Sari's approach is that it is personal, humble, funny, and real. She avoids the stilted prose one so often reads in dry journals and instead provides warm and supple words, words that capture the spirit of ADD from a woman's perspective and offer positive and practical approaches to making life better.

I am always skeptical about the women vs. men dichotomy. After all, we are each human, more alike than not alike, and it can be misleading to suggest that women lead an entirely different life from men. And yet, in some ways, they do. Sari captures the unique female experience without overly generalizing the separation between men and women with ADD.

I love her humor, her sensitivity, and her warmth as she details the trials and tribulations in life with ADD, as well as how she celebrates the potential triumphs of this interesting kind of mind. Sari knows from firsthand experience how embarrassing and difficult

ADD can make life, but she also knows from personal experience what an advantage ADD can be if it is managed properly. She captures the fun, the pizzazz, as well as the fizzle and disappointments. But above all she captures the reality of the experience of being a woman who has ADD.

What is it like to be embarrassed to look into your pocketbook for fear of others seeing what a mess it is inside? What is it like to feel so ashamed of your living room that you don't invite people over? What is it like to feel stupid even if you "know" you are smart? What is it like to worry that you can't be a good enough mother because you have ADD? What is it like to get distracted at just the wrong moment . . . like in the middle of making a presentation, or when trying to remember an important number, or even in the middle of making love? Sari will tell you about all this and much, much more.

It is wonderful to see this classic book in its new incarnation. I trust it will help as many thousands of readers as the first book did.

Edward Hallowell, M.D.

Edward (Ned) Hallowell, M.D. is a child and adult psychiatrist and the founder of The Hallowell Center for Cognitive and Emotional Health in Sudbury, MA. He was a member of the faculty of the Harvard Medical School from 1983 to 2004.

A graduate of Harvard College and the Tulane School of Medicine, Dr. Hallowell is an expert at offering practical ways to approach some of life's most difficult challenges. He is the co-author of the national best sellers, **Driven to Distraction** (Pantheon, 1994) and **Answers to Distraction** (Pantheon, 1995) and **Delivered from Distraction** (Ballantine Books 2005), all of which discuss attention deficit disorder in children and in adults.

ORIGINAL FOREWORD
by John J. Ratey, M.D.
(1993)

Current developments in cognitive science are enabling researchers to uncover the many secrets of the brain. Techniques such as neuro-imaging allow us to observe, measure, and analyze brain activity as it occurs, leading us closer and closer to an understanding of the brain's tremendous complexity. For many individuals, however, the excitement of this progress is accompanied by the threat that ultimately everything will be defined in terms of matter, and the more ethereal category of the human spirit will no longer by acceptable.

Most recently, neurological discoveries have been complemented by advances in genetics. Yet this advancement is met with resistance as well as by those who oppose the idea that we may be controlled by the past or defined in any way by our genetic destiny. To many, this idea seems to invalidate the core of our very existence, namely, the quest to achieve our own individuality. If even our most subtle characteristics were determined by our genetic history, this achievement would be impossible. What we are beginning to learn, however, is that genetic guidance is exceedingly sensitive to the environment. In fact, neuroscientists, along with others who are delving into the mysteries of human consciousness, emphasize that individuality is apparent throughout the brain. This variation is, for the most part, due to each individual's unique experience of the world. We are learning that everything counts, that everything we experience impacts brain development. While the brain remains susceptible to environmental influences throughout life, the greatest impact occurs in utero, during the first stages of existence.

Of particular interest is the role of hormones in the development of the brain, especially in regard to gender differences.

It is now a commonly accepted fact that men and women's brains differ as a result of exposure to different hormonal environments in the womb. This difference does not imply that one environment is preferable to the other, but simply that they each produce unique effects. After birth, the brain continues to develop and is constantly reorganized through the experience of the environment, especially that of the interpersonal and social milieu. Thus, along with the furious pace at which we are gaining knowledge about the brain and genetics, we are also reconfirming scientifically the belief that the social environment contributes a great deal to the development of the brain and the mind.

For example, these social influences may cause a genetic condition such as Attention Deficit Disorder to be expressed quite differently even among members of the same family. By examining this interplay between genetics and environment, Sari Solden has broken new ground in *Women With Attention Deficit Disorder: Embracing Disorganization at Home and in the Workplace*, a book that follows that dictate of Dr. William Osler, who stated: "Ask not what disease the person has, but rather what person has the disease." On both a personal and professional level, Solden explores just how women deal with the neurologic difference that is ADD. She at once narrows our perspective and broadens our understanding by revealing how the genetic composition of this disorder is manifested in women. Until recently, most disorders had been considered only from a limited perspective, one that explained how the condition was expressed in men. When data was presented regarding both sexes, gender differences at the level of genetics and development were rarely, if ever, reported. In examining the gender differences of ADD, not only hormonal but also social influences are important as well, especially as this disorder is often subtle and hidden from view.

For a woman, the ADD traits of impulsivity, carelessness, forgetfulness, changeability and procrastination extend far beyond the environment of work or school to include every aspect of her life. They exist at the very core of a woman's expectations of herself and of society's expectations of her as well. The expectation that she will be the rock, the dependable, steady force in every situation causes her to be much more susceptible to the confining and crippling emotion of shame. This dynamic acts subtly, yet is extremely persuasive and often inhibits the growth from every direction of a woman who has ADD. *In Women with Attention Deficit Disorder,* Sari presents us with a number of meaningful anecdotes and a wealth of invaluable clinical lore. Her work represents one of the first attempts to broaden our perspective by focusing the experience of the genetic disorder on that of women alone. She provides us with a crucial understanding of a woman's experience of ADD within a complicated social matrix.

Dr. John J. Ratey, M.D., is an Associate Clinical Professor of Psychiatry at Harvard Medical School and has a private practice in Cambridge, Massachusetts. Dr. Ratey has authored the best selling book, *A User's Guide to the Brain*. He has also co-authored *Driven to Distraction* (1994) and *Answers to Distraction* (1995) and *Delivered from Distraction* (2005) with Edward Hallowell, M.D., and *Shadow Syndromes* (1997) with Catherine Johnson, Ph.D.

INTRODUCTION TO THE NEW EDITION
by Peggy Ramundo and Kate Kelly

A decade ago, we were happily writing the introduction for Sari's groundbreaking book, **Women with Attention Deficit Disorder**. The subtitle, **Embracing Disorganization at Home and in the Workplace**, was a topic near and dear to Peggy's heart, as she could be the poster child for the society for chronic disorganization. Kate, on the other hand, was organized, but at great cost. She simply limited her life severely, so that she was never caught in disarray, disorder or failing to meet a deadline. Kate also had a host of somatic symptoms that would give her an honored place in the hypochondriacs hall of fame. These ailments were the result of stuffing down the angst of trying too hard to keep it all together.

Today, ten years later, we are confronting the organizational demon again. It is the eleventh hour and the partially completed new and improved introduction to Sari's book is nowhere to be found. Not on our hard drives, in multiple email boxes or in the many piles we have sifted through in the search for this treasure. In the past, before we read Sari's book and began the process of de-toxing those crippling layers of shame, it might have been time to get out the cyanide, or tar and feathers or something like that.

So, after all the years of ADD recovery work, we are back at groundzero. All the systems in the world couldn't save us from this last minute scramble. The same old-same old, but with one important difference—we are laughing. Joking our way through the process of letting go of the misplaced text, and starting over. But first, giving ourselves a virtual hug infused with a liberal dose of acceptance and approval.

We have been ADD coaches for the past ten years, our clients mostly women. Almost without exception, these women talk about the book (*Women with ADD*) that "saved my life." They are not kidding, and they are not being hyperbolic. They weep as they describe their profound sense of relief upon reading the book and finding that they are not alone; that there are sisters out there who are similarly oppressed by mountains of "stuff," both physical and psychological.

Perhaps the most important contribution Sari made, was to honor the heroic struggle of ADDult women, who are trying to keep themselves and everyone else in the family together while handicapped by weak attentional skills. One of the most devastating experiences for women with ADD is feeling you are drowning in a sea of trivia that everybody else can manage with their hands tied behind their backs. We women with ADD then feel not only that we are inadequate, but also that we are just whining about really silly stuff.

Here are some of the comments our clients have made:

> "Did Sari install a nanny cam in my kitchen? How does she know so much about my life?"

> "I never realized that being a homemaker was such a difficult job when you have ADD - I just thought that I was a complete loser."

> "I was able to schedule my first coaching session after reading Sari's book. Before that I was too embarrassed and ashamed to talk to anyone about the reality of my life."

In the years since the first adult ADD book appeared on the horizon, there has been a whole host of excellent books written that offer a glimpse into the ADD mind and the ADD experience.

None, however, has touched our hearts in the way that Sari did, when she laid bare her emotional experience and those of her clients in *Women with Attention Deficit Disorder*. Before Sari's book came out, women with ADD were an invisible population. No one was talking about the possibility that the female form of the disorder presented very differently from the mostly male subjects profiled in the literature. The book inspired others to write about and begin researching the issues of women and girls with ADD.

In this second edition of *Women with Attention Deficit Disorder*, you will find new, up-to-date information on medication and how to make decisions re: medical treatment. A special section on friendship challenges will help you, the reader, find ways to take down the walls of isolation and connect authentically with others. We are certain that you will appreciate the wealth of new information on how hormones play a critical role in the female ADD experience.

If you are a new reader, you have a big treat in store for you. If you are a loyal fan of Sari's work, you will be delighted with the new material that will add another dimension to your understanding of how ADD plays a role in your life. It may be time to give the book a second read in any case. Or a third, fourth . . . twentieth, etc.. Rereading a pivotal book like this one after more growth and life experience can lead to fresh insights. Give yourself, once again, the gift of healing laughter and tears. We did.

Warmly,
Kate Kelly and Peggy Ramundo

ORIGINAL INTRODUCTION
by Peggy Ramundo and Kate Kelly

Dear Readers,

When Sari sent us her completed manuscript for review, we were honored and delighted that she had asked us to write an introduction to this important new book.

When we began writing *You Mean I'm Not Lazy, Stupid, or Crazy?!*, there were no books available written specifically for ADD adults. Because there was so little written information out there, we felt compelled to attempt the impossible - to create an encyclopedia of ADD!

With such a huge task in front of us, the writing process seemed to go on endlessly. But we did manage to complete the book after more than two years of effort. The book was not finished as quickly as Kate would have liked, nor did it fit Peggy's idea of perfection.

However, we managed to produce a fairly comprehensive self-help guide for ADD adults. Still, we knew that there was so much we had yet to learn about ADD and so much that we didn't have time or space to address.

Although we are women with ADD, we did not address women's issues in any depth in our book.

Sari has used her personal and professional experience to shine some light into the dark closet inhabited by far too many ADD women; a closet of shame and despair and invisibility.

Women's voices have not been heard loudly enough in the world of ADD, reflecting women's situation in society at large.

We do not intend to dishonor the valuable contributions made by men to the field of Attention Deficit Disorder. But we feel that understanding of ADD has been hampered and dominated by a tendency to rely too heavily on objective means of viewing it.

As Belenky et.al, (1986) found in their massive study of women's intellectual development, experiential and subjective learning is an important step in women's developmental process. In comparable studies with male subjects, the subjective piece was noticeably lacking.

ADD is a complicated disorder that does not fit neatly into the usual diagnostic boxes. Trying to describe it in terms of the three classic symptoms of hyperactivity, impulsivity and inattention gives us a one-sided and overly simplistic view of the problems faced by persons with ADD.

Too much of the available literature is written from the standpoint of the ADD expert looking at the disorder from the outside.

And the view from the outside tells only part of the story. ADD is a subtle handicap that can impact in ways we are just beginning to understand.

When we were first exploring the impact of ADD on our own lives, there was almost nothing known about ADD in adults. We had to read the child literature and extrapolate mainly from accounts of hyperactive boys. It was a starting point, but it did little in terms of helping us to make sense of our experience as ADD women.

We found that the personal stories of other ADD adults provided the missing puzzle piece that made a more complete picture of our own lives and struggles.

Sari has taken this perspective a step further in her book. She empowers ADD women by validating their experience as worthwhile human beings who struggle with serious organizational problems in many areas of their lives. She illuminates the heavy burden placed on the shoulders of ADD women, who face additional demands for organizational skills by gender role expectations imposed by our culture.

Girls and women with ADD have been socialized to suffer their problems in silence. Or at least in a quieter version than that of the classic picture presented by AD/HD boys and men. Hyperactive girls learn to either inhibit their behavior to an unnatural degree or suffer the consequences of being labeled as unfeminine. And those who have ADD without hyperactivity fade into the background.

The problems of ADD women are often trivialized or dismissed. Because they are hidden, locked up in a closet of shame.

Do not be misled by the title of this book. It is not merely another self-help book on how to get organized. There are practical suggestions for dealing with the concrete messes of women's lives, but the heart of the book deals with the much larger issue of the impact of chronic disorganization on all facets of life.

The "messy closet" is a metaphor for a brain that is locked up and hidden because its owner is overwhelmed by the chaos of too many expectations and the inability to sort and prioritize them.

By sharing her personal experiences and those of her clients, Sari will help countless women begin to acknowledge and wrestle with the crippling shame that prevents their emergence from that dark closet.

Kate Kelly and Peggy Ramundo are the co-authors of the classic ADD adult books, You *Mean I'm Not Lazy, Stupid or Crazy?!*, and *The ADDed Dimension*. Kate is an advanced practice psychiatric nurse and Peggy is a professional educator. Both Peggy and Kate have worked professionally with ADD adults for more than a decade. Currently, they both practice as ADD life-coaches. Their most valuable credential, however, is that they have learned to live and love successfully as ADD adults. Visit them at their website – www.addcoaching.com

Peggy Ramundo and Kate Kelly

INTRODUCTORY SECTION

AUTHOR'S PREFACE

Many women have an extremely difficult time organizing themselves in their daily lives. They frequently feel overwhelmed and may have been struggling with relationships, depression, and underachievement all their lives. Some of these women are hyperactive and fit the stereotyped notion of what most people (even mental health professionals) think that AD/HD is: fast-talking, hyperactive, non-attentive, bouncing-off-the-wall people. Many more women, however, have what is now called the inattentive type of AD/HD. They may have never been hyperactive, but because they don't fit the more common notion of what AD/HD is, they have never considered AD/HD as a way to explain their difficulties.

Before I first wrote this book in 1995, the standard quoted ratio of AD/HD in boys and girls varied from 6:1 to 10:1. At that time, however, experts were just beginning to discover that this difference was because these studies did not include the quiet, non-hyperactive child. In *You Mean I'm Not Lazy, Stupid or Crazy* (1995) Kate Kelly and Peggy Ramundo said that if you count girls without hyperactivity, the corresponding ratios approach 1:1. Also back in the early nineties, Dr. Daniel Amen, in his video of *Windows into the ADD Mind* said that "girls are overlooked, and that this huge under-diagnosis would, if corrected, even out the statistics that regularly report so much larger an occurrence in boys." Another expert in the field, Dr. Larry Silver, author of *The Misunderstood Child* (1992), wrote at that time that the ratio of girls to boys with AD/HD was probably much closer to equal because girls who are doing poorly in school are more likely to be withdrawn and quiet, thus appearing disinterested or depressed instead of AD/HD.

In the years since *Women with Attention Deficit Disorder* was originally published, it has become even more commonly accepted to acknowledge that girls and boys are affected equally when counting

xxiv

the inattentive type of AD/HD. Although there is much overlap between boys and girls in terms of the childhood characteristics of inattentive AD/HD, the struggles they face in adulthood, albeit equally challenging, are often very different because of the gender role expectations that women struggle to meet.

Even though I focus in this book on women who have never been hyperactive, much of what I say about them applies to those who are or were hyperactive, as well. Hyperactivity is not the only or critical element of AD/HD. Other executive functioning deficits challenge women who identify with the symptoms of AD/HD.

Why I Chose to Write a Book on Women with AD/HD

1. Women with AD/HD had not been the focus of an entire book before and the topic had not received adequate attention.

2. AD/HD inattentive type (that means without hyperactivity) is the most common form of AD/HD in girls and women.

3. AD/HD inattentive type was and still is the least commonly understood and identified form of AD/HD.

4. Those who have this kind of AD/HD usually remain undiagnosed longer than those with hyperactivity.

5. Those who have remained undiagnosed the longest often have the most serious consequences, especially in the way they internalize their problems, which often results in depression, anxiety, and self-image struggles.

6. Even after diagnosis and medical treatment, women continue to have serious inner barriers to getting the support they need with their real life problems. This is due to the shame they feel about not being able to meet gender role expectations because of their AD/HD challenges.

7. Many women still see their disorganization issues as a character flaw.

8. The partners of women with AD/HD needed a resource where they could get a deeper understanding of what both they and their partner were struggling with.

9. The mental health professional trying to help the women with AD/HD also needs to understand the complex emotional issues involved in order to more effectively guide these women and their partners.

There are many women out there struggling with serious organizational problems who have no idea that something neurobiological like AD/HD could be at the root of their difficulties. A few years ago I read an article about women who formed a self-help group for "disorganized women." They met in private to protect their anonymity and describe themselves as "self-confessed slobs." Ever since then, it became very important to me to try to reach these kinds of women, to help them understand that in the absence of any serious mental disorders, there may be another explanation for severe disorganization. Since this book was first published, it has been overwhelmingly received by women all over the world who were previously completely isolated, thinking their problems were the result of personality flaws.

Perspective

This book was written from three perspectives: that of a psychotherapist, that of a woman with AD/HD, and that of someone involved personally and professionally for many years with other adults and professionals in the field of AD/HD. As a psychotherapist, I am specially trained in the impact of life experiences on relationships, interpersonal difficulties, and self-perceptions. This book was originally based on six years of clinical observation and work with AD/HD adults with a focus on the special challenges facing women. Now I have had 10 more years experience, and I feel more strongly than ever that the unique experiences described in this book are shared by countless women who are impacted greatly by the cultural expectations they face and the idealized roles they have internalized. Secondly, as a woman with AD/HD, I observed my own personal process as I began to understand what it meant to live successfully in this culture. Thirdly, the material in this book was drawn from all the talks and meetings I've had with women across the country and around the world who have shared their feelings about AD/HD, disorganization, and how it affects their lives. Integrated within all of this are the wonderful writings of many experts, as well as the currently available literature on AD/HD diagnosis and updated treatment options and recommendations. Some of the references first used in this book are out of print or circulation. Many of the quotes still in this edition were from the very beginnings of discussion on this subject; from seminars or tapes no longer able to be referenced. When I am able to I will let the reader know this in the reference section.

The Scope and Focus of this Book

There is great diversity in this thing we call AD/HD, from those who are hyperactive to those who are hypoactive, from obviously impulsive individuals to those who are more shy and withdrawn. There are men with AD/HD, women with AD/HD, those who have been diagnosed since childhood, and those who have just been diagnosed in mid-life. There are those with AD/HD who are well educated, who have work and relationships they enjoy, and those less fortunate, who struggle just to get by. I do not attempt to speak to all the facets or elements of AD/HD, especially the medical and neuropsychological aspects. Although I will touch on the biological issues that impact women, such as PMS, pregnancy and menopause my perspective as a psychotherapist is to trace the emotional journey that women with AD/HD embark on as they try to understand their experience.

There have been many fine books written, virtual textbooks, which address a wide and diverse AD/HD population, their subject matter covering diagnosis, testing, medication, and treatment for both children and adults. These are listed in the resource section at the back of the book.

The Characters in the Book

To illustrate my points, I've used material drawn from my clients, as well as interviews with other women with AD/HD. Most of the examples are in the form of composites, which are representative of actual stories that many women with AD/HD have shared with me. Other examples are true stories from specific clients who have given me permission to share their experience with the reader. Of course, I have changed the names and other identifiable information for the purpose of protecting their privacy.

In addition, I've created two fictional composite characters named Jodi and Lucy to represent the major struggles reported by women with AD/HD. I use this technique in order to provide certain information in a more narrative and interesting form. I trace them through their formative years to help the reader understand the journey of women with AD/HD on a more personal level.

Overview

Women with Attention Deficit Disorder includes A Pocket Guide to AD/HD, which lays out the basic concepts for those not familiar with AD/HD and serves as an easy reference throughout the book.

PART I, *Surviving*, starts out with my personal and professional AD/HD story, explaining the beliefs I have come to hold regarding living successfully with AD/HD as a woman. I then trace the development of a little girl in order to examine the effects of being undiagnosed at various stages of a girl's life; this will help the reader understand the challenges and struggles she may face as an adult before diagnosis.

In PART II, *Hiding*, we go beyond the primary AD/HD symptoms and explore the collision between these symptoms and the cultural expectations placed on women. We will then begin to understand the emotional legacy of "shame" that often results from this life experience. We will also examine the complex and painful "secondary effects" an AD/HD woman may experience such as underachievement, depression, and relationship difficulties.

In PART III, *Emerging*, I present an overview of diagnosis and treatment issues especially for women. We'll explore the ease with which women are overpathologized and misdiagnosed. We will travel the variety of roads one might take on the way to understanding their AD/HD and/or disorganization, and we'll discuss the tools they will need to start this journey such as moving through the AD/HD grief cycle. I will outline the MESST model of treatment I have devised, an acronym for Medication, Education, Strategies, Support and Therapy. I also include an AD/HD screening tool I designed especially for women.

Finally, PART IV, *Embracing*, focuses on the essential "three Rs" required for anyone to live successfully with AD/HD, but specifically for a woman. These include the following: restructuring her life, renegotiating her relationships, and redefining her self-image. Doing these things allows a woman at some point to embrace her AD/HD. She crosses a certain line where she is able to become proactive in order to access the help that she needs. This, in turn, leads to a new "cycle of success" in which she can begin to thrive instead of just survive.

AUTHOR'S INTRODUCTION
TO REVISED EDITION

"There is no greater agony than bearing an untold story inside of you."
—*Maya Angelou*

I recently discovered this quote, and it immediately became one of my favorites. It captures what has been one of the most gratifying experiences for me in the years since I first published this book. When I meet women who have resonated with my book, they proudly show their copy to me—raggedy, well worn, with pages folded over, underlined, highlighted, bulleted, marked with Post-its, multicolored markings, writing in the margins—all to say "This is me. This is *my* untold story." They read and reread it, not so much for particular facts but to relieve themselves of this *untold* story they have carried inside them their entire lives . . . not even really knowing that this was a story, thinking instead that it was just their own little shameful secret.

They tell me, "You must have followed me around", or "You must have stolen my diary," realizing that if I was able to describe their inner world so exactly, then it must be true that so many other women really do share their experiences. With that realization, they begin to feel part of something bigger, not alone anymore. After so many years of being dismissed, discounted, and told they were over-reacting or oversensitive—they feel validated. They offer the book to their therapists, their partners, their families, and their doctors to let them know "This is my story."

Over the last several years, these same women have helped shape and define what the experience of living with this difference called AD/HD is about by banding together to speak the truth of their collective experiences. Their courage to stop hiding has made it possible for other women in more remote areas of the world to break their chains of silence and get diagnosed and treated.

What has also struck me with increasing frequency and conviction since I first published this book and began to hear from women across the world is how much the way women with AD/HD struggle with cultural expectations is similar to the way that other women struggle with things such as growing older or body image. The challenge for all women is to break free from the cultural ideals they have internalized and begin to define for themselves what it truly means to be a competent and valuable woman, mother, or partner.

Although this inner struggle remains the core of this new edition, much has changed in the field since I first published this book in 1995. The options for the medical treatment of AD/HD have vastly expanded and improved, the fields of AD/HD coaching and professional organizers have also grown tremendously, and the work on women's AD/HD issues has increased dramatically along with the opportunity for women to connect, be supported and informed by books, magazines, online resources, and conferences all over the world. Of course, the official name of the condition has also changed since I first wrote the book. I debated about whether or not to continue using the less awkward and more vernacular term ADD instead of the more formal AD/HD. But in the end I decided to go all the way with the update and use and explain the official term and present how readers can equate the current subtypes with other more familiar names. I expect the terms will change again by the time I write the next edition. Who knows what it will be called by then?

When I began this new edition, I thought I would simply update these name changes and rewrite and update the sections on medication, women's issues, and resources that were either obsolete or incomplete. But then, of course, in true AD/HD fashion (in a good but much longer process), the project became like renovating a beautiful old house: as each layer of wallpaper was removed, it revealed more problems and new things to attend to, and so I kept going.

I am grateful for the chance I have had to update, expand, and edit this book. This new edition retains the same voice and basic material, but now I have had time to *reorganize* it for the better! There is a great deal of new information and adjustment of the original material woven throughout. Some of it may be hard for you to detect, but it is there, sometimes with subtle but important changes and improvements.

In addition to this, there are brand new sections drawn from pieces I have either created over the years or presented on but never published, as well as new things I created just for this book. Some of these include the following:

- I am proud and grateful to have a new introduction by Kate Kelly and Peggy Ramundo and a brand new foreword by Dr. Ned Hallowell, in addition to the wonderful, original foreword by Dr. John Ratey and introduction by Kate and Peggy.

- In the pocket guide and throughout, I have woven in the new terminology about AD/HD with new explanations of executive functioning as a way to view these challenges.

- Another new highlight is the friendship chapter in Part Two. Included is a new *Friendship Inventory* to help you discover how your AD/HD may be affecting your relationships and some simple solutions.

- Part Three contains updated, expanded treatment sections on *Medications and Women's Issues*, including a discussion of hormones and AD/HD.

- The chapters on diagnosis and treatment have been expanded and clarified and include my new *Strategy Grid* to help you plan and personalize new approaches.

- Chapter 18 on therapy includes new information on couples counseling intended for both couples and mental health professionals.

- Look for my new *AD/HD Work Decision Tree* in Part Four, Chapter 20.

- Also, updated, expanded *Resources* and *Bibliography* sections are included in the back of the book.

- Finally, a new *Woman's Voices* section has questions and answers from my online columns over the years so you can hear from other women who may have had some of the same questions as yours.

My hope for this new edition is that the material will remain accurate and relevant for a long time to come. And for women who have already read the first edition, they can revisit those original concepts and get a fresh perspective. I also hope that a whole new group of readers will begin to identify with other women with AD/HD, thus breaking their habits of isolation and hiding. As they begin to integrate the AD/HD more deeply and positively into their self-concept, they can push away some of the shame they may still be holding onto. Finally, I hope that another group of women will be helped to share their *untold story*.

Sari Solden
June, 2005

A Pocket Guide to AD/HD

This section can be used for important information about AD/HD before reading the rest of the book. It is useful for people who are not familiar with AD/HD and can also be consulted as a handy reference throughout the book.

Defining AD/HD

Most people start out by telling you what AD/HD is. I'd like to start out by telling you what AD/HD is *not*. Because so many people who don't fit the common picture of AD/HD rule themselves out prematurely, it is important to clear up the misconceptions and stereotypes that surround AD/HD.

AD/HD is *NOT*:
- Just for kids
- Just for boys
- Just about hyperactivity
- About a "deficit of attention"
- About being irresponsible or having a character flaw

AD/HD *IS*:
- A neurochemical condition (not a psychological one) that affects behavior on various levels:
  - *attention*
  - *activity*
  - *impulsivity*
- A diagnosis of AD/HD requires that these behaviors be:
  - *chronic* (meaning you have had them a long time)
  - *severe* (impacting your life negatively in serious ways, more so than other people)

Diagnosing AD/HD is Complex

However, even if you have had challenges all your life, they may have been masked by structure or support or because you were very smart or creative. You may have compensated all your life in ways that kept the symptoms under control, or you may have self-medicated without knowing that's what you were doing.

What can be even more confusing is that even though you may have these difficulties over time, you may not have had them *consistently*. As Thomas Brown, Ph.D. puts it "they may be chronic but not constant." (1999, pg. 3) They may vary from situation to situation. You may have done some things very well and have had significant gaps in other areas. To complicate the diagnostic picture even more, no two people with AD/HD will have the exact same problems.

AD/HD can be best understood by explaining the executive, or management, function of the brain. Thomas Brown, Ph.D. leading expert in adult AD/HD from the department of psychiatry at Yale University illustrates this condition as he lectures about executive function with the metaphor of wonderful musicians trying to play together in an orchestra without a conductor! Executive functioning is described in more detail in Chapter 5, but it has to do with shifting, starting, dividing, stopping, and starting your attention. It includes the following:

- Activating your brain to begin to work.

- Maintaining attention in the midst of distractions.

- Sustaining attention when energy and interest fade.

It is extremely important to understand that while AD/HD is a serious disorder, it is not characterological or psychological, but *neurobiological*. This means it's not your fault, but it's how your individual brain works. It does not mean you have brain damage.

While no one knows *exactly* what causes AD/HD, it is commonly understood to be genetically transmitted. You are born this way, and there are probably others in your family who either have or have had these difficulties.

The Information Highway in Your Head

The brain uses multiple chemical substances called neurotransmitters to act as messengers, sending information to and from the different parts of your brain. Three neurotransmitters that have been linked to behavioral and emotional conditions are *Dopamine, Serotonin, and Norepinephrine.* While low levels of Serotonin are linked with clinical depression, AD/HD appears related to the other two neurotransmitters, Dopamine and Norepinephrine. Most people agree that AD/HD symptoms are connected to the inefficiency and inconsistency of this *chemical information transmission system* in the brain. The brain itself is fine. There is no damage, and actually people with AD/HD are often quite bright or creative. It is just that for some reason these chemical messengers are not firing consistently or efficiently. It's logical that if the regulators aren't firing properly in the part of your brain that regulates attention, activity level, and impulsivity that these areas of behavior would also be inconsistent.

In his 2004 article on the basics of the neurobiology of AD/HD, Terry Dickson, M.D., an expert in the field, likens the difficulty of communicating inefficiently across nerve synapses in the brain to talking on a cell phone with bad reception. I liken this neurotransmitter inconsistency to problems you may experience with your computer. Even if you have the most expensive, well-built computer with the ability to process and store great amounts of information, your desktop can get too full, or something can go wrong with the operating system. Or your computer could have great long-term information storage capability but inadequate operating capability to match. Those of us who use computers have all experienced the frustration when an error message suddenly appears without warning—the screen freezes, and the system crashes. In a sense, this is what AD/HD is like; not being able to use the potential of the fine tool that is there.

The inefficient and irregular transmission of information in the brain causes a host of unique difficulties in each person affected. The huge number of variations and limitless possibilities of combinations that exist in these chemical connections makes what we now call AD/HD so confusing to understand. It's hard for many to accept, especially because the symptoms manifest so differently in each person. AD/HD even looks different in the same person at various times.

Seeing is Believing

Promising technological advances have allowed us to actually see the brain in action thus bringing us closer to a true understanding of how it functions. In the same article by Dr. Dickson mentioned above, he tells us about three functional brain imaging techniques—MRI, Pet and Spect—used to take pictures of the metabolism of brain chemicals. Dr. Dickson says that these functional brain-imaging techniques have played a vital role in understanding the AD/HD brain.

One of the leading scientific discoveries was made by Dr. Alan Zametkin (1990) of the National Institute of Mental Health. Through the use of a special brain-imaging technique called Positron Emission Tomography (PET) scans, he has been able to measure and document the glucose metabolic process in individuals. These tests show fairly conclusively that during tasks that require concentration, the brains of individuals with AD/HD have a markedly lower level of brain activity in these areas as compared with those without AD/HD.

There is no clear agreement on the exact process by which AD/HD symptoms are produced in the brain. However, researchers surmise that because certain medications that affect the specific processes in the brain work so well in the reduction of AD/HD symptoms that these brain chemicals are also the ones involved in the creation of AD/HD symptoms. With the promise of these new brain-imaging techniques, we will better understand the great variations in human brains in the future.

The Many Faces of AD/HD

For many years, when people thought of AD/HD, the picture that came to mind was of a hyperactive, troublemaking little boy, running around causing a lot of problems and was identified with these overt behaviors: not being able to pay attention, having an overactive activity level, and impulsively acting out. These disruptive behaviors were impossible to miss. In reality, AD/HD has many more dimensions than this common stereotyped picture.

We used to believe that children with these behaviors outgrew their AD/HD when they became adults. However, we eventually learned that a large percentage of them continued to struggle as adults even though their hyperactivity diminished. Even though their difficulties were often less visible as adults, their poorly regulated attentional system caused them just as many perplexing and frustrating problems. Since the first edition of this book, we have become more aware of another group of adults with AD/HD who *never were* hyperactive. These people, largely consisting of women, continue to be under identified in childhood and often remain undiagnosed as adults.

AD/HD by Any Other Name . . .

The Names Change, but the Facts Remain the Same

It seems that the official labels used by the professional community to diagnose Attention Deficit Disorder change every few years, thereby confusing many people in the process of attempting to more accurately describe this syndrome and capture its variations, as well as its core characteristics. Individuals in the professional community may differ on the wisdom of some of the nomenclature, but the general characteristics they are trying to describe stay the same.

To confuse matters further, it is common for many people, especially the general population, to use the terms ADD or AD/HD without differentiating types since it is awkward to specify types in normal conversation.

Different Types of AD/HD (as of this writing)

AD/HD Hyperactive/Impulsive Type

These people used to be called AD/HD with hyperactivity and are the speedy, hyper, bounce-off-the-wall children and multi-tasking adults.

AD/HD Inattentive Type

These people used to be called AD/HD without hyperactivity. They can be dreamy and under active and work and move slowly. Much of the focus of this book is women with inattentive AD/HD. Again, there is much variation. Many women who were hyperactive as children have lost the hyperactivity yet still experience the effects of attention problems. Many who are under active on the outside are hyperactive in their thoughts and experience an internal feeling of being driven even if it is not translated to hyperactive physical activity.

There are also combined types of AD/HD who share characteristics of both.

Detailed Breakdown of What AD/HD is and What It's Not

AD/HD Does NOT = A *Deficit* of Attention

Instead it means attention irregularity and inconsistency. This includes difficulties with the following:

- Distractibility or excessive shifting of attention.
- Activating, deploying, and directing one's attention.
- Containing and maintaining one's attention.
- Screening out unimportant matters from one's attention.

And contrary to the meaning of deficit, there are many positives attributes that tend to come along with AD/HD, including a surplus of ideas, creativity, excitement, and interest.

AD/HD Does NOT = Hyperactivity

Instead it means a dis-regulation of activity and arousal levels that involves extremes of activity levels from high to low or from hyperactive to "hypoactive," or what I call *overly underactive.*

AD/HD Does NOT = Impulsive Troublemaking

Instead it can be a quieter, less obvious kind of impulsivity with excessive shifting of tasks or life directions.

A Deeper Dive into the Complexities of AD/HD

What we call AD/HD is often confusing because AD/HD looks and feels so different for each person. For example, the AD/HD inattentive type presents differently on the outside than does the more commonly understood and more easily recognized AD/HD hyperactive type. It also feels very different on the inside. In fact, women often internalize their difficulties rather than acting them out, which may result in depression or anxiety. Despite the outward appearances, it is by no means a *mild* case of AD/HD as Thomas Brown, Ph.D. who has written and spoken extensively about this kind of AD/HD emphasizes. Both forms of AD/HD share the same core difficulties and are just as extreme but are experienced and expressed in various ways with different effects in a person's life. The important thing to remember is that none of us have perfect control of our attention, regulation of our activity, or impulses. However, as you can see from the following spectrum, AD/HD is defined by symptoms that are extreme, chronic, and severe.

Can You Have These Symptoms and Not Have AD/HD?

Yes! Not everyone who has these symptoms has AD/HD. Let's say you have these problems to a severe level, and you have had them for as long as you can remember (chronic), and even if they weren't highly visible, they had great impact. Does this mean you have AD/HD? Not necessarily! You can have these difficulties *at particular times, even severely,* and not have AD/HD.

Other Reasons for Symptoms that Mimic AD/HD

- Perhaps you have just experienced a major change in your life such as a divorce, a move, a loss of a job, or you are under great deal of stress. As a result, you may become very disorganized, depressed, or feel bad about yourself *for a while.* To have AD/HD these symptoms must have been there *most of the time and over a long period of time.*

- You may say things like, "I lose my keys all the time," or "You should see my closets," or "I procrastinate." This may be somewhat of a problem, but if it's not severe enough to be *the* problem causing tremendous difficulty in all important areas of life, then it isn't AD/HD.

- Other kinds of neurological, psychological, and physical disorders such as head injuries, thyroid imbalances, post-traumatic stress disorder to name a few can account for the same kinds of symptoms and must be ruled out.

Family or environmental conditions such as growing up with a chaotic family life, an abusive home, a mentally ill parent, or an alcoholic family can all contribute to such intermittent symptoms. Sometimes a person can have had these family backgrounds *and also have AD/HD*; this takes expert diagnosis. It's also possible that your parent's difficulties may have been a result of *their undiagnosed AD/HD.*

For all of the reasons listed above, it is especially important to get a diagnosis by a mental health professional who understands AD/HD (with and without the symptom of hyperactivity), as well as other conditions that look like AD/HD.

Effects of AD/HD

We have just looked at the three core symptoms of AD/HD and its many variations. The conditions you might actually see as a result of these symptoms in the lives of adults with AD/HD are as follows:

- Disorganization

- Emotional reactivity

- Under-achievement

- Low self-esteem

- Impaired relationships

- Depression

Since AD/HD individuals operate with their gates wide open, they have difficulty screening out unneeded information or irrelevant internal and external distractions without effort or thought and easily become flooded, bombarded, and overwhelmed. It is easy to see how living like this would lead someone to be *emotionally reactive*. It is also easy to see how this kind of shifting attention could lead to *severe disorganization* and feelings of being out of control or that things are about to fall apart. On the other hand, as a compensation some people spend an inordinate amount of time organizing to the detriment of their relationships and enjoyment of life. They may look organized to others, but that is not the criteria by which to judge the struggle. Instead, it is the process they go through to achieve this level of organization that must be explored and understood in order to fully appreciate the impact and impairment.

The Impact of AD/HD on Lives

All this can impact *relationships*, choice of partners, and *self-esteem*. These feelings can lead to a growing sense of *desperation*, hopelessness, and depression, making it difficult to stay on track or pursue meaningful goals. This could also lead to the *underachievement* of the individual, causing a person to be emotionally reactive once more and thus beginning this negative cycle over again.

It is a myth, however, that if you have AD/HD you cannot go to college, get an advanced degree, or achieve success. You may, however, need support to help you with your challenges and help you find your strengths.

Basic Treatment

The cornerstone of treatment for AD/HD is medication, usually stimulant medication, which is increasingly combined with other medications such as anti-depressants. While low levels of serotonin are linked with clinical depression and treated for that reason, antidepressant medication increases the availability of the serotonin neurotransmitter in the brain, which is why stimulant medications are known to increase the production of the two neurotransmitters, Dopamine and Norepinephrine, associated with AD/HD symptoms by boosting their levels into the normal range. Joseph Carver, Ph.D. in his article called *Attention Deficit Hyperactivity Disorder* found on his website www.drjoecarver.com describes it as follows: "If we imagine using a 'dipstick,' like the dipstick used to check oil/transmission fluid levels in our automobile, we might be able to check the neurotransmitter levels in our brain, finding which neurotransmitters are low, within the normal range, or high. "Medication is thought to improve the transmission of messages in the brain through the neurotransmitters."

While medication has proved to be quite effective in reducing many of the primary symptoms of AD/HD, it is just the first step. Education, support, strategies, coaching, and organizing can all play important roles in long-term successful outcomes. Counseling can also be extremely helpful in addressing how people think about their AD/HD and what they think about themselves.

Take Away Message

It is critical to remember that despite all the problems discussed in this section, there are many strengths associated with the kind of brain that produces symptoms we call AD/HD. These individuals when diagnosed, treated, and supported, can and do lead exceptional lives. When they come to accept and value their differences and find a way to use their strengths in the world, they can and do find fulfilling work and meaningful relationships. This is the real take away message of this book.

The Buried Treasure

Millions of people have this neurobiological condition. When undiagnosed it can be devastating and debilitating, silently robbing them of their dreams, their hopes, their self-esteem. These people spend their lives trying to solve a riddle—the mystery of their lives must lay somewhere out there, just around the next turn in the road. They remember that they have glimpsed it, that special something once felt or envisioned, before things got so overwhelming and they became trapped and lost—wandering aimlessly in a forest looking for clues as if from an old treasure map. They know the treasure is there somewhere, but perhaps deeply buried or locked behind a fortress. They have incredible perseverance and determination to keep going, often pulling an enormous weight. The remembrance of that special feeling, the knowledge, deep inside, that they have something important of value to do, to create, to contribute, keeps them searching. They continue on, though the memory, that belief, grows more faint each year as despair begins to replace hope. Hope that they will ever find the treasure, that they will even find their way out of the forest and back to the road.

Still, they trudge on, clutching that old, crumpled, faded map, holding on to the hope they will find that buried treasure chest and reclaim their abandoned hopes and lost dreams.

PART I

SURVIVING

CHAPTER ONE

Coming Out of the (Messy) Closet

Introduction to My Personal and Professional Story

It wasn't until I went to my first Adult AD/HD Conference and spent three days under the same roof with hundreds of other adults with AD/HD that I developed the concept of "being in the closet" as applied to individuals with invisible disorders. It wasn't until I saw hundreds of people not in the closet, being themselves in front of others for the first time, that I realized how much time and energy is spent hiding, pretending, and carefully monitoring one's behavior. I especially enjoyed seeing women tearing through oversized, overstuffed purses, hunting furiously for something they needed and couldn't find but without the usual embarrassment or self-consciousness. I stood in delighted wonder as I watched them throw things on the floor in search of that certain piece of paper or phone number they couldn't find, scribbling on their hands when they couldn't find a piece of paper, talking fast, interrupting, laughing— finally finding people who could keep up with them. Sure, there were angry feelings and frustration when things didn't go smoothly, but the picture of adults with AD/HD being themselves, obviously bright and interested but often confused or disoriented, warm and exciting though struggling, brought home to me in a vivid way the extent to which these invisible disorders are hidden in everyday life—how much of the time these folks spend hiding, pretending, or just plain controlling their symptoms to present themselves well, to pass as "normal."

Even though I had been diagnosed and was on medication at the time, not many of my family, friends, or people at work were aware of my "secret." I knew I was living in two worlds: my AD/HD world and my so-called "straight" world. Although for years I had been

1

talking to other women and clients about the concept of shame, I didn't even realize the extent of *my own* shame until the following incident. I was scheduled to deliver a speech about women and AD/HD when a flyer announcing the speech (prepared by the sponsoring organization) was sent out all over town, including my colleagues, associates, and friends. In describing the speech, the flyer announced that I would discuss my *personal* experiences with this condition and that my husband would comment on life with an AD/HD woman. There it was. I was "outed." I was mortified and ashamed. I felt as if it had been just announced to the world that I was some kind of awful criminal. I wasn't aware until that moment that I, too, was still so affected by these deeply embedded feelings of shame.

I'd like to take you back to before that pivotal moment in my life and trace my personal and professional AD/HD story, which led to the writing of this book. I was working at a large counseling agency as a therapist, seeing adult clients in the general population for issues such as relationships, depression, anxiety, and self-esteem. At the same time, I was fortunate to be part of an unusual project within this agency that also served adults with "invisible" disorders such as learning disabilities and Attention Deficit Disorder (ADD), as it was called at the time. It soon became clear to me that there was a major difference between these two groups of clients. *The very thing that caused the most pain and severely impacted the lives of the adults with hidden disorders, the core of what was discussed week after week during the therapy hour, was very different from my other group of clients without these invisible disorders.*

What AD/HD individuals talked about in therapy was the confusion, frustration, and pain of ordinary, daily life. The difficulty they had in organizing themselves in life was monumental compared to people without these kinds of disorders. By the time they reached mid-life, they described it as a kind of desperation born of not being able to achieve what they had originally planned to do. The double whammy seemed to be that coupled with this severe disorganization, they often felt that they had "thousands" of exciting ideas started, lying in rubble, unfinished in their rooms, taunting and haunting them. And even when the AD/HD clients were struggling with relationships and depression, these difficulties were often the *result* of the underlying disorder.

These people were not alike in their behavior. Some were impulsive—getting in trouble, blurting out words, interrupting others, reacting too quickly, or getting angry at the wrong times.

Others were withdrawn and shy, not causing problems at all. Some couldn't get off the couch, direct their energy from an idea to take action, or mobilize themselves. At the other extreme, some people couldn't stop moving. They were driven and needed to do ten things at once to stay alert and focused. There were those who sought out very high stimulation while conversely others felt bombarded by any stimulation and could only do one thing at a time in a very controlled, quiet environment.

From the outside, the personalities of these individuals didn't resemble each other. In many cases, no one could tell them apart from people without these particular kinds of problems. But during the therapy hour, they all described the same kind of pain and told the same story in one form or another. They told tales of unusual twists and turns in their career paths and life directions. They talked about the difficulty of working for large organizations with the inherent paperwork and details; many wanted to be independent and on their own but were vulnerable to falling into an abyss of emptiness without any structure at all. Most of them felt trapped and blamed themselves. Most of them, by the time they were adults (especially if not diagnosed early on), had some deeply embedded notion that a character defect or fatal flaw was at the source of their problems. And even *after* they were diagnosed and treated, they still berated themselves with words like irresponsible, lazy, unmotivated, slob, or failure. Even *after* they were on medication and had some idea that a neurobiological condition was at the root of these difficulties, they were still unable to automatically wipe away the years of low self-esteem and feelings of failure.

In the same way that I could clearly see the difference between the AD/HD and non-AD/HD groups, I also started to notice significant differences between men with AD/HD and women with AD/HD in my clinical work. This was both in terms of the special challenges they faced in living successfully after diagnosis and in accessing the help they needed to rebuild and restructure their lives. The patterns that women reported were similar to each other, especially regarding their level of difficulty in taking certain kinds of actions to help restructure their lives. I began to look at these attitudes as somehow being culturally transmitted. The struggles around cultural expectations seemed to go beyond individual psychology. There seemed to be some unique vulnerability that these women faced that made learning to live with these kinds of difficulties a special challenge.

Men with AD/HD certainly faced their own painful difficulties such as the cultural expectations of being a stable provider, the successful breadwinner, and a strong, solid force in the family. But it seemed women faced a whole host of other problems. Observing and understanding these other difficulties became very important in my learning how to help women move through a successful course of treatment. I was able to see that on the one hand, the women were very motivated to help themselves. On the other hand, the moment they tried to ask for an accommodation at school or at home, these women froze. They couldn't go any further. For example, at school they might have wanted more time on an assignment, at work they might want to move to a quieter area, or at home they might have desired help with the piles and clutter. *But they hit a wall of shame, guilt, or embarrassment so strong that it needed to be understood, and worked through first before they could employ the strategies suggested for organizational difficulties.*

These internal barriers impacted women differently than men, keeping them locked on a treadmill until they were depleted, overwhelmed, and feeling like failures, even after diagnosis. I watched as these women struggled to overcome these barriers by becoming proactive and taking control of their lives. It was an exciting process to witness these women slowly coming to life. It was as if they had opened a door and started to walk into life again in quiet but dramatic ways. Their lives didn't suddenly become stress free; they didn't turn into perfectly organized, different kinds of women. But they *did* begin to access help, repair feelings of low self-esteem, and get their lives back on track.

Personal Discovery

At the same time that I was engaged in counseling these clients, I was reading, attending conferences, and digging in the literature to understand all I could about AD/HD. I began to see references for adults with severe organizational problems to use Ritalin, just like it was prescribed for children. I began to wonder more and more if some of the difficulties I had experienced my entire life could have had something to do with AD/HD. I certainly had done well in school and had never had any behavior problems, yet still. . . .

At that time (and all my life), I had a little room in one part of the house in which I spent each night and weekend trying in vain to "get organized." I had no idea that other people weren't spending each weekend as a bridge between Friday and Monday, trying frantically to dig their way out of the "rubble" before Monday arrived again. As I began to understand AD/HD, I began to notice small things; for example, I heard other people making plans to go to the park on the weekend or to a concert. To me, it was like hearing people from another planet. Each Friday at the agency where I was working, my friend and colleague, Lisa, would ask me, "What are you doing this weekend?" I would say, "I'm getting organized." After a few months of hearing this response, Lisa finally said to me, "Oh, you must be working on a major project!" And I said, "No, I'm just getting organized."

It started to dawn on me that others weren't living the same way, but I had no idea how they did it. I started watching Lisa as she went through her workday. She had a large, loose-leaf notebook with multi-colored, labeled dividers. Each day at the agency what seemed to me to be thousands of pieces of paper put in our boxes would wind up perfectly divided into their proper sections of Lisa's notebook. What amazed me even more was that she seemed to accomplish this effortlessly with little extra thought or energy expended. She had virtually nothing to bring home with her each day. I watched as she sat every day in the busy, noisy staff room, writing her notes as she chatted with the other women. This was absolutely unfathomable to me, as the many distractions in the room made it impossible for me to concentrate on even the simplest tasks, let alone my work.

I, on the other hand, behind closed doors, locked in a little office, spent a great deal of time trying to organize all those pieces of information. But first I had to move the ticking clock in the room and stuff it into a drawer to muffle the sound. Then I had to close the windows and turn up the fan to block out any extraneous sounds.

Invariably, at the end of each day, still unorganized, I would stuff all my papers into my briefcase and take them home. I would put them with the other accumulated stuff in that little room downstairs and spend the evening, trying again in vain to organize them. It's not hard to see that I was rapidly becoming buried. At the same time, no one at the agency had any idea what I was coping with, and I certainly wasn't about to risk their favorable opinion of me by letting them in on my embarrassing lack of organizational ability.

It seemed that the dilemma I faced up to that point in my life was that I could either *not* achieve my potential and stay somewhat organized, or I could continue to achieve but get overloaded and buried, eventually hitting an organizational wall so hard that I would have to change course. As I looked back over the years, I realized that every major decision up until then, every move I had made in my career, relationships, or geography was based on my inability to cope with organizational demands after they increased to a certain level, not on my true interests or abilities.

Through more research and my growing understanding, I was eventually able to get diagnosed and treated. Since that point, I've carefully observed my life and my process as I've continued to learn to live successfully as a woman with AD/HD.

Living Successfully as a Woman with AD/HD

I said I've learned to live *successfully* as a woman with AD/HD. The definition of the word successful is very important because women often get locked into a fruitless search for an unachievable goal. When I say I'm living successfully, it doesn't mean that I'm living stress free or that I'm perfectly organized. It doesn't mean that I don't have to constantly strategize and struggle. And it doesn't mean I'm never overwhelmed or that I don't sometimes still hide.

What it does mean, for me, to live successfully with AD/HD, is that I've found a way to move the focus of my life onto my strengths, my talents, and my abilities and to increase my choices and options. It means that through medication I am awake, alert, and able to maintain my energy and attention throughout most of the day. It means I can sort out my neurology from my psychology and figure out what things in my life I can change and what I just need to control or live with. It means that I've learned to separate out my strengths from my weaknesses and to embrace both of those as part of myself, even though it's a long stretch. I've come to accept the fact that I do have deficits out of proportion with the rest of my abilities and that these do severely impact my life. I've learned to separate out the shame, embarrassment, and guilt surrounding these difficulties from my core sense of self. Now when my AD/HD symptoms do appear, I don't add to them a negative self-barrage that creates a downhill cycle.

I have learned that to be successful with AD/HD you must eventually restructure your life. You move through Shame and Guilt and must ultimately redefine your sense of what it means to be a mature, confident, competent woman, even if after treatment you are still somewhat messy, disorganized, or forgetful. For me, it means I have learned to value myself as a creative woman who will never match some culturally sanctioned image I may have internalized a long time ago about what a woman should be or be able to do.

CHAPTER TWO

An Equal Opportunity Disorder
Girls and AD/HD

Mrs. Collins' fourth grade class is sitting quietly doing their math problems. Billy's pencil breaks for the fourth time that day; he jumps out of his seat and runs to the pencil sharpener on the other side of the room. On the way he notices a cool picture of his favorite basketball star on the cover of a friend's notebook and picks it up to admire it. His friend yanks it out of his hand and, without thinking of the consequences, Billy blurts out, "You stupid jerk," interrupting the whole class. Since this is the twenty-fifth incident in the last two weeks, Mrs. Collins has finally had enough and banishes him to the principal's office. He gets upset and starts arguing with her, not knowing why he's in trouble again. He just wanted to sharpen his pencil to get his work done.

Sitting quietly in the back of the classroom, Jodi hasn't noticed any of this commotion. She is looking at a bird outside the window, wondering where it was for the winter and where the rest of its family is. She is startled back into reality by the sound of Mrs. Collin's voice calling out her name and asking her for the answer to problem number seven. She panics because she has barely gotten through problem two. She smiles sweetly and says softly, "I'm sorry Mrs. Collins, I haven't finished yet." Mrs. Collins says, "That's ok honey, try to work on it now," thinking to herself that Jodi is "such a nice little girl" but she is a bit slow in math. Thinking of Billy, she wishes she had a whole classroom full of children like Jodi.

By the end of the month, Billy has been tested by the school psychologist and is diagnosed with Attention Deficit Hyperactivity Disorder

(AD/HD). He sees his family doctor who starts him on the medication, Ritalin. Mrs. Collins and Billy's parents all see a big difference in Billy's behavior and schoolwork.

By the end of the school year, Jodi has barely made it through math with a C minus average, but she receives an A in citizenship and gets a great report from Mrs. Collins about what a sweet little girl she is. Over the next few years, Jodi's parents continue to get similar reports from her teachers; her grades continue to go down in many subjects, even though her parents think of Jodi as a bright girl. The teachers keep telling them that nothing is wrong and not to worry that Jodi is just an average student, implying that they, like most parents, have an inflated view of their daughter's intelligence. At home, they see Jodi becoming more and more overwhelmed by the amount of schoolwork, unable to organize her work or her personal belongings, and more withdrawn and unhappy.

Up until recently, when most of us heard the phrase "AD/HD," what came to mind was the picture of hyperactive little boys, like Billy, tearing around the room, bouncing off the walls. Because they made trouble for people, they were noticed and consequently got diagnosed and treated. Even though life for these individuals and their families continued to be challenging and stressful, at least everyone knew what the root of the problem was. Attention Deficit Hyperactivity Disorder (AD/HD) with hyperactivity and impulsivity is what Billy has and what we commonly think of as AD/HD.

But little girls like Jodi, sitting in the back of the class, not bothering anyone, were and are still easily overlooked. Jodi belongs to a group of individuals that we now know do not and never have had *hyperactivity* and yet still have AD/HD. Kathleen Nadeau, Ph.D. has called these kinds of girls' people pleasers, especially to parents and teachers. (2000) They try hard to conform to teacher and parental expectations. She said at the national ADDA (Attention Deficit Disorder Association) conference that their AD/HD symptoms often only show up at home after an exhausting effort to "hold it together all day." (1995)

AD/HD (Minus the Hyperactivity)

Even though we now officially call Attention Deficit Disorder AD/HD, the simple explanation is that some children have attention problems who have never been hyperactive. We used to call this AD/HD without hyperactivity, but now we call this the inattentive type.

Children with AD/HD who are not hyperactive have been described by Dr. Dale Jordan, (1991) a psychologist who has written a great deal about this kind of AD/HD as "lost youngsters who drift and float quietly on the edges of the environment." As I said in the pocket guide, Thomas Brown, Ph.D., from the Yale Department of psychiatry, who has contributed so much to the body of knowledge about AD/HD of this type, has emphasized for many years that this is not just a mild form of AD/HD but is itself is a severe condition.

These children have extremes in some of the same areas as children with hyperactivity but on the other side of the spectrum. Instead of being hyperactive, they are often *hypo*active, i.e., extremely underactive. Instead of not being able to stop moving, they have trouble starting to move. Instead of acting impulsively without thinking, they have difficulty moving from an impulse to an action. And instead of seeking high stimulation, these children feel bombarded by stimulation. Rather than doing many things at the same time in order to concentrate, these children can only concentrate on one thing at time.

AD/HD can sometimes be confusing for the individual as well as the people around them because we usually associate intelligence with quick processing speed. AD/HD symptoms such as distractibility to both internal and external stimuli and difficulty with synthesizing and organizing ideas coupled with general fogginess and confusion make it difficult to process information in an average amount of time. Not only will this mask their level of intelligence, but people might even think they are less intelligent than they really are. On the other hand, though, just because a girl is a good student and is thought of as smart, *doesn't mean she doesn't have AD/HD!* It may just mean one of the following: (a) processing speed may not be one of her problems, (b) she may have a good support system, (c) she may be working extraordinarily hard to do a good job, or (d) her difficulties might impact other areas of her life more than academics. These will probably show up later in life. *A woman who is now the mother of four children says of her own childhood, "My kindergarten teacher told my mom that I wanted to know all about the moon and the stars, but that I couldn't remember to button my coat the right way or where I put it."*

> These girls are easily misdiagnosed. Girls are more compliant, and are not as easy to spot. Often they are left to drift along from one school year to the next, never working up to their potential. (Nadeau for ADDvance)

One of the most telling signs of the child with this type of AD/HD is disorganization. One look at her locker, desk, room, or maybe even her handwriting might give you a clue that she may be struggling with this disorder. They might also be extremely sensitive to visual stimulus and physical movements and be highly distracted by both their internal and external worlds.

Girls with AD/HD (inattentive type) may have trouble socially, as well. Because they have problems with small talk and with figuring out the rules of social interaction, they tend to become shy and withdrawn. Kathleen Nadeau, Ph.D. (ADDA, 1995) says that little girls like this often appear awkward, painfully shy and unable to fit in.

AD/HD GIRLS
(with the hyperactivity and impulsivity)

Lucy as a Girl

Lucy is sitting in the back of Mrs. Collins' room next to Jodi. Lucy is talking nonstop to some of her friends. She passes notes back and forth to her girlfriends about the cute boy two seats away. She is not paying attention to Mrs. Collins' long and boring lecture about the location of countries around the world. Instead she is giggling with delight at the thought of recess five minutes away when she can try out the new hop-scotch game she just thought of. At recess, however, another girl laughs at this new game and won't play. Lucy is mortified. She breaks into tears, throws down the chalk, and stomps away. Mrs. Collins sees this, shakes her head, and thinks this is another typical "overreaction" by Lucy. Mrs. Collins attributes this behavior to the recent divorce of Lucy's parents.

Why AD/HD Goes Undiagnosed Longer in Little Girls

AD/HD goes unidentified longer in girls with both kinds of AD/HD than in boys. Even though girls who are more hyperactive are more noticeable than girls who aren't hyperactive, they too are identified and treated later than hyperactive boys because they don't act out as much or cause as many problems. The hyperactivity of girls with AD/HD is often manifested differently than in boys. Often these girls are hyper-talkative rather than hyper-active. They are "silly", excitable and over-emotional. They chatter constantly in class and have trouble staying quiet even when they are disciplined for talking. They interrupt others frequently and jump from topic to topic in conversation. (Nadeau for *ADDvance*)

Rather than having an attention disorder, many times their behaviors are attributed to emotional or family problems. For instance, in Lucy's case, if she is still undiagnosed by the time of her parent's divorce, it will be especially difficult for her to get an accurate diagnosis. In addition to her AD/HD, she will be reacting to this upheaval in her life.

Because girls who do not display hyperactivity aren't behavior problems, they often aren't identified at a young age, unless they also happen to have obvious learning disabilities. Another reason they don't get diagnosed, according to expert Dr. Daniel Amen, psychiatrist and author of many books on AD/HD, is that the cultural stereotypes that we have of little girls contribute to their under-identification. As in Jodi's case, the school system tolerates underachievement in girls that it wouldn't in boys. Also, I feel that these girls usually fall into the "nice little girl" stereotype. Because they are nice, quiet, or shy, they meet cultural expectations so people either don't notice or are not as concerned with their subtle information processing problems.

Another reason that AD/HD in girls often goes undiagnosed is that AD/HD in boys is often detected during a school evaluation for learning disabilities. According to Drs. Hallowell and Ratey in their book, *Answers to Distraction*, since girls with AD/HD have fewer learning problems in the early grades in math and reading than boys do, these girls are less apt to be diagnosed through this avenue.

The reason early identification of girls is so important is that years of being mislabeled, misunderstood, or just plain missed can lead to serious long-term impacts on their self-esteem, relationships, achievement, and emotions. We will see these consequences as we trace the lives of Jodi and Lucy through childhood, their teenage years, and into adulthood.

Twelve Years Old and Still Undiagnosed . . .

It's 3:30 pm. Twelve-year-old Jodi is lying exhausted on her unmade bed, trying to recover from a normal day at junior high school. Her clothes from the last few days are lying in heaps on the floor. Her books and papers are in total disarray all over her desk. She is unable to rest, however, because she is distracted by the bouncing basketball next door and is growing more and more upset by the minute. Her mother comes in, looks around, and gives her the familiar lecture of starting her homework on time and cleaning up her room. Jodi is thinking about the seventh grade history project and how stupid she must be because she can't figure out how to do it even though her classmates are doing it easily. Besides the project, she is facing another long night of homework. Jodi is hoping for the phone to ring, but she knows it won't. In junior high, it seems harder and harder to figure out what to say to people or how to make friends. After she analyzes a conversation at school, studies the cracks in her ceiling, and makes a futile attempt at cleaning her room, she is dismayed to hear her mom call out, "Jodi, I hope you're doing your homework. It's 5:30 and almost time for your appointment with Dr. Evans." Dr. Evans has diagnosed Jodi as depressed and has suggested family therapy to find out the reason why.

So how do we know that the psychologist wasn't right and that Jodi isn't just depressed? It's not always easy to tell AD/HD inattentive type from depression because many of the symptoms of depression look like it such as low energy levels, disorganization, and difficulty concentrating, as well as social withdrawal. However, in lieu of formal testing, which we'll talk about later, there are important clues, which can be strong indicators of this type of AD/HD. Additionally, Jodi *may* be depressed, having had to cope with all these difficulties for years now and feeling more like a failure every year. The important thing to find out is this: Is she depressed because she's disorganized, or is she disorganized because she's depressed?

Complicating the picture further, the psychologist is partly right. There may well be family discord as well as an over focus on Jodi's problems that no one has been able to solve. Again, this would be a *result* of Jodi's undetected AD/HD, not the cause of the problem.

So what are the important factors to consider when sorting all this out? In Jodi's case, this is more than just a reaction to starting junior high, albeit a big adjustment in her life. Signs of her difficulty were apparent from early on. In Jodi's case, there is no chaotic family history such as alcoholism or abuse to account for these ongoing difficulties. Another important factor is the severity of Jodi's symptoms. If you compare Jodi to other children her age and ability level, you'll see that her difficulties are extreme, severely impacting her ability to work up to her potential. As we will see throughout the book, while all of us may have some of these symptoms some of the time, for those with AD/HD the symptoms are *severe and chronic*. And remember that even though AD/HD symptoms are severe and chronic, AD/HD symptoms in girls, like Jodi, can also be *subtle, quiet, and invisible*.

When girls have these strong emotions and reactions to the world, they are more apt to internalize these difficulties and develop depression and anxiety rather than acting out. Their stories are more likely to be of quiet failures coupled with self-esteem and self-doubt. These are the seeds of the emotional legacy that will continue to grow as these children become teenagers and women.

Teenage Years: Lucy in the Sky (without protective factors)

Lucy is now a teenager and has been living with her mother since the time of her parent's divorce. Her mother is highly disorganized and probably has undiagnosed AD/HD herself. They don't have any extra money for tutors or for after-school lessons that could have helped Lucy develop her special interest in art. After school each day Lucy is pretty much on her own. She tries to study before her mother gets home every night from work, but she usually gets bored and ends up watching a lot of television, eating junk food, and subsequently gaining a substantial amount of weight. When she is about fifteen, a friend offers her some diet pills, which also happen to be stimulants. For the first time, she feels awake, alert, and focused.

Around the same time, she also begins experimenting with marijuana and alcohol. She feels so relaxed at these moments, and it feels so good to be with a group of people who seem to like her and with whom she doesn't feel any pressure. By this time she is fed up with school anyway, since no matter how hard she tries she somehow manages to "mess up" and get bad grades.

During the teenage years, organizational demands increase for adolescents. High school can be confusing; it can be overwhelming to have to move to many classrooms. The work itself demands more independent organizational skills. The social life of the teenager also requires more independent thought as the teenager is less dependent on the parent. As all variables in the lives of girls with AD/HD increase, they find it increasingly difficult to handle the demands of their environment. In *Answers to Distraction*, Drs. Hallowell and Ratey discuss the changes that occur in AD/HD girls around puberty. They say that this upheaval combined with hormonal changes make these girls more vulnerable to the underlying

AD/HD symptoms. They say that girls who have been quietly dealing with their symptoms up until this time often begin to display more drug and alcohol use, teenage pregnancy, shoplifting, eating disorders, and high-stimulus activities.

Girls with AD/HD who struggle with impulsivity and high stimulation seeking behavior might find themselves turning away from school and may turn toward boys or socializing to compensate. Girls with inattentive type AD/HD might just move more into their own shell and become absorbed in their own ideas. Both groups of girls might turn to drugs, alcohol, or coffee self-medicating themselves unknowingly in an attempt to concentrate, stay awake, relax, or ease social difficulties. *This is different than normal teenage experimentation because it is often actually an attempt to gain control rather than lose control.* They also are prone to other addictive behaviors such as promiscuity or over/under eating. They do this in an attempt to self-soothe or be stimulated or as a way to seek structure and focus.

As their coping mechanisms become strained, some of these girls will be identified as having some sort of problem, although they may not always be accurately diagnosed as having AD/HD. For instance, they might get help with their anxiety, depression, or communication with their family. Other girls, however, will continue to struggle even more and remain undiagnosed for a variety of reasons.

One reason teenage girls are often not diagnosed is because protective factors in their lives can delay the full force of their difficulties until adulthood. In his article, "Attention Deficit Disorder Without Hyperactivity,"(1993) Thomas Brown, Ph.D., emphasized the effects of having a high IQ on the diagnosis of AD/HD. Special talents as well as a high degree of family support and structure might also mitigate and mask the effects of AD/HD. For example, a girl might have a family that provides her with tutors and guidelines for homework and a structured activity schedule. Or maybe she has the kind of family that helps her find the right niche to allow her talents and abilities to flourish. Another girl may develop a coping strategy of working extremely hard so that she is able to get by with average marks.

These protective factors, however, are a double-edged sword for a girl with undiagnosed AD/HD. Even though they protect her from the full force of her difficulties as she's growing up, they also prevent other people from understanding her difficulties and consequently getting her appropriate help.

The Seeds Of Self Doubt

The seeds of negative self talk and self -doubt are taking root in Jodi and without explanation and guidance they will continue to grow.

"What is wrong with me? I must be an idiot," Jodi thinks to herself. "I'm sixteen years old, and I guess I'm just not college material. I don't understand; I got high test scores, and my art and drama teachers think I'm so bright and creative, but I keep getting D's on my English papers. My teacher says that I'm just not trying hard enough. Whenever I open my mouth to express my ideas, nothing comes out right. On top of it all, I can't go to the party Saturday night because I haven't studied for the exam, and I don't even know where my notes are, and my dress for the party is dirty, and I lost the directions, and I can't call again 'cause she'll think I'm stupid, and I'm just so tired all the time, and I act like a two year old. I said the stupidest thing in class yesterday. . . . Even though my mom helps me every night and gets me tutors, I still don't see how I'm going to make it through college. And if I don't go to college, I don't know what I'm going to do. I'm so confused, I'm just going to take a nap . . ."

Even though Jodi is struggling so much, an outsider might write her off as a typical teenage girl, as most are confused about their future, tired, or struggling with issues of self-esteem. Again, what is important here is *the chronic nature and severity of her symptoms.* Looking back, we see this has been a continuous thread throughout Jodi's life. While the AD/HD symptoms themselves are not changing, what is new and developing is her negative self-evaluation, as she is unable to understand her experience in any other way.

Every year that she remains undiagnosed, a girl with AD/HD becomes more vulnerable to emotional, social, and academic problems. As we have seen with Jodi and Lucy, the difficulties begin as *primary* AD/HD symptoms. Each year that passes, the difficulties are compounded, resulting in *secondary* emotional effects such as depression, low self-esteem, underachievement, and relationship difficulties. These effects will continue to grow and take on a life of their own as she becomes a woman, adding another complex layer to the original AD/HD symptoms she has already been coping with for years.

At some point, the demands on these girls and the pressures they feel and carry inside increase to the point that they are over their heads. No one knows what is going on: not their families, not their teachers, not their friends, and not even themselves.

For more on girls with AD/HD see the resource section in back of book.

CHAPTER THREE

"Dance with the Lady with the Hole in Her Stocking"

A Portrait of Women's Lives before Diagnosis

The Secret World

Women with AD/HD often live in a secret world. Some people call it passing for normal. I call it being locked in a (messy) closet. Whatever the cute expressions, the painful reality is that many women with AD/HD have moved away from relationships or have at least kept a part of themselves locked away from other people, usually without even realizing it. Often their lives have taken on a secret tone, as if the way they live is in some way shameful. This feeling of secrecy and shame wipes out the possibility of enjoying or appreciating all their other abilities and qualities. Their inner world is a place that outsiders couldn't fathom, where the simplest activities—getting dressed, planning the day, or running a simple errand—are extremely difficult and frustrating. The cumulative effect of these daily experiences makes them feel like outsiders, separate from the world in some important way, spending their days coping with this silent thief of time and dreams instead of living life.

In this chapter, we will explore the inner world of women with AD/HD in order to better understand the complexity of their lives. We will then be better able to appreciate what happens when they meet up with the expectations of the outer world.

The Good News Is . . .

Once these women are diagnosed and treated, many of the qualities they have developed along the way can help them get back on track. As a result of their struggles, they have often developed a reservoir of strength, perseverance, and determination. The creative problem-solving ability they have developed as a result of not being able to do things "the regular way" can be of help when strategizing about effective solutions to their difficulties, especially once they understand what they have been coping with. As a result of their experiences, they often are compassionate and sensitive to others with difficulties.

More good news is that AD/HD is closely correlated with creativity because one has the expanded ability to see connections that others don't always see. Without diagnosis and treatment, that creativity can sometimes go wild, creating the chaos that contributes to the feelings of being bombarded, overwhelmed, and out of control. The good news is that with treatment this creativity can be directed and harnessed. This natural abundance of ideas and fresh outlooks combined with the positive qualities developed along the way, allows these individuals to access their strengths and talents and move ahead in new, personally meaningful directions.

All Grown Up and Still Undiagnosed

Whenever I give a speech or seminar about AD/HD, I usually relate a story my friend Adriane told me about frogs because I think it is applicable to people who are coping with invisible disorders. This story goes that if you put frogs into cold water and then very *slowly* turn up the heat that they won't notice that the water is boiling until it's too late to jump out and by then they've boiled to death. If they had known they were in trouble, they could have easily jumped out and saved themselves.

Unfortunately, this story demonstrates what some adults with undiagnosed AD/HD cope with. They don't know how hard they are working or how much of their energy is going into just *surviving*. They don't know that living is not supposed to be *that* hard. Too often, like the frog, by the time they discover this is not the way it's supposed to be they're already depleted, depressed, or overwhelmed.

For women who have grown up with undiagnosed AD/HD, it's as if their thermostat for enjoyment and sense of normalcy has been completely thrown out of kilter, much in the same way that too much yo-yo dieting throws off the body's metabolism. Eventually, this makes it impossible to eat almost anything without gaining weight. These AD/HD women have spent a lifetime trying to keep their heads above water so their internal gauge, which registers how hard one needs to work to stay afloat, is seriously "out of whack." Unfortunately, there is no time for them to really reflect on the reality of this. They are too busy either trying not to drown or trying to hide their problems from other people who might be able to throw them a life jacket. Surviving becomes the only goal. If they do survive, they feel they are doing well. Their goal becomes to "not feel bad" instead of to "feel good."

This is understandable because they have never known any other way of living. Women say, "I can cope," "I can get by," "It's okay." And they do. They cope, they compensate, they have systems, they hide, they cover up, or they self-medicate with food or other substances. They overwork or severely limit their choices in life in order to control their lives. They organize their days around keeping their lives together to the exclusion of friends, family, work, or recreation.

AD/HD is such a full-time job that some women have never had the opportunity to stop and figure out a way of doing things differently. They haven't discovered how to change the rules, what it means to feel comfortable, or how to live without feeling overwhelmed. They just don't have the concept.

"We've Only Just Begun"

There are obviously a great variety of life paths that a young woman with undiagnosed AD/HD can take. As we said previously, the double-edged sword of protective factors often enables women to pass for normal: they go to college, develop a career, or have a family. The protective factors such as parental structure or high IQ can prevent these individuals from getting identified or feeling the full force of their symptoms at an earlier stage in their life. This makes it much more difficult for them to understand the load they're carrying and to make sense of the tremendous difficulties they face. The more they've achieved, the more confusing it is for them and others close to them, to see the complex process they go through in order to maintain this success or achievement. We will examine this scenario in more detail as we resume Jodi's story later.

Other women, even if they've had little support in high school, still manage to go to college. Unfortunately, because they have no idea what is wrong and what accommodations they could get to succeed, they are soon overwhelmed and either drop out or change schools several times.

Others continue to self-medicate with drugs or alcohol to counteract their low self-esteem and bring them some form of needed relaxation, as well as a way to feel focused. Other young women might act out sexually with multiple partners or even tolerate destructive relationships in order to have the security of some kind of structure to come up against.

Let's Look At Lucy's Young Adult Years

By senior year in high school, Lucy had had it. She dropped out and moved in with her boyfriend who didn't seem to mind the way she was. He didn't get down on her like her mom did for making a mess. Secretly she believed her mom when she told Lucy she would never amount to anything and that she was a lazy, irresponsible slob. Lucy just tried to get through each day and worked hard to forget the "stupid" dream she once had of becoming a fashion designer.

For a while she liked living with her boyfriend because even though he was becoming increasingly domineering, it felt good in a way to have someone tell her what to do. She took a job at a fast food restaurant and was soon overwhelmed. She got the orders mixed up, she was confused when handling money, and she got upset when customers got impatient. Everything seemed to be happening at once— people yelling, lots of noise, and multiple demands for her attention. She often forgot important procedures, which made the manager angry. Then she was late for work a couple of times. Eventually, she was fired. Her family wondered how she would ever be able to do anything in life if she couldn't even hold on to this seemingly simple job. The experience confirmed for her what she had feared for a long time—that she was just plain stupid. She tried to figure out how to do what they all told her she must do:

"Change your ways."

"Change your attitude."

"Try harder."

"Concentrate on what you're doing."

"Be responsible."

Mostly she kept trying to figure out the answer to the question that kept ringing in her ears, "What's the matter with me?"

The Many Roads Taken . . .

Up until recently, before the growing public awareness of adult AD/HD, Lucy probably would not have had the opportunity to recognize her symptoms for herself. Her life could have taken one of several different directions. She could have continued to spiral downhill, drinking more and more, going from one bad relationship to another, and never getting the help she needed. If she were lucky, she might at some time get help for depression and low self-esteem. This might bring her some relief and some needed direction for a while. With this kind of intervention, maybe she could wind up working in a department store around the fashions she loved. If things continued to go well, she might eventually start a community college program. If she were really lucky, an observant college instructor might pick up on her difficulties, especially if a learning disability became obvious. In this way, Lucy eventually could get some help for her AD/HD. On the other hand, she might go undiagnosed until she had her own child, who, when identified as AD/HD, caused her to recognize the symptoms in herself.

Without the benefit of education, women like Lucy often have to work at unskilled, low-paying jobs that are either too fast-paced to manage or too boring for them endure. Either way, their talents, abilities, and strengths are pushed underground, their self-esteem plummets, and they often find themselves living with a chronic, low-level depression.

Other women in this situation, even in unskilled jobs, may find a good match between their personalities and a certain kind of working environment. Hitting the wall may be postponed for them. In the book, *Diagnosing Learning Disorders*, (1991, p. 98) Bruce Pennington, Ph.D. states: "Lower-status work can be highly structured and routine and not tax executive functions too much, but other aspects of adult development that require initiative, planning, flexibility such as career development, intimacy, marriage and parenting may pose other problems."

Finally, if a young woman happens to be very talented in a particular area, and she's lucky enough to find a niche or an environment in which she can thrive, she might have a better outcome at this stage. She could continue along with a minimum of problems for a longer period of time.

"Hey, Jod . . . Take a Sad Song and Make it Better . . ."

Jodi's story is a representative history of an undiagnosed woman. Despite her previous difficulties, Jodi had a different experience than Lucy. Even though she was struggling on the inside, she did get some help from a psychologist who suggested tutors and facilitated family support, even though he didn't diagnose her as AD/HD. This turned things around enough for Jodi to get through high school and develop her interest in drama enough to derive some sense of self-esteem.

College

After high school, Jodi went on to a small private college where she discovered that she liked the field of communications, especially radio and TV. Since she didn't have to work to support herself in college, she took her time graduating, taking the minimum required number of credits each semester. Some of the required courses in science, for instance, were very difficult for her, and she received a few D's. In other courses, such as history, she devised elaborate systems for studying and processing the information. She knew that sometime around two in the morning her brain would turn on and she would study incredibly well. She got hooked on coffee and cigarettes and often stayed up all night, but she got through. Her teachers in the TV courses thought she was talented and she felt "really alive" in front of the camera. She didn't do much socializing but instead put all her focus and energy into finding a way to show the world her real abilities.

After College

After college, a friend of her parents who had "connections" made arrangements for her to get an entry level job at a local TV station, mostly as a "go-fer" at first but later as assistant to one of the writers. Her parents were proud of her and bragged to their friends about Jodi working in an exciting field like the television industry. Everyone agreed it was perfect for a creative girl like Jodi.

At first Jodi was excited, too. After all, this had been her dream. What she soon found out, however, was that talent and interest in a field were apparently not enough. What seemed to be equally critical to success were the day-to-day, real-life working requirements that didn't always match her skills, strengths, or interests. This entry level job required a great deal of paper work, keeping track of details, responding to multiple demands in a distracting environment, and a lot of boring tasks like filing. She was motivated, though, and was determined to stick with it long enough to move up in the ranks to where she could really shine—in front of the camera.

Finally, her big first break came and she was promoted to junior copywriter. Jodi had many great ideas for stories but she found she had a very difficult time communicating the depth of her ideas to anyone. In addition to this frustration, writing remained difficult for her. She found that in order to meet her deadlines, again, as in college, she had to stay up very late waiting for her brain to turn on so she could deliver the goods.

Her family thought she was doing very well. Every time they praised her, however, Jodi felt dishonest, as if she were fooling them. She knew how much harder she had to work than other people. Even though the final product was good, no one else saw the mess she created and coped with behind the scenes. Her anxiety mounted. She was growing exhausted. Each day she wondered, "Will today be the day I let down my guard and have my mask ripped away? Will someone ask me to do something I haven't prepared for enough and expose me as the fraud I really am?"

Junior copywriters didn't have assistants; they did their own filing and typing and they didn't have their own offices. They worked in the middle of the room surrounded by ringing phones, typewriters, and lots of activity. Eventually, Jodi couldn't find the important papers and information she needed for the stories she was working on. She spent hours searching for statistics or phone numbers she had misplaced and needed in order to verify sources.

The demands increased. People started teasing her and making comments about the state of disarray on and around her desk. She started hiding, taking as much work as she could home, in the hopes that she would be able to concentrate better there.

One day, to the total bewilderment and disappointment of her parents who thought she was doing so well, Jodi just quit. Not knowing what the problem was, she had no way to solve it, and no way to understand what had just happened to her. She had no idea what went so wrong in a field she loved so much. Maybe it was her. Maybe she just wasn't cut out for a career in TV. . . .

Married without Children

A year later, Jodi married a man who seemed *very organized* and had a *secure job*. Jodi secretly felt relieved to be out of a demanding work environment. Her husband was supportive of her creative instincts, and Jodi happily began to explore all her many interests— writing, photography, acting, and drawing. Before long she had ideas for many projects that would combine all these abilities in a new, exciting entrepreneurial endeavor. Now that she had the time and space, she just knew she would be able to put it all together.

Jodi took art classes . . . and then wanted to put words to the creations, so she took a class in haiku poetry . . . there she met a very interesting person who told her about the local political situation, and she felt compelled to write an editorial on the subject . . . she realized she needed more computer skills so she took a class at a local adult education center and realized that she could teach a more interesting class than that . . . and then she found out that she could become a producer at the local cable station on a volunteer basis . . . and that was exciting because she could finally get her ideas across in the way she wanted to, on TV. . . .

Five years later she looked around her bedroom floor and saw there were about twenty uncompleted dreams sitting in piles strewn across her floor—and another five or ten stuffed in boxes in the closet.

Married with Child

Jodi soon had a baby girl named Jessica and began to hope that maybe her true talents lay in childrearing and caretaking. She and her husband both agreed that it was important for her to be at home during these preschool years. She threw herself into the role and fell in love with the baby and with being a mom. She read every book on childrearing and enrolled in all the mother-daughter baby classes. Then came:

- *Co-ops and nursery school*
- *Volunteering and baking*
- *Driving and making clay*
- *Halloween and birthdays*
- *Christmas cards with baby photos*
- *Little girl's schedules and mom get-togethers*

All of a sudden there was a whole lot more than "you and me, and baby makes three." And her little girl didn't seem like the others. She wasn't as easy going as the other little girls. Jessica cried all the time, overreacted, withdrew, and got upset very easily. Gradually, Jodi felt more and more overwhelmed, out of control and depressed.

School Daze

Finally, Jessica entered first grade. Jodi's husband was supportive at first when she returned to work part-time, but when Jessica began to have trouble in school, coupled with her husband 's increasing complaints about her lack of organization around the house, Jodi quit her job. But things didn't get any easier. Secretly, she wished that she could get a housekeeper, but how could she justify that since she only had one child and wasn't working? Her days felt like a nightmare. She found simple errands incredibly overwhelming and boring. No one understood why an errand that should have taken only a few minutes meant hours of frustration and confusion. By the time she found her keys and an unwrinkled shirt to throw on and assembled all the "stuff" and the lists she needed, and by the time she stopped to get money because she was out of cash and didn't have her checkbook, she was already frustrated and upset. Just going to the grocery store bombarded her with too many decisions. The lines irritated her to such an extent that by the time she got home she felt she had just returned from battle.

When her daughter was in school, she would go out to have a cup of coffee, write in her diary and try to relax, but the conversations around her in the cafe overwhelmed Jodi, and she couldn't block them out. She'd wind up moving several times, but again, she'd become irritated by someone at the next table tapping his cup in an annoying way. She would go back home to try to get some peace, but the dog next door would bark, and the war zone effect would start again. No wonder, then, when her husband got home and said, "Didn't you get to the cleaners?" she would blow up, slam the door, and start to cry. He had no idea that she'd been to a war and back.

The Mother of Child with AD/HD

When Jessica was in the third grade, she started to fall behind the other children scholastically. At the parent-teacher conference, they asked Jodi to help keep her daughter organized and suggested an elaborate reward system to check off every day in order to structure Jessica's schedule. Jodi found herself unable to maintain this kind of structure, and her daughter continued to fall more and more behind. She and her husband began to fight more and her entire extended family began to blame her for being a bad mother and being too lazy to take care of the house and her daughter. As she began to spend more and more time lying on the couch, she began to believe they were probably right. What seemed like millions of obligations swept through her mind, as well as millions of ideas for new projects, but she felt paralyzed to move or take action. All the creative ideas that she had accumulated through the years lay strewn in piles all over her room. Her feelings of hopelessness increased, and she dreaded the moment that her husband would arrive home every day, knowing that a barrage of criticism would follow when he saw all the unfinished tasks.

Every couple of days, though, and for a few minutes each day, Jodi was surprised to find that she felt great. When it was just the right time of month, when there was just the right amount of stimulation without too much overload, it was as if a light switch had gone on inside her brain. She could easily get up, direct her energy, and get her errands done effortlessly. During those times, she would sit down at the computer and start filling in a new calendar/planner. She felt in control and was determined to stay that way. The next day, as mysteriously as it arrived, the feeling would disappear. Her husband suggested that this obviously meant she wasn't really motivated or didn't really care.

She went into therapy to resolve the anger toward her husband that was obviously, as she and therapist agreed, related to unresolved conflicts with her father. A couple of years of therapy later, she had resolved all the conflicts with her father and her husband, but she still spent ninety percent of her time rummaging through her purse, looking for matching socks, or searching for those organizer/planners that were going to be so much help! Most perplexing of all was why, after all this therapy did she still have this low-level feeling of anxiety, inner chaos, and depression?

Choice of Partners

As you can see by the story of Jodi and her husband, AD/HD impacts a couple a great deal, especially before diagnosis. In addition, the undiagnosed AD/HD also impacts a woman's choice of a partner in many subtle ways. Jodi, in the above example, says she liked that her husband was *very organized and had a secure job*. She also said he was supportive at first of her creative pursuits. They may have been attracted at first by these opposite qualities in each other but then over time, these became points of irritation.

Lets look at the variety of choices women with AD/HD often make for a variety of reasons when choosing a partner, usually without fully understanding why at the time. Women like Jodi and Lucy who have grown up with undiagnosed AD/HD are often influenced by their experiences to choose particular kinds of partners. What follows below are patterns that I've noticed in the choice of intimate partners for AD/HD women.

Chaotic Partners

A woman with AD/HD's outer life can often look chaotic and her inner life can feel chaotic. As we know, however, when viewed through the "lens of attention," a phrase coined by John Ratey, M.D., and Andrea Miller, (1992), this appearance can be a result of their attention deficit problems and not of a deeper psychological disturbance. Before she understands the reason for her often chaotic lifestyle, though, a young woman may find herself attracted to partners whose lifestyles are also chaotic. First of all, these partners might be more likely to accept the chaotic environment that the AD/HD woman often creates. These individuals might also be as confused and as lost in a fog as the AD/HD women feel that they are. Unfortunately, these partners are often leading chaotic lives for other, more serious reasons. For instance, they might have a serious mental disorder that might cause disorganization or a personality disorder that makes them unpredictable or erratic. In many cases, AD/HD women might be attracted to someone with a serious substance abuse problem. The probability of becoming involved with someone like this is increased because many individuals with AD/HD self-medicate with substances before they are diagnosed and medicated. This increases the likelihood that they would socialize with others with the same problems.

It's easy to see how disorganized people can appear similar on the outside to some extent, even if the disorganization stems from a different source. The emotionality and reactivity can also look very similar in these potential partners, but they are due to very different experiences—they are not the same kind of people. Once women with AD/HD become diagnosed and begin to get treated, they understand these differences and realize their partner isn't the one they belong with. In time, they will often move away from these kinds of partners, but it's often a difficult process. It takes these women a long time to understand just where they do belong and what kind of people they really want to be with. It can be very confusing for a long time.

Unavailable Partners

Some women with AD/HD choose partners who are unavailable, either physically or emotionally, because such partners place fewer demands on them. *I worked with a woman whose husband had a demanding professional life and who was home very little. Her friends used to say to her, "You're so understanding and patient!" but this woman experienced his absence as a relief. "If he were here all the time, I wouldn't be able to handle it. I wouldn't be able to meet all those demands." Women with AD/HD feel they have to find extra time anywhere they can so they're either going to take it out of their own hides, as we've seen earlier, or pick a partner who is not going to come with a full plate of expectations.*

A variation of this is a woman who might have become involved with someone who is available emotionally and then, for the same reasons, she finds herself keeping her partner at a distance. On a deep level, this woman might feel that if a partner got too close to her, she would be found unacceptable in some way. The partner might now see her outside mask, but if he got too close and saw the way she really lived, if he saw the real mess, he'd see how difficult any life together would be. She may feel that if this side of her were revealed, she would be so unacceptable that he would ultimately reject her. It's easy to see how a woman who feels like this might keep a potential partner at arms' length. This harkens back to the deeply-ingrained feelings of shame from childhood that leave women believing that their "failure" to meet traditional role expectations, their discrepancies, so disproportionate to their abilities, are sufficient to wipe out all the good things they can bring to a partnership. They might believe that it would be so impossible for them to create a way of working it out or living together that they take themselves out of the running. It takes a long time to work toward this in a relationship when a woman has such depths of feelings about the personal way she lives. But once women integrate and accept these kinds of difficulties in themselves, they are able to work toward letting their partners know them fully and allowing other people to help them.

Caretaking Partners

Both women and men with AD/HD will sometimes find that they have unconsciously chosen partners who function as caretakers. These partners structure and organize their lives for them so much that these AD/HD adults might not even hit an "organizational wall" until something happens to disturb this relationship. If the woman herself doesn't understand the actual, real-life functions that the partner has been providing, it will be very difficult for a mental health professional who might be working with her to understand what seems like an intense overreaction to the loss of the relationship. The loss of a caretaking relationship for an AD/HD adult, then, involves more than the "normal" sense of loss at the end of a relationship. In her case, the vital structures of daily life are disrupted.

Of course, this kind of caretaking can cross the line into dependency and co-dependency. It's critical when getting the help she needs from her partner that a woman doesn't accept what I call "toxic help" along with the assistance and that she doesn't give away too much of her sense of power and control. When this partnership works well, it can help a person achieve and get the kind of coaching functions they need from their spouse. It can also, though, overprotect them for so many years that they develop a sense of incompetence and set them up for a huge fall if something disrupts the relationship.

Controlling Partners

Another form of intimate relationships involve controlling partners who are drawn to a woman who feels that she is floundering around with no sense of internal structure. Someone who can provide a strong structure may seem quite attractive. This can work up to a point if a partner is able to provide firm limits and structure or is very systematic and organized. The danger is that he might cross the line to become controlling and dominating. A woman might get involved with someone who's organized to the point of being obsessive-compulsive and who, because he can't tolerate her disorganization might be abusive or subtly put her down. As we saw with the caretaking partner, both of these kinds of partnerships can work up to a point, as long as the interactions remain positive, complementary, and consciously worked out.

Summary

Living with AD/HD has a great effect on every area of a woman's life, especially her intimate partners, friendships and relationships with family members. When trying to understand Jodi, Lucy, and women like them with undiagnosed AD/HD, it is important to remember that almost all women, not only women with AD/HD, have difficulties meeting the complicated demands of today's world. For the women with untreated AD/HD, however, the demands of daily life can be crippling to their self-esteem, families, work, and relationships. With undiagnosed and untreated AD/HD, there will be some serious effect somewhere in their lives, even if it's invisible and/or hidden. They don't always talk about it. Only those closest to them may know the level of difficulty they confront each day of their lives. In the next chapter, we will examine the meaning of these experiences on a woman's developing self-concept.

CHAPTER FOUR

"Who Am I?" and "What's the Matter with Me?"

The Impact on a Woman's Developing Self-Image

Let's think back and consider the development of that little girl growing up undiagnosed with such a puzzling array of attributes and experiences. One of the most basic areas of impact from these kinds of childhood experiences is on a woman's self-image. She often wonders, "Who am I? Am I smart or am I dumb? Am I talented and creative or incompetent? Am I successful and interesting or immature and childish? Warm or intrusive?" These women often have difficulty developing a cohesive self-picture that makes sense because as they grow, the pieces just don't fit together.

As you see in this picture of the Mona Lisa, the pieces that make up her self-picture don't always fit together easily or naturally. Usually other people without these kinds of wide ranges in abilities go through life unconsciously putting together a picture of who they are, formed from their experiences. These experiences make sense to some extent; they're in a range that isn't out of the ordinary. Most people have some successes and some failures as they go through life. They develop some abilities, and they notice some difficulties in other areas, but for the most part their experiences fall within a fairly narrow range. They might not be exceptionally gifted, but they aren't way off the scale in the other direction either. A person with AD/HD might have a wider range between their weaknesses and abilities.

As the non-AD/HD person continues on through life, the pieces continue to make sense. They don't get A's one day, and F's the next; they aren't called creative one day and lazy, unmotivated, and irresponsible the next. When people without these difficulties try to do something, their efforts usually pay off. In other words, there's a direct relationship between the effort and the results. This is because they have the necessary underlying, supportive organizational skills that help them pull it all together. This allows them to translate their ideas or abilities into the real world. They can then communicate those ideas cohesively to other people.

Because their discrepancies are much larger, people with hidden disorders are confusing to themselves and perplexing to other people. Because their range can be very wide, individuals can't easily encompass and incorporate both their strengths and their weaknesses into their self-image. This is especially true before they know the nature of this challenge. On a day when things are going well, when they're "on," they may feel, and everyone else may think, that they are very competent or even talented. The next day, when a different kind of skill is called for and/or they're not "on," people might feel they have turned into selfish, preoccupied, unmotivated individuals. Have they suddenly become dumb, odd, hopelessly mean or controlling? If they only could just reach out and *embrace* both sides of themselves. Everybody could then perhaps see that they have both abilities and difficulties. Acceptance would be easier for themselves and others.

When someone is diagnosed with AD/HD as a child, it wreaks havoc in their lives because of school and relationships. There is still tremendous stress, and it still impacts self-esteem. But when it is explained and understood, at least it makes sense and is comprehensible.

The problem for women is that most of them were *not* diagnosed as children. Even if they were hyperactive, they usually did not act out in the same way that boys did. They were apt to be labeled tomboys or written off in some other way without understanding the underlying attention deficit disorder. And for those dreamy girls without hyperactivity, it was even less likely that they would come to anyone's attention. Parents and even professionals would not have any way to understand their subtle information processing problems, confusion, or disorganization. These women often grew up with absolutely no way to make sense of this baffling self-image. The wonderful pictures that they had inside didn't match the kind of reactions they got from the world. For them, these labels meant that no matter how much they tried, despite having equal abilities with other children, they weren't able to show what they really knew. Despite how hard they tried, they weren't able to measure up or please people.

A woman client tells of spending many Saturdays in her room as a child because she wasn't allowed to go out to play until she cleaned up her room. She knew she couldn't figure out how to clean up her room, but she couldn't figure out why she didn't know how. She just knew that for some reason she wasn't doing it, so she spent all day locked in her room, unable to go out to play until she finished her work, but . . . she couldn't finish her work.

The Inside and the Outside Don't Match

One beautiful woman I know said she feels like Pigpen with a little cloud of dirt around her all the time. This poignantly demonstrated to me the difficulty women have of integrating opposite images into one self-concept.

In addition to the gap between what you feel like inside and what other people see, there is also a gap between the ideas someone has inside and what one is able to verbally express. It is painful to have wonderful thoughts with no way to organize or express them. It is as if the ideas of these women are padlocked shut, like having a beautiful car but no keys and no gas—all dressed up and no place to go. Many of my clients express what one woman summed up as follows: "It's as though I have a symphony inside me, but all that comes out is a plunk on a broken-down old piano."

One more discrepancy in these women's lives is between their level of academic or professional achievement and how they carry out the details of daily life. *I once went over to a woman friend's house who was "AD/HD with a Ph.D." She was standing frozen in the middle of her room, staring blankly at a tangled web of clothes and clutter. She had absolutely no idea of how to proceed to clean up the room.* Another women client of mine has just passed all the requirements for her Master's degree, but she forgot to file the papers that would have allowed her to graduate. For all these women such difficulties often unfortunately wipe out any sense of their real achievements. As we'll see later, the goal for women is to understand and hold onto opposite ideas about themselves at the same time.

These problems are often invisible, and even when there are visible signs, the level of internal difficulty is invisible. Since it is the daily tasks that are hard for the AD/HD woman, the routine ones that no one likes to do, it's even more difficult for anyone to understand that this is more than what all women struggle with. Until recently, no one ever heard about the neurological issues that cause AD/HD symptoms. No matter what conventional advice she hears, she's still not able to maintain any semblance of order in her life. As long as there are no other answers out there, she will continue to feel depressed, hopeless and fall back into the three "I am's," described in the next section.

What's the Matter With Me?

By the time these women have grown up and lived without diagnosis for many years they have been asking themselves the question, *"What's the matter with me?"* for a long time. I call these negative self-labels that women often use to describe themselves the three "I am's."

1. I am incompetent

2. I am immature

3. I am an impostor

Let's examine these three basic areas.

I Am Incompetent

Women with these kinds of difficulties incredulously ask, *"How do other women do it?"* meaning life. They look at women who are able to lead regular, consistent lives as if they're from a different planet. They just can't fathom it. As Hallowell and Ratey say in *Answers to Distraction*, "They just don't have the equipment" because "the AD/HD brain lacks the internal organization that naturally leads most people to structure their lives." As one client of mine said when it finally dawned on her that her friend had free time on the weekends, "You mean this woman doesn't have six months worth of unfolded clothes piling up around the house? She doesn't have stacks of unopened mail to wade through or unpaid bills to confront? You mean she's not constantly worried that the phone or electricity will be turned off or that the rent check will bounce?" For these women, it's unimaginable that these things don't happen to other people. Unless and until they've truly integrated the belief that this is part of the AD/HD, that it is the way they're built, and this is part of a disorder, they will continue to feel very confused and attribute their difficulties to some immaturity or lack of character. Two reasons these women feel incompetent are as follows:

- They only compare themselves to non-AD/HD women

- They feel that there is absolutely no way they can keep up with the demands of life

We'll be looking at this more when we talk about the actual *Job Description for Women* in Chapter 6 when we see what a poor match it is for a woman with AD/HD.

I Am Immature

Many women ask, *"When will I ever feel grown up? When will I get over this? When will I stop being so irresponsible?"* They berate themselves because the discrepancies between their levels of abilities and their difficulties are so much larger than average. Despite great maturity and competence in other areas, some parts of their lives do match this same level. It is difficult to accept this in oneself or in one's partner as anything other than being stuck in childhood or still acting like a messy, irresponsible teenager. As we saw when we looked at the kind of discrepancies an individual with AD/HD struggles with, we can understand why it's so easy to attribute them to a character flaw, and not just by others, but more significantly, by adults with AD/HD themselves. Even after diagnosis, without successful treatment these kinds of negative self-concepts are difficult to erase.

I once heard Dr. Ned Hallowell say that he doesn't think that balancing your checkbook should be the measure of whether you're mentally healthy. In the same way, I feel that women have to understand that being able to keep your house a certain way or staying organized a certain way isn't the sign of whether you're grown up or mature. Is it a sign of maturity to be able to see if you're blind or walk if you have a broken leg?

One professional woman said in an interview, *"I feel like a stupid jerk. I feel like a two-year-old."* She berates herself with criticism for not being able to manage the details of her household or her business anywhere close to the way her other friends or associates do. She asks herself the questions, *"Why can't I get it together? Why am I so undisciplined? Why do I say I'm going to do something and then can't do it?*

I Am an Impostor

Many women feel that no matter how competent others think they are, or no matter how much they achieve, they are really just fooling everyone. This stems partly from the large disparity between their inner and outer worlds. Other people often see the *real* competence of these adults but don't see the conflict inside. They don't see the "mess" in other areas of their lives or how hard it is to achieve that outer picture. These women often believe they are fooling anyone who thinks well of them because without any warning the switch inside their heads could turn off and their feelings of inadequacy would be exposed. They worry that they won't have enough time, that their systems won't work, or that people will drop in unexpectedly. Any minute things could fall apart.

This accounts for the sense of impending doom that often is reported. Even if the achievement for these women is real, it feels tenuous and scary to them; they still feel like impostors. One person describes this inner/outer disparity as *"the counters are all clean, but the inside of the drawers are a mess."* This is a great metaphor for the exteriors that women often present while experiencing the interior feeling of messiness, disorder, and confusion. Instead of taking credit for their "clean counters," they just feel that it's a cover. Even when they do take a risk, and let down their mask by letting people know what's going on inside, they are met with disbelief, invalidation, or ridicule. *The irony is that the more they achieve and the better they do, the less people are inclined to believe them, and the more they feel forced to then stay in the closet.*

Unsolved Mysteries

Throughout their lives, these women cope, compensate, and unconsciously devise ways to get by, to cover up, and to keep their heads above water. They don't even know they are doing it. They cut back on sleep, on friends, fun, or achievement. If they do go ahead and socialize or work, they then cover up what a toll it's taking. They often have an exquisite sense of not belonging, of hiding, pretending, and waiting to be discovered. *They are trying to solve a mystery without knowing what they're trying to solve.* Even the ones who do it best and longest—well compensated, often self-medicated adults—eventually hit a wall, physically or emotionally. They may eventually seek and accept psychological explanations for their difficulties. They either get help at that point, sink more and more into depression, or become determined to use more will power.

Trying Harder

- *I'm just going to try harder*
- *I'm going to go home and DO it this time*
- *I'm going to clean that desk*
- *I'm going to get through those piles*
- *I'm going to be on time this week*
- *I'm going to balance my checkbook every month*
- *I'm going to maintain those systems*

They are determined to work harder. They are trying to solve the problem in the same old way, but when this doesn't work, it can become demoralizing and debilitating. Remember, it's not that these women *can't* do the same things that other women do, or that they don't have the ability, it's just that they can't do it *and* also lead a regular, balanced life without a tremendous strain on their resources, without staying up to all hours of the night, without sacrificing all their free time.

Some of these women's lives are spent "secretly organizing," just the way some people secretly eat or drink. They often feel that their dilemma is deciding between two equally bad choices. The first is to tell or to hide and the second is to achieve or not to achieve.

To Tell or Not to Tell

To Tell

If they stop hiding and let more of their disorganization show, they will get written off as spacey and irresponsible. They fear they won't be taken seriously and will be judged by their exterior difficulties rather than the strength of their ideas.

To Not Tell

On the other hand, they can hide. This means many extra hours working behind the scenes with a tremendous toll on their time and energy.

To Be or Not To Be

The other way women feel trapped between two bad choices has to do with their own achievement and ambitions.

To Be

One choice is to give up trying to control the uncontrollable and instead try to maintain a higher level of achievement and self-focus. Unfortunately, this then often creates chaos for themselves and those around them. If they focus on their own strengths without the structure and support of coaching or organizational assistance and have not yet accepted or understood their difficulties, chaos will reign and overwhelm them, ultimately destroying their feelings of success. It feels like a terrible trap because they perceive the other choice as holding themselves back as described below.

Not to Be

With this choice, they *cut back* on their ambitions and achievements or give up the idea altogether in order to try to control the demands coming at them fast and furious. They give up the idea of focusing on themselves because it seems like an impossibility given the fact that they can't even keep up with the demands of daily life. So they spend their lives focusing on the routine tasks, which is actually the "hard stuff" for them. They wait to get that under control before they move ahead and attend to their own needs or their own lives. But that's not possible without somehow changing strategies because they're focusing on their areas of difficulty rather than focusing on their strengths. Without some help, they will never get things under control and focus on their strengths. This is the treadmill from which they can't get off.

Other Options

Women with AD/HD don't have to make these impossible choices. Later in the book, in parts three and four, we will examine the process whereby a woman begins to expand her sense of choice, options, and control.

So far, we have discussed the feelings of *internal* disorganization. In the next chapter, we will take a look at how disorganization manifests externally—in other words, we'll take a deeper look at the mess, the piles, and the clutter.

CHAPTER FIVE

The Disorder of Dis-order
Understanding Disorganization

"Disorganization causes the gifted and the well-motivated to fail. . . . It takes many forms and invades every aspect of daily life. It is pernicious. It is self-perpetuating. It builds on itself, and it dooms fine minds to menial work."

This is how Sally Smith, in *Succeeding Against the Odds* (1991, pg. 86) describes the effects of disorganization. In one form or another, disorganization is the subject that women with AD/HD talk about the most in counseling, either the stress of living with it, strategies for dealing with it, or the emotions surrounding it.

It is important to take an in-depth look at disorganization as it will help us understand how the experiences of women with AD/HD collide with cultural expectations for women. We will see that the real-life effect of the primary symptoms of AD/HD is often disorganization, which leads to many of the internal conflicts and feelings of failure for women. With disorganization as their constant companion, further emotional complications result for women as they go through life.

Listen to how some people have described their everyday struggles with disorganization and the level of difficulty with which they are coping:

- *"I disorganize so quickly. I turn around after a few minutes, look back at the kitchen I just walked out of and see all the drawers and cabinets open, the milk carton still left out on the counter. And I have no idea how it happened. People think I'm doing this on purpose or I just don't care."*

40

- *"I spend ninety percent of my time looking for things."*

- *"They tell me to get a planner. I have twenty of them and can't find any of them."*

- *"They say to make lists. I have hundreds of notes scribbled on pieces of paper. I find them in my pockets, everywhere."*

Disorganization is a severely misunderstood and underestimated problem in the lives of millions of people. Every single thing in life takes organization from doing the dishes and organizing your bills or your social life to getting through the day on time and organizing your grocery list. Equally important is the ability to organize your thoughts and ideas such as when writing a report or holding your own in an argument.

Disorganization Affects Cognitive Abilities as Well as the Physical Environment

Without good organizational skills, it is easy to accumulate a huge amount of clutter, which can overwhelm you by the end of the day. Poor organizational skills, combined with the extra ideas that the AD/HD mind generates, exacerbate the problem into one of constant expansion rather than pulling things together and controlling them.

Remember again, these are not ordinary difficulties with disorganization. These are severe and chronic difficulties. And they are inconsistent. They enter a person's life in a pervasive, invasive, and insidious way. The ease with which other people organize just isn't part of an AD/HD adult's wiring. Dale Jordan, Ph.D., says in his book, *Attention Deficit Disorder*, that disorganization is the "earmark of AD/HD in adults." (pg. 25)

Disorganization isn't a disorder worth getting treatment for unless it's creating serious problems or consequences in your life. That's how we distinguish it from creative or busy people who have these problems but aren't bothered by them to the same extent. For people with AD/HD, it's causing serious problems, impacting their ability to achieve their goals or to have any time for friends or family or serious relationships; it's seriously affecting their mood or self-esteem.

For a person with these difficulties, there is a constant drain on their resources of time and energy, often to the exclusion of the rest of life. A simple ten-minute task, with no emotional component (such as washing the dishes) turns into a long, drawn-out affair for the AD/HD individual. Besides taking up valuable time, it can also contribute to a sense of emotional overload. Even women with AD/HD who say they are very organized are often obsessively so. These people are still centering their entire lives around the effort to "keep it all together," knowing if they let up on their vigilance in this area, they will be lost, like a blind person groping in the dark. For these women (and men) who must have everything in place to function, disorganization is still taking a toll on their lives, as the imbalance of focus on this area keeps them away from other creative, productive, or recreational pursuits.

My Left Hand

During the initial writing of this book, I hurt my left hand and had to wear a brace. People were solicitous and sympathetic, constantly asking if I needed any help. This was startling to me because it was nothing compared to my AD/HD and my organizational problems. The solution to this physical problem was simple—I just didn't use my left hand. But I can't just "not use" part of my brain. I can't just say, "Well, today, I'll just leave that part of my brain out of things." Not using my left hand was inconvenient, but people obviously understood there was something physical that I couldn't do. There was no self-recrimination or hiding. No emotion was attached to it. Again, it was nothing compared to the invisible disorder I can never get away from.

Organization affects everything you do, say, and think. It doesn't matter how many creative ideas one has if they can't organize them or communicate them. It permeates every moment of your life. There is no getting away from it.

Do You Suffer from TMS—Time, Money, and Stuff?

When I talk about disorganization, I mean a variety of things for a variety of people. For women as well as men, time, money, and stuff can dominate their lives, impacting their abilities to achieve their goals and feel like mature individuals.

Time

"Time is just a white, wide open empty space with no markers and no way to know how to piece it out." You may have more trouble with

time than stuff, as the above quote expresses, feeling that there is no way to proceed successfully through your day. This obviously affects arriving on time, as well as short- and long-term planning. It also affects prioritizing and sequencing your day, week, and month. Not being able to plan one's day effectively can be very demoralizing. Poor time management adds a great deal of effort to any project and obviously reduces the odds of finishing a project at all. Even if the project is finally finished, and even if it's on time, the process you have had to go through to accomplish this may be filled with anxiety and tremendous stress. It can create an atmosphere of chaos, negatively affecting families or co-workers, as well as taking a toll in other areas.

Problems with time can seriously affect relationships and jobs. For instance, if you are chronically late for either personal appointments or work responsibilities, it sends the unintentional message that you are not taking a person or a job seriously.

It is like traveling on a long journey with no road map or like walking on a balance beam, one foot in front of the other, having to consciously and carefully plan the placement of each foot, monitoring the placement of each step for fear of falling off. It can be done, but it is painfully slow.

Money

You may also experience difficulty with controlling and keeping track of *money*. For instance, the boring routine and attention to detail of balancing your checkbook makes this a task that many with AD/HD just don't do. Combined with the impulsivity of overspending or overcharging on credit cards, this can leave you with a chronic feeling of being immature and out of control. *"My bills are in unopened piles all over the place. I live with the constant feeling that the gas and electric will be turned off any moment."*

As anxiety mounts, even less attention is given to this area, creating a dead end cycle of avoidance and disorganization. This eventually results in real-life problems, such as shutoffs, final notices, and bad credit. It also creates problems with relationships and trust.

Even today with most women working, even women without AD/HD have issues around money and taking care of their financial affairs. They aren't as knowledgeable about financial matters as they'd like to be and often have control, power, and dependency issues. Combine this with AD/HD and feelings of being overwhelmed, and it creates an even greater tendency to shut down and tune out in this area.

Stuff

For some, disorganization is centered around *physical stuff* such as papers, books, files, dishes, boxes, clothes, common physical objects that you come in contact with. This leads to a basic sense of confusion and of feeling trapped, almost as if your hands were tied together. Your life is haunted by Disney-like, animated pieces of "stuff." People describe it as surreal or Kafka-esque. You may feel that you are bombarded by "billions" of things that you can't control.

"I look down at my feet after a couple minutes of sitting in a room, and I see papers and all sorts of stuff accumulated in disarray, a mess all around me. How does this happen? Why doesn't it happen to other people? It's embarrassing."

"We have to just push all the stuff and papers to one side of the table to eat."

I've heard many people express frustration that they "disorganize quickly." Other people in their environment might ask, "Why do you leave everything open? Why don't you put things back?" They don't understand that it was not a conscious decision. People with AD/HD say that they have no idea what has happened, or how it has happened, until they turn around and see that all the cupboards are open, that they've left out all the food and milk, and that there are things dropped on the floor.

Why Do People With AD/HD Have Organizational Difficulties?

The reasons adults with AD/HD have difficulty with disorganization goes to the core of AD/HD. We will look at these in a few different ways because some of you may think of your challenges in one way whereas some of you may have a different name for the same kind of struggle. There is much overlap between different ways of thinking about your particular difficulties or categorizing symptoms.

In the following sections, we will look at how problems with executive functioning, problems related to regulating attention, activity and impulses as well as cognitive differences and processing speed can lead to organizational problems. These can be with time, money, and stuff as we just talked about but also can also lead to great difficulties with organizing, expressing, and storing ideas.

Executive Functioning

In the fall 1999 issue of *Focus Magazine*, Thomas Brown, Ph.D., from the Department of Psychiatry at Yale University, said that current research is recognizing impairments of *executive functions* as a core problem of AD/HD. He explained: "Executive functions are management functions of the brain. They activate, regulate, and integrate a wide variety of other mental functioning. An individual's ability to perform many important daily tasks of school, work, family and social interaction may be markedly impaired relative to others of the same age and mental development. While everyone has problems sometimes, AD/HD adults have significant chronic impairments that are persistent and more pervasive than their peers" Brown identifies functions that are affected by this impairment in executive functioning as "severe difficulty in mobilizing and sustaining their attention, alertness, effort, and working memory functions for less interesting, though important tasks."

These problems, as Brown describes them, have to do with activation, (the ability to organize your brain to begin to work), distraction (the ability to sustain attention on tasks), and effort (the ability to maintain energy, alertness, and processing speed). Difficulty with sustaining focus when affected by emotions such as frustration and difficulties with working memory and recall also are components of executive function.

Activation

Some individuals with AD/HD, especially without hyperactivity, have an activation problem as described by Thomas Brown, Ph.D. in his article *AD/HD without Hyperactivity* (1993). Rather than a *deficit* of attention, this means that individuals can't deploy attention, direct it, or put it in the right place at the right time. He explains that adults who do not have hyperactivity often have severe difficulty activating enough to start a task and sustaining the energy to complete it. This is especially true for low-interest activities.

Often it means that they can't think of what to do so they might not be able to act at all, or, as Kate Kelly and Peggy Ramundo say in *You Mean I'm Not Lazy, Stupid or Crazy?!* (1995), they might experience a "paralysis of will" (pg. 65).

"The clothes from my trip—a month ago—are just still lying in a heap in the suitcase."

"I spend a lot of time in bed watching TV but my mind isn't watching TV. I'm thinking about what I should be doing, but I don't have the energy to do it."

Sequencing, Prioritizing, Planning, and Categorizing

You can imagine the great impact that problems with sequencing, prioritizing, remembering where you put needed materials, starting to work, and finishing up a project would have on maintaining an organized life. Putting things in piles results from the fear that you won't find them if you file them, that they will disappear into a "black hole" without this needed trigger for your memory. The build up and accumulation of stuff just adds to the confusion of knowing where to begin and how to proceed, which leads to frustration and more disorganization.

Turning your attention to very small categories is difficult and frustrating for many AD/HD adults. It is problematic to process all the information that comes into a household and put it into the right places, particularly with sorting and filing. Most of these chores fall to women, and most people do it more or less automatically. Adults with AD/HD don't. Kelly and Ramundo (1995) attribute this in part to AD/HD adults' tendency to consider a multitude of options that make these small distinctions incredibly difficult.

"I am an executive at a large company where I must excel at long-term strategic planning. My husband doesn't believe me when I find it agonizing to have to sort the newspapers, bottles and cans for recycling."

Many people have difficulty figuring out what the next step in a task or project should be or how to plan. They may look at the whole picture but don't know how to proceed with a job. They just can't figure out a good plan of attack (*executive functioning problems*).

"I get up in the morning with no idea how to choose from what seems like millions of possibilities of things I need to do, how to organize my day . . . so I just sit there. My non-AD/HD husband tells me how to clean the kitchen after a meal. First, put all the perishables in the refrigerator. Then you put away any other food in the pantry. Then you throw out everything that can go into the trash. Then you stack dishes and glasses together. Then you clean out the sink. At that point, you start rinsing the dishes, stacking them again in categories before you put them into the dishwasher."

This is how non-AD/HD people do tasks and organize their lives. This is exactly what an AD/HD person has such difficulty with. To them, life contains millions of equal stimuli, with no order, no categories, and no priority. Finding a particular bill or matching pair of earrings could be as baffling and frustrating as writing a report. It's all the same."

Visual Memory: Loose, Shifting Mental Images

Dr. Dale Jordan in *Attention Deficit Disorder* describes in depth some of the reasons for disorganization in adults with AD/HD. He uses phrases throughout like "they can't maintain organized mental images. . . . Their mental impressions change immediately. . . . They have loose internal patterns . . . the brain [of the AD/HD adult] does not maintain an organized impression of time, space or things within a given space." Even if these people have the activation needed to organize, they often can't remember where things go or how things should look. Some people don't have a strong image in their mind, which would allow them to put an object back in a particular place or in a particular way. Forgetting where things are can be extremely frustrating as one goes on a wild goose chase, wasting time looking for earrings, stockings, belts, notebooks, or keys.

"I have a Ph.D., but I can't figure out how to clean my closet. I just stand there and stare at it. I don't remember where things go or what to do. I get so confused and overwhelmed."

In *You Mean I'm Not Lazy, Stupid or Crazy?!*, (1995), Kate Kelly and Peggy Ramundo discuss the impact on organization from what they call "the erratic [memory] storage system" in AD/HD individuals (pg. 282). They emphasize that in order to organize one must first be able to remember where one's belongings are and then be able to figure out what to do with them. They talk about the spatial problems often associated with AD/HD and point out that even when AD/HD adults have the motivation and slow down enough to confront their organizational tasks, they often "face the nightmarish task of figuring out what to do with his/her chaotic surroundings" (pg. 60).

In addition, associated motor difficulties such as bumping into or dropping things often creates more mess in the process of trying to clean up than existed before. Kelly and Ramundo (1995) also speak about a "distorted sense of how one's body moves in space in relationship to other objects' (pg. 60). This can add to the organizational difficulties of individuals with AD/HD.

The Traditional Triad

Before discussion emerged about executive functioning, people traditionally thought about AD/HD as problems with three different areas: attention, impulsivity, and activity levels. Let's take at look at it from this framework to understand the relationship between these symptoms and disorganization.

Attention

Difficulty Focusing on Routine Tasks

People with AD/HD need *high levels of stimulation in order to focus.* The brain's neurotransmitters, those information messengers, aren't functioning efficiently or consistently. It is during these routine tasks without any high stimulation that one becomes day-dreamy, unfocused, and unproductive. Susan's story emphasizes this.

Years ago, before Susan was diagnosed, she lived in a house with an apple tree in the back yard. Every autumn the apples would fall off the tree, and Susan's family would have to pick them up or they would rot on the ground. (She wasn't the type that looked forward to this—picking up the apples, making apple sauce, canning them for the winter—very un-AD/HD-like activity). Her husband insisted at least for the sake of the neighbors that they pick them up. It was torture for her. She was slow, upset from the second they started, and obviously non-productive. This became an annual source of conflict between them.

Tasks like this with very little external stimulation or structure create a situation, which can be of extremely low interest to the individual. This is where medication can often be very helpful. It turns on the brain and helps one focus when there isn't anything externally exciting going on.

Inability to Filter Out Distractions

For people with AD/HD, this often means that there is not an effective filtering system with which to block out all the internal thoughts and external stimuli. The result is that you feel bombarded by excess information: this includes sounds, smells, noises, movement, and even internal ideas. Between work life and home life, things can mount so much that it feels like a tornado inside your head. The distractions at work can increase so much that you may be trying to catch up on office work at home. But being at home is filled with such distractions, especially with children in the house, that not only does the extra work from the job not get done, but the household work isn't accomplished either. You can see how this could lead to another overwhelming sea of distress.

"When I'm inside my house, it's like I'm right in the middle of a busy street. Each noise from down the block throws me off. If I have a thought and then the phone rings, I'm lost. Each tick of the clock drives me over the edge. People say, 'Just ignore it,' but I can't block it out."

"I was in Atlantic City for a conference. I had to keep taking time out to go back to my room so I could get away . . . from the noise, the clicking, the coins; I was ready to lose it. It was a nightmare."

For women with AD/HD, every day feels like the height of the Christmas season: the kinds of stress and demands that all women report this time of year are just regular days in the lives of AD/HD women.

Impulsivity: Excessive Shifting of Attention or Activities

In a woman's home there are so many distractions, choices, and variables, so many things to grab one's attention that it can be difficult to pick out the most important thing to do first. It leads to tremendous inefficiency. Many women just can't figure out the proper sequence of events in order to accomplish a task.

"I start out to straighten the house, but I notice we are out of towels so I go downstairs to get some more, and I forget why I'm there when I reach the bottom of the stairs, but I notice my shoes so I take them upstairs to the bedroom, and then I see the travel article open on the bed because I wanted to plan a trip and since I remember now about the deadline, I go to find the travel agent's number, but I am confronted by a mass of papers and scribbled illegible numbers so I start to dig around, and then I see the bills I haven't paid and think maybe I should go buy some stamps, but I remember I don't have any gas, and I can't find my keys. . . ."

"I just wander around all day, it seems. I don't get anything done. I just move things from one place to another."

Activity Regulation

Even though traditionally thought of as problems with hyperactivity, many adults with ADHD struggle with just the opposite, *hypo activity*. Both ends of this deregulated spectrum impact challenges around organization because a woman is either speeding from one activity or thought to another, or she is too slowed down to carry out the tasks before her.

Cognitive Challenges

In addition to visible disorganization, an individual with AD/HD often has extreme difficulties with internal organization, especially ideas. Taking in information, organizing and storing ideas, and expressing them efficiently can be a struggle that consumes a great deal of time and energy.

At the 1995 National Attention Deficit Disorder Association (ADDA) Conference, Tom Brown, Ph.D. emphasized that AD/HD causes significant but subtle diverse cognitive impairments. In Chapter 6 on women in *Answers to Distraction*, Drs. Hallowell and Ratey also point to subtle information processing problems in women with AD/HD. Let's look at some of the ways women with AD/HD may be impacted by these cognitive challenges that further increase their disorganization.

Synthesizing Ideas

For many people, trying to find the ideas inside their head that they need for a particular purpose can be as difficult as finding papers on a messy desk. Many creative people with AD/HD find it difficult to pull all their ideas together in an organized, logical, linear manner, especially in written form. Many have an extremely difficult time creating structure or a skeleton on which to build their ideas, thus leading many to overwork. They often have to spend many more hours behind the scenes to pull together what is usually an excellent product. The level of difficulty involved is way out of proportion to the person's ideas or ability to address the subject. It's as if they have to go through many more cognitive processes to arrive at the end product. For example, a very bright young woman in college reports that she spent fifty hours to produce a five-page paper. This kind of difficulty is something I often hear reported by bright individuals with AD/HD.

There is often a limitless drive for information that leads to feeling overwhelmed because the person cannot organize the amount of material that they can generate mentally. This seems to come both from being unable to ignore any idea or connection that they make in their minds as well as a need (which I have observed) to understand the whole of a subject before they can understand any part of it.

Often AD/HD people just need a "bridge over troubled waters"—a coach, a partner, or a professional—to help them structure their day and pick out a few things to focus on. Without that small bridge, they're trapped hopelessly alone on the other side of an island, not even knowing that they can signal for help. We will look at this need to ask for help in more detail later in the book.

Next we will examine the "jobs" our culture requires of women in the course of a regular day and the expectations that even the most "liberated" women have internalized and hold sacred. We will look at the effect of disorganization on a woman as she tries to live up to this cultural ideal.

For good resources on organizing from an AD/HD perspective see the resource section in the back of the book

PART II

HIDING

CHAPTER SIX

The Job from Hell

A Woman's Job Description

Can you imagine finding the following ad in your local newspaper?

"Woman wanted to coordinate multiple schedules in an unstructured, distracting atmosphere. Must be able to process great numbers of details quickly and maintain a neat, well-organized environment. Must keep track of all important occasions, including social obligations, birthday cards, and thank you notes, as well as be responsible for all subtleties and niceties of life. Must be able to choose quickly and easily from a great number of options. Applicant will be responsible for all recordkeeping and for maintenance of all systems in the organization, as well as the upkeep on all equipment. For those interested, please call 911-N-O-T-A-D-H-D."

Even today, there still exists an unwritten job description for women both at home and at work that requires great organizational skills. These job expectations create an internalized image of the "culturally ideal woman." Difficulty in matching this "ideal image" continually confronts the AD/HD woman leading to frustration and failure on a daily basis. This makes it difficult for her to be assertive or to ask for what she considers to be "special" help. All women are exposed to and often struggle with these expectations, but for AD/HD women, whose difficulties form the very basis of these expectations, the problems are compounded and intensified.

We have looked at the various symptoms of AD/HD and traced the development of the inner world of the AD/HD girl growing up into a woman. Now we will place that woman in the middle of the cultural context in which she lives each day. We will see how AD/HD symptoms and disorganization collide with the role expectations for women in our culture.

Why AD/HD Impacts Women Differently Than Men

Men with AD/HD face their own painful challenges and struggles in not meeting cultural expectations, for example, of being the stable, solid, breadwinner in the household. Below is a list of some of the ways AD/HD impacts women differently than men.

Women tend to:

- *Have more varied responsibilities and tasks from different areas of their lives to coordinate and organize*

- *Be more diffuse and have multiple role conflicts and more distractions*

- *Have more of the responsibilities for structuring the daily lives of their children (who often also have AD/HD)*

WHY ADD IMPACTS WOMEN DIFFERENTLY THAN MEN

- Women have more tasks to do.
- Women's lives are often more diffuse.
- Women with children have more responsibilities.
- Men more often have partners who organize their lives.
- Men more often have secretaries or other assistants organizing them.
- Men are often encouraged to focus on a narrow area.
- Men don't feel the same sense of shame about their disorganization.
- Men with the same difficulties are more often seen as endearing or absent-minded.

Men tend to:

- *Have wives or partners who organize their personal lives*

- *Have secretaries or other assistants organizing them at work*

- *Be encouraged from an early age to focus on a narrow area of strength and to pursue that*

- *Not feel the same sense of shame about their disorganization because they have not internalized these organizational cultural expectations to the same extent as women. As a result, they ask for help more easily, which allows them to focus on their talents and abilities*

- *Men with the same difficulties are more often seen as endearing or absent-minded whereas women with these difficulties are seen by themselves and the external world as defective or deficient in some basic way*

The Ideal Candidate

Upon calling for more information about the job posting (at the beginning of the chapter), you might receive a more detailed description of the ideal candidate as follows. "Much of the work is boring and routine so applicant must be able to function well without needing high level of interest or stimulation. Appearance is important; applicant must have a variety of well-coordinated outfits. This job requires keeping up the appearance and maintenance of the building as well as attending to the subtle details in order to make the surroundings attractive for others. This position involves a great deal of entertaining so one must know the socially correct things to say at all times. Must excel at small talk, never interrupting or saying the wrong thing at the wrong time, never going blank, and always remembering people's faces and names. One must be able to converse on a variety of topics, remembering details from movies and plays, and of course be well read and able to comfortably discuss both the recent bestsellers in fiction and nonfiction, as well as the current political situation.

It is also important to not be reactive to people but instead to maintain a calm demeanor. The position may include the opportunity to care for children who have severe problems with attention and behavior. It could require the ability to be able to carefully structure their lives in order to give them the calm, supportive, organized atmosphere they need. The candidate will be held accountable for the children's success.

Finally, the perfect candidate for the job will go above and beyond the actual performance of the tasks themselves and be an example to others of how best to perform these particular tasks. Slow, careful folding of napkins would be applauded. Enjoying grocery shopping, carefully picking the best vegetables, and finely chopping them would be most preferred. Of course, excellent calendar and scheduling skills would be most appropriate. We also prefer that you never say no to requests from volunteer organizations, charitable events, or, of course, friends or family. It will be important to attend as many of these organizational meetings as possible. Merit raises will be given to those who spend no time on themselves, and instead focus all their time and energy on others. Going that extra mile means always saying yes and not asking for special favors. You must know how to cope and get by and certainly keep any difficulties to yourself."

Would anyone with AD/HD (or even without for that matter) deliberately apply for a job like this? Of course not. Yet women with AD/HD cling steadfastly to this image and often remain determined to achieve this ideal standard.

Summary of a Woman's Basic Job Description

- Multiple task coordinator
- Central household information coordinator
- Household maintenance manager (responsible for creating a comfortable and attractive home atmosphere)
- Bill payer
- Budgeter
- Housecleaner
- Cook
- Time Manager and Scheduler
- Event Planner (manager and staff)
- Grocery shopper
- Clothes shopper

- Clothes coordinating
- Social Coordinator and Hostess
- Packer for trips
- Travel Coordinator
- Interior Designer
- Holiday Coordinator
- President of the Social Occasion Obligations Club
- Secretary of the "Hallmark" committee (responsible for getting the right card to the right person at the right time)
- Chairman of the "Volunteer" committee
- Coach and organizer for children with AD/HD
- Charter Member of the "Welcome Wagon" ("We willingly open our doors to friends and neighbors.")
- Household "Mood" Engineer (setting the emotional temperature of the household)

All this is often in addition to working outside the home all day!

The job description of running a home and family requires multiple task coordination that can be disastrous for women with AD/HD. You can see that such expectations bring them right up against their areas of deficit that we described previously. As Lynn Weiss, Ph.D. says in her book *Attention Deficit Disorder in Adults* (1992, pg. 119) "an ordinary day for a woman is a nightmare for a woman with AD/HD". Kathleen Nadeau, Ph.D., psychologist, author, and international expert on women AD/HD, says that mothers with AD/HD "may be viewed by others as a 'bad mother' rather than as struggling valiantly with demands which are difficult if not impossible to meet." (ADDA, 1995)

Feelings of Failure

These are the three main parts of the *job description* in which women experience feelings of failure: 1) performing and conforming to role expectations, 2) identifying themselves as women, and 3) fulfilling their role as partner and mother.

Feelings of Failure to Perform and Conform to Role Expectations

Whether a woman is married and/or taking care of children at home and/or working at an outside job and/or is single and trying to keep up with the demands of a social life, women with AD/HD often express feelings of failure to perform and conform to job expectations. *Dorothy really loved staying home and taking care of her four children, but she was not able to take care of her domestic responsibilities anywhere near to the level required. The distractions were overwhelming, and she could not filter out the multiple demands on her attention to attend to cooking or cleaning while the children were present. She asks poignantly, "Why am I a failure at the one thing I want to do?"*

Another example comes from Joan, a single woman, who says, "My friends don't understand why I'm so exhausted and overwhelmed after working all day that I can't go out with them at night. I don't really understand it, either. What's the matter with me?"

Feelings of Failure in Feminine Identity

The feelings that women often express about the impact of these failings go to the very heart of their identity as women. Compounded over a lifetime, these experiences of failure in this role have a great effect on their sense of "femininity." As one client said to me, *"I can't make small talk or shop. These are two things that make me feel that I'm not like a woman."*

A beautiful young client named Lani also expressed this feeling of not being feminine. Because accessorizing, coordinating, and dressing in the morning were such chores, she always chose very basic clothes. This interfered with the full and natural expression of her personality, coloring her self-perception for many years.

For Nancy, going to the grocery store often made her feel like ducking for cover from all the stimulation and choices. Going to a department store where she was confronted by piano players, flashy displays, and a dizzying array of colors, fragrances, and choices was even worse.

Nancy has a very difficult time trying to hold in her mind what she needs to in order coordinate an entire outfit. She often just wanders around department stores for hours, leaving without accomplishing anything. Not only does she feel that she has wasted time and doesn't have anything to wear, but most importantly she feels like an abysmal failure—a woman who can't even buy an outfit, let alone enjoy it in the way that other women seem to do.

Feelings of Failure as Partner or Mother

Rose was in tears as she asked me, "Aren't wives supposed to take care of the couple's social life, like setting up dates with other couples? I'm afraid my husband will leave me eventually because I don't perform these basic kinds of functions. I just can't keep up with all of that."

An accomplished professional woman, Rose admitted with a painful sense of "confession" her profound feelings of failure in her role as a wife and her fears that she is unacceptable to her husband, almost as if she had betrayed him. Even though her husband says he doesn't care about her role as social organizer, she still has managed to have received this message from the world around her. She constantly observes how other women manage their lives and perform these roles well or at least adequately.

Parenting raises a whole host of other problems for women trying to fulfill their basic role expectations, especially when this involves structuring the life of an AD/HD child. More specific suggestions for approaching this will be explored later in the section on the Three R's. For now, we can begin to appreciate the huge collision that results when the woman with AD/HD is confronted with these parenting expectations.

Kay, a woman with AD/HD, had a son diagnosed with AD/HD and attended a meeting intended to help her provide proper structure at school and home. One of the goals was to make sure that her son, Mark, completed his homework every night. On the nights that it wasn't done and Mark went to school the next day with it uncompleted, Kay was the one who felt responsible for this failure. Kay was the one whom the teacher confronted with the "bad news" at the end of the day when she came to pick Mark up. Kay's husband, Jerry, didn't feel the shame, embarrassment, frustration, or daily stress of completing that homework, even though he didn't have AD/HD and might have helped Mark more easily. Mark certainly didn't feel the pressure of not getting the homework done either. Kay, who had extreme difficulties with organizing her own life, became driven to the exclusion of all else to get that homework done so that she could avoid a negative report from the teacher each day. She wound up being responsible for the homework and basically took over emotional ownership of this task. Obviously, the result was overload in an already overtaxed area of operation.

Women's (Unspoken) Job Descriptions at Work

Even at work, women face their own particular difficulties. While sometimes it is easier for women with AD/HD to be more successful at work than at home because there are fewer distractions and they are able to zero in on a specific talent or ability, work can often present its own particular set of challenges.

Women's Basic Job Description at Work

- Making small talk in the coffee-break room

- Serving on committees for fund raisers

- Baking or contributing food to special events

- Remembering co-workers' birthdays

- Sending get well cards

- Spending extra time with someone in need

- Picking out going away presents or arranging going-away lunches

- Socializing over lunch (engaging in non-work related conversation)

- Attending or arranging co-workers baby and wedding showers

Even if a woman has found some measure of success in her job, it is often a painful reality for her to discover that it is often assumed (without question) that she naturally enjoys, is good at, has desire for, or has time for the kinds of activities listed above. A woman may feel subtly pressured to fulfill these kinds of non-work-related cultural expectations. The assumption is that because she is a woman she has these natural inclinations. This situation keeps these women swallowing feelings of failure and feelings of disappointing other people despite other successes. This keeps them from being able to feel the full flowering of their success in the workplace. They are still keeping parts of themselves hidden, "in the closet," saying yes to these "extracurricular" requests that eventually result in a feeling of being overloaded.

A woman on the job may feel a subtle pressure to be involved in volunteer work or being on special committees. It's especially difficult to say no to "charitable" causes that fundraise or aid others in some way. "Sunshine committees" that take care of the niceties of life and help people who are ill or out of work can put a dark cloud over the woman who is already overloaded but continues to smile and hide.

A man these days is often asked to sign a card or even pick up a dish for a potluck, but he is rarely expected to take charge of or organize an event. If he takes on the responsibility and fails to do an adequate job, he is affectionately tolerated, thereby meeting the cultural expectations for a man.

Women are less able than men to compartmentalize their relationships at home and work, so they might feel more pressure to invite business associates into their personal lives or to accept others' offers of such personal relationships.

One of the worst things for many women with AD/HD is having to go to a business lunch and make "small talk." When men go to lunch, they are more likely to be focusing on "deals" and business. Women are often expected to discuss outside interests such as shopping or the theater or bestsellers, even if they have no interest in or knowledge of them. Women with AD/HD feel they have been unable to acquire or remember this kind of popular cultural information but that this reflects as a personal failure. When this happens with business associates whose good opinion is of critical importance to them, they may spend most of these social occasions covering up what they feel are their inadequacies rather than feeling good about their areas of excellence. It particularly feels like a trap when a woman has worked hard to achieve excellence in her field only to have to either "do lunch" badly or else refuse these social occasions and be thought of as a snob or a little weird.

The areas that women with AD/HD struggle with are often those largely required to satisfactorily or easily perform the basic "job description" that today still exists for women. These difficulties are compounded by the cultural messages she receives as she grows up. As a result, she struggles daily, often with intense inner pressures and conflicts.

Summary

Without even realizing it, the woman with AD/HD often deeply internalizes culturally transmitted images of behavior and performance that culminate in her pursuit to match the standard of the "culturally ideal woman." A woman with AD/HD, no matter how successful she might be in other areas of life, when confronted continually with her areas of deficit, can experience a daily diet of stress, or frustration, or even failure.

We trace this legacy and see how over time this small daily washing away of self-esteem adds to the feeling of not measuring up in some fundamental way. Over the years it silently erodes a basic sense of competence and self-worth, instilling a strong need for self-protection.

CHAPTER SEVEN

The Emotional Legacy
Shame and Guilt

At this point you might be thinking, "I just want to pay my bills, be on time, and be able to see my desk again. Why do I have to understand the emotional implications of all this?" Well, I could tell you just to go out and get a new, fancy date book but this time, just try harder! But I imagine that you've done this about a zillion times and guess what? You're still disorganized, and you probably feel worse each time one of these systems doesn't work. Only by understanding the emotional components of disorganization will you then have the tools to live successfully with AD/HD.

We have seen the difficulties that many adult women have in fulfilling their job expectations and the sense of failure that often develops as they struggle to keep up with these overwhelming tasks. This is coupled with their attempt to match the dead-end pursuit of the idealized, culturally approved image of what a woman should be.

In this chapter, we will explore the two kinds of messages that women collect throughout their lives. The first are those general, *culturally transmitted messages* that a woman absorbs as she grows up. The second are more personal in nature, which she receives from the significant people in her life. I call these *maligning messages*. We will see how these messages can eventually result in the emotional legacies of shame and guilt.

Culturally Transmitted Messages

Cultural messages are deeply ingrained rules of acceptable behavior that are often transmitted both through society at large and

Cultural Messages To Women

- Be "Nice"
- Help Others
- Don't Say No
- Don't Ask for too Much
- Don't Hurt Anyone's Feelings
- Don't Set Time Limits on Projects
- Don't Try to Get Out of Work By Asking for Special Favors

through the family of origin. They sound so simplistic that most women might think they are ridiculous and that they can readily overcome them. But, in fact, they are very powerful and can easily slow or stop even the most determined person. They often involve these four areas: helping other people, asking for help, acting special, and asserting one's own needs.

Such cultural messages are frequently articulated, in some form, by women in therapy, trying to make changes in their lives. For women with AD/HD, these cultural messages can have an even greater impact. It is absolutely essential for them to confront these messages in order to create the necessary changes to make their lives work for them. These changes have to be made at home, at school, in their jobs, and in their relationships.

General Messages to All Women

- *Be nice*
- *Be accommodating rather than asking for accommodations*
- *Help others rather than ask for help*
- *Don't say no to requests from people in need*
- *Always lend a helping hand*

Here are some other cultural prohibitions or warnings women have come to believe:

- *If you ask for too much, someone will get angry or think you are trying to get away with something*

- *Don't try to get out of work by asking for special favors*

- *If you say no, you'll hurt someone's feelings*

- *You should never hurt someone's feelings*

- *If you set limits on your time and projects, people will think you just can't cut it*

- *Don't complain; keep your problems to yourself*

- *Don't act like you're better than anyone else*

The following deeply held cultural values, transmitted through the family of origin, become ingrained in women's minds as children and continue to exert strong influence on them as they consider getting help or making changes in their lives. In addition, everyone's family has certain rules, rituals, and traditions that they hold sacred. These are extremely hard to confront and break. Below are a few of these often deeply held ingrained messages:

- *Will power and hard work will get you through anything*

- *Put up a brave front*

- *Cleanliness is next to godliness*

- *Don't start something you're not willing to finish*

- *This is the way it's always been done*

- *There's a right way and a wrong way to do things*

One of the first women with AD/HD that I worked with in therapy was a young, bright, college student named Carla. She was enrolled in a highly technical course of study in which it was absolutely essential that she have extra time on exams. It took her months to be able to ask for the accommodations she needed. It was the first time I witnessed how, despite great motivation and legal documentation of a disability, something more powerful going on internally held this young woman back.

For Carla, like many women, this had a great deal to do with asking for special privileges or special favors. She had a deep belief that she didn't deserve what she viewed as an unfair advantage. Moreover, she felt that even if she were granted this help, it would somehow diminish her in the eyes of her instructor. Carla didn't truly believe she was only asking for a level playing field. She believed that she was trying to "get away with something," to get out of work, or to fool someone. All these scripts from earlier days were swimming around in her head, causing tremendous conflict about asking for accommodations.

I've seen this play out repeatedly in my female clients. Women with AD/HD grow up hearing attributions and admonishments from parents and teachers. They are used to explain mysterious gaps, as well as to motivate change in performance. These messages continue to exert strong influence over them as adults as they contemplate change or consider measures to help them restructure their lives. They need to get help with their difficult areas so that they can move ahead with their strengths. Unless the depth and source of these barriers are fully appreciated, a woman with AD/HD (as well as anyone trying to intervene in helpful ways) will have a hard time understanding her apparent lack of follow through.

After her initial resistance, Carla did make a cursory attempt to ask for help at school, but she was rebuffed. At this point, instead of pushing through the process, she backed away. Carla, like many women who find themselves in this position of needing to confront a closed system with their needs, faced even greater internal resistance than external. A woman with AD/HD has struggled for years to get into a position of fulfilling her potential or beginning to feel the possibility of success. To have to admit vulnerability at the point of greatest hope would understandably be very threatening.

When women with AD/HD are afraid to ask for changes that would help make their life better, it is often because they feel this kind of stance will be seen as demanding or aggressive. They think this would lead other people to reject or resent them.

All the small talk and constant chatter made it impossible for Diane to do her work, and she knew there was an area away from her current workstation that would be a less distracting place for her. But she hesitated to request this move. She felt the other women would think that she was standoffish, better than they were, or special in some sort of way.

It took a long time and a lot of support from the AD/HD group Diane was in before she could express these kinds of feelings and confront these internal barriers. After a few months of getting support from the other women with AD/HD, she became more desensitized to the reactions of the people in her office and was able to consider the option of moving to another location in the office.

After a lifetime of hearing and seeing what a woman should be or do, *cultural messages* tend to become virtually unshakeable thoughts that stay in a woman's mind. Although women often don't believe these ideas intellectually, when they are pushed to take action that runs counter to these messages, they find themselves confronting powerful internal barriers. It is at this point that AD/HD treatment can become slowed or halted, even with diagnosis and medication.

Guilt

We've seen that exposure to cultural messages makes it difficult to ask for help. When a woman with AD/HD considers asking others to help her with things she believes she should be able to do on her own, she often feels guilty as if she is asking for "special" accommodations. To take time away from helping others and to focus on herself keeps her on a treadmill fueled by guilt. Women with AD/HD are often afraid that assertiveness (as they were indirectly taught on their way to womanhood) will be met with anger. On an unconscious level, they expect retaliation, confirming their worst fears. I hear this from women with AD/HD of all ages during counseling.

If they do manage to take the first halting steps, they are often rebuffed and then have difficulty in going on to the next level. This difficulty is partially from a lack of assertive skills, but also from a lack of belief that they deserve these accommodations. They haven't yet fully integrated the reality of AD/HD or discounted the internalized messages below:

- *Don't make trouble*
- *Be grateful to be here at all*
- *Don't bother anyone*
- *Keep your problems to yourself*
- *Just blend in*
- *Don't make waves*

Women with AD/HD, like many women, may feel uncomfortable putting their needs before others, saying no, or not contributing to the group or team. They put their own lives and needs on hold for as long as possible in order to avoid saying no to others or having to ask for special help. Even if they feel confident enough to defer a task or to make a space for themselves, they don't enjoy the resulting free time. They remain focused on what they have left undone and feel guilty about it. If the daily tasks are too difficult for them to complete, they're often unable to participate in other kinds of nourishing, fun, or replenishing activities either because they've failed to do their work first. Certain kinds of work are never finished (because the tasks are so overwhelming and unending) and they never feel justified in blocking out any time for relaxation or fun.

An important part of the process of change, as we'll examine in more depth later, is to push that envelope and become gradually more comfortable enjoying life, even though some work is still undone.

Shame

A woman develops *shame* as the result of the cumulative effect of the kind of messages that have been used to describe her. No matter how bright or competent a woman is, the reminder of these negative messages continues to hold quite a sting. They create an internalized sense of self-blame, of not being good enough.

This following story of a former client of mine, Sharon, demonstrates poignantly how AD/HD symptoms can send waves of shame through a person, instantaneously triggering intense reactions. Despite maturity and success, an individual exhibiting her AD/HD symptoms in front of someone who thinks she is competent can send her into a state of anxiety and shame.

The Rhodes Scholar

Sharon was a fifty-two-year-old woman with two grown children, divorced after twenty years of marriage. All her life, she had heard *maligning messages* such as, "You're as slow as molasses. You'd forget your head if it wasn't attached." In spite of this, she went back to community college and started both to do very well and to have great difficulties. For the first time in her life, she became identified as having learning disabilities. When she finished community college, she went on to enroll in a well-respected, competitive university. She received accommodations for her learning disabilities and achieved high grades, despite having an extraordinarily difficult time in the process. She found that integrating and synthesizing a huge amount of material, continuously having to juggle, (e.g., figure out whether or not to drop a particular class, whether or not to get extensions, etc) contributed to her feeling overwhelmed and anxious. In one way, she was thriving in this stimulating, exciting, challenging world; in another way, she was constantly feeling as if she were about to drown.

Through counseling she began to learn how to hold onto her successes, even when the process was difficult, and she felt that disaster was around the corner. Sharon eventually also became aware that she had AD/HD, but at the time, she felt she was merely a bumbling sort of person. She used to call this her "much-ness," because she was overflowing with ideas, enthusiasm, books, and papers. She did have difficulties but she also had corresponding qualities of being excited, interested, curious, and involved. She was beginning to be able to integrate and express the ideas she was being exposed to.

The pinnacle of her success came in her senior year when she received a letter that invited her to apply to become a Rhodes Scholar. She learned later that this honor had been offered in error because only students under a certain age were eligible. This technicality disqualified her but that didn't matter to Sharon. This moment of triumph was naturally intense for her in the light of all her struggles. She experienced it almost like an internal earthquake because it didn't match her inner experience of herself. For instance, just that day she had asked for an incomplete in a course because she was unable to complete the required work on time. She had papers all over her room and books spread over all the tables. She was interested in and following up on so many ideas that she wasn't always able to meet her deadlines. Of course, she was thrilled with the honor on one level but was still struggling to integrate this great accomplishment into her picture of herself.

Sharon grabbed the award letter along with the rest of her things and rushed over to the hallowed halls of the great university. She caught up with a distinguished, old professor, an imposing figure whose opinion of her meant a great deal. Excited and a little out of breath, she said, "Professor Churchill, I want to tell you something very important. I was invited to apply to be a Rhodes Scholar! I want to show you the letter." She looked down at her feet, in horror, to see an array of papers, books, notes, her purse overflowing—and she couldn't find the letter.

She got down on her hands and knees and started going through everything, searching in vain as he towered over her. At that moment, sitting there, all the feelings of an ashamed, incompetent, bumbling little girl flooded her. The feeling of shame, she said, started at the tips of her toes and traveled up her body to the top of her head. At that moment, it felt as if everything—all her successes—were just wiped out. The extremes of that pivotal moment demonstrated both sides of the AD/HD coin: on one hand, there was the success, the brilliance, the creativity, and the competence, and on the other hand, there was the bumbling, the fumbling, the disarray, and the confusion.

Sharon looked up at Professor Churchill in tears and said, "Huh! What a joke! How could I be a Rhodes Scholar? Look what a mess I am! I even had to take an incomplete in your class today!" In her mind, she had undone for herself all the great success that she had achieved. Her professor, however, understood that they give Rhodes Scholarships to people who have overcome great adversity and have shown great perseverance in order to achieve. They are given to reward people who are committed to the pursuit of knowledge. Even though he knew she had taken an incomplete in his class, he realized it was her intense love of knowledge that led her off in so many directions. With all the wisdom of his years, Professor Churchill looked down at Sharon and said, "Listen to me, Ms. Oppenheim. It is because of everything that you are that has made them select you for this honor. Your thirst for knowledge and your perseverance cause you difficulty, but they're also what make you a Rhodes Scholar."

In that moment, this man had summed up the essence of this kind of discrepancy. The difficulty with staying on track because of an intense interest in many things, the drive and excitement, even though they may cause severe difficulties, had also made Sharon a special person in many ways.

A few years after this incident, Sharon was able to say, "Now when something like that happens, I don't fall all the way to the bottom. I still feel embarrassed sometimes, but those feelings don't bleed into my self-concept the same way."

Personal Maligning Messages

As we can see in the above example, in addition to the culturally transmitted messages we discussed earlier, other deeply embedded and more personal "maligning messages" also may exist and affect

MALIGNING OF MESSY AND DISORGANIZED WOMEN

"She's a slob."

"She has no pride in her home or appearance."

"She doesn't take care of the children well."

"She's self-centered."

"She just doesn't care."

many women. Because they are more personal, they are also inherently more toxic. A woman with AD/HD has often been unconsciously collecting maligning messages since childhood. These stay with her and emerge at the most seemingly ordinary times.

Maligning messages come in the form of both "*you*" messages and "*she*" messages. "You" messages have been spoken directly to a woman since childhood and are interpretations and evaluations of her performance and behavior. "She" messages are descriptions she has heard about other girls or women who have the same difficulties she may have. She takes these as indirect criticisms and indications of her own failings, becoming painfully sensitive to these kinds of statements.

"You" Messages

We've seen how a girl with AD/HD can present a confusing picture to other people. As a result, she collects many negative labels and attributions along the way. AD/HD behaviors can look like something that she is "doing to" other people. Many negative labels absorbed at an early age remain tender, sensitive "hot spots," even when these children become adults. Children with AD/HD were blamed for things that they didn't know how to change; they were blamed for just being themselves. The following kinds of questions conveyed "you" messages to them:

- *Where were YOU raised? In a pigpen? This is a mess!*

- *Why are YOU being so stubborn?*

- *Why don't YOU clean up your room?*

- *Why are YOU so slovenly? Why don't YOU care about the way YOU look?*

- *Why don't YOU try harder?*

Women with AD/HD fear even when they become adults that if they push too hard to get what they need, they will hear some "awful truth" about themselves thrown back at them.

- *You are stupid*

- *You don't belong here*

- *We made a mistake. You fooled us for a while*

- *You are too much trouble. You cause problems all the time*

"She" Messages

"She" messages are those words one hears to describe other girls and women, who, like you, fail to meet culturally sanctioned standards:

- She's a slob

- She has no pride in her home or appearance

- She doesn't take care of the children well

- She shouldn't have had children

- She's self-centered

- She just doesn't care

- She's a space cadet

- She's let herself go

- She's just not very interesting

- She doesn't take the time to take care of herself

Jodi is out to lunch with a group of women (all college graduates) who are discussing the latest bestseller. Jodi hasn't read a complete book in years. No one would guess this secret about Jodi. She's working hard during this lunch to keep up the illusion that, although she hasn't read this particular book, she still is well read.

All of a sudden, the subject of Donna comes up. Jodi cringes inside because she knows that what will follow is the standard "she" message line about Donna, how irresponsible she is, how selfish, self-centered and lazy. She always seems to be too busy for anything. The kids never get a decent meal. Her husband has to do all the housework. She never sent a thank-you note for a present sent months ago. She hasn't reciprocated any of their dinner invitations. "Can you believe that she's a lawyer? I can't imagine how any of her clients put up with her! She's so disorganized."

Jodi's anxiety level increases. She is sure that they must talk about her like this. "How should she react?" she wonders. Should she say, "I have those problems, too," or just keep quiet and stay undercover?

Hiding the "Shameful" Secret

Even if Jodi considers telling other people about her difficulties in order to get close to them or to get help, she might hear, "Oh, don't be silly! You're so smart. I have that problem too. I lose my keys all the time." All her feelings about being invisible, of not being able to make herself understood, and of being discounted become activated, and she often retreats to the relative comfort of the closet. Inside her head, she hears her inner voice repeating:

- *You're just trying to get sympathy*

- *You're overly sensitive*

- *You're inventing problems*

- *Who are you trying to fool?*

- *What are you trying to pull?*

- *Who are you trying to kid?*

Women grow up constantly exposed to messages about what's right or acceptable behavior. When they fail to meet these standards, women often move into a "closet," hiding themselves from other people. This results in great difficulty in ever getting help. If she feels it is shameful to be disorganized, so shameful that she would not let someone see the kind of disarray in which she lives, naturally, she would keep people away from her. This is a perfect setup for depression and depletion and has a negative effect on relationships and achievement, leaving women feeling isolated, alone, and disconnected.

A client named Joan would not permit a friend, let alone a coach or a family member, to come to her house in order to help her get through the piles and backlog of materials, bills, and stuff. She especially wouldn't let a baby-sitter in her house to care for her child even though it would allow her to start a lucrative career. When contemplating the idea of getting some help, the imagined feelings of embarrassment and hiding that would occur if someone helped her go through her things brought her up against a huge wall of shame.

This makes sense if one considers that every pile, every piece of paper examined, and every unpaid bill discovered brings up a new feeling of failure, a new recognition of opportunities abandoned, another reminder of a way she didn't measure up. These kinds of feelings prevent her from having the kind of help necessary to move ahead. Unless these kinds of emotions are understood by the individual and by everyone trying to help her, she will eventually run into a brick wall. Before a coach, a friend, counselor or family member can effectively intervene, they must understand the level of difficulty that a woman may have employing strategies that sound completely reasonable to the person suggesting them.

Emotional Flow Chart

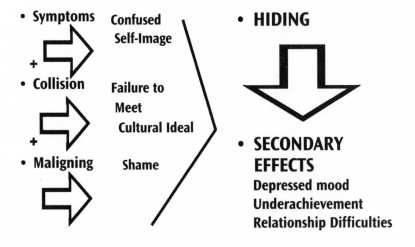

Summary

Going With the (Emotional) Flow

As you see in the Emotional Flow Chart, AD/HD symptoms of inconsistent attention, impulsivity, and activation can lead to a confused self-image, laden with disorganization. Quite often the woman's job description and the cultural expectations set a woman up for failure to meet the cultural ideal. Along with this, she hears maligning personal and cultural messages that create emotional legacies of shame and guilt.

The cumulative effect of this experience often leads a woman to hide a large chunk of herself from other people in order to protect herself. This keeps her locked tight inside that closet for fear she will be scrutinized, found out, publicly exposed and humiliated. She then becomes trapped on a continuous treadmill, unable to get the help she needs to restructure her life and unable to break through the guilt and the cultural messages against asking for special treatment.

The lack of time and energy, feelings of depletion, and hiding all combine to create "secondary effects" on women's lives. Three of these that we will examine more closely in the next two chapters are underachievement, a depressed mood, and difficulties with relationships.

SECONDARY EFFECTS

Depressed mood
Moving away from relationships
Underachievement

CHAPTER EIGHT

Secondary Effects
Underachievement and a Depressed Mood

The shame, guilt, and need for self-protection that we've just examined contribute a great deal to what I call the secondary effects of AD/HD symptoms. The primary symptoms of AD/HD (inattention, impulsivity, over or under activity level) often manifest themselves in struggles with routine tasks such as housework, schoolwork, jobs, and organization. The secondary effects of AD/HD result from these and impact women primarily in three areas: achievements, mood, and relationships. In this chapter, we will discuss these first two issues, achievement and mood.

Underachievement

Shelly was a good student in high school. She did well in college also though she overworked herself almost to the point of exhaustion. After she graduated, she took a job with a local social agency. She did all right there, however, the paper work became overwhelming and eventually she left in frustration. She changed careers a few times, looking for just the right fit but never really found it. She would always bog down at a certain point and never stayed long enough in one place to really move forward. She took a few other jobs through the years usually with the same results. She got married, had a baby, and a few years later went back to work again. However, she never could excel at anything. Shelly started seeing high school and college classmates' names in the paper—president of this company, director of that agency. "I was as smart as those people," she thought. "I wonder why they made it, and I didn't."

With each fleeting year, the woman with AD/HD becomes more aware of other people passing her by, people of equal or lesser abilities. These others have been able to proceed in a single direction, stay on course, and mobilize their energies in order to build a career. The woman with AD/HD has no way to figure out, especially before diagnosis, why that happens or how to get herself on track. We can see how the web she feels tangled in traps her in the same place instead of allowing her to move back on track. Each person she meets or hears about who relays a history of achievement often causes a stab, a pain of diminished self-esteem or grief over lost opportunities and eventually a feeling of hopelessness. Without diagnosis and treatment, she continues to feel trapped. A woman's inability to extricate herself from her entanglements and expectations, makes her despair of ever finding a way to achieve and pursue meaningful goals. In *Driven to Distraction*, Hallowell and Ratey listed the pain of underachievement *number one* on their list of common themes heard from people with AD/HD.

The woman with AD/HD may shy away from making a phone call to get the information she needs to move along in her career. She fears that she will be called stupid or scolded if she has already received this information and misplaced it. She may fear being laughed at or thought weird if she has an interesting new approach to a problem, and requests assistance in carrying it out.

Below are three ways that the secondary effects of AD/HD particularly affect women in areas of achievement. The first I call *Getting Stuck*, the next is *Assertion Blues* and the other is *The Mask of Competency*.

Getting Stuck

Even though women obviously are in more positions of power now than in previous years, they still find themselves confronted with having to do more paperwork and more detail work as they advance than do men of the same ability level. Once AD/HD women can rise above entry and mid-level positions, they often are able to do quite well; they can see the "Big Picture," conceptualize wonderfully well, and they (finally) have secretaries. There is often a double organizational wall that confronts women; they may face both the traditional "glass ceiling" in organizations as well as difficulties with organizing, which keeps them trapped in the position of having to organize for those in higher positions.

Sometimes women feel that when their organizational skills do not match the requirements of their jobs, the mismatch is a personal failure rather than just a poor match between an individual and a job. In these cases, women usually assume that they are "not good enough" and should therefore move downward to an "easier job." In reality, it may be that they need to move upward to a job that does not require them to scale down their thinking to match the limits of the job. They may need to develop a support net beneath them to handle the detail work that would allow them to express or present their ideas in an organized way.

Maggie had an entry-level position in a service business. She constantly berated herself for not being able to do small tasks even though all her ideas, projects, and concepts were so big. She used to say to herself, "I'm a failure. I'm not even able to do these basic tasks. How am I going to be able to move ahead?" instead of thinking, "I need to do a different kind of job where I can shine and grow and use assistance to do this other kind of work." Maggie eventually took the examination necessary to enter a very demanding professional field and obtained an almost perfect score.

Women often confuse their strengths with their deficits. They see them as one big glob of ability that defines them. It is critical that women continuously sort out and isolate their strengths from their weaknesses. Many women seem to operate on the premise that "Something's wrong with me." They say, "I can't think that small. I can't do that kind of slow, boring work. I can only write huge reports. I can only think of big ideas. Something's wrong with me. I need to get smaller and smaller. I need to give away the exciting, big parts of this so I can do the small, required, detailed tasks."

Without any kind of organizational assistance, they either quit the jobs that require larger conceptual thinking (which is their strength) and find jobs where they can manage the organizational demands (not using their conceptual abilities), or they keep thinking they're bad because they're not able to meet the demands for smaller thinking. These women don't need to get smaller, they need to find ways to continually get bigger and discover how to provide a cushion of support underneath them as they use their real abilities and conceptual strengths. They must constantly find ways to keep pace with their achievements so they can continue to grow. Of course, this applies to men as well as women, but usually men are in a position of having more support, both at home and at work.

Think of "The Organizational Package." This is a separate set of duties that need to be handled but perhaps they are only ten percent of the essential function of a job. They shouldn't dominate your choice of careers if ninety percent of your skills are a great match that would let you fulfill your dreams. When you understand this, you can then present yourself with confidence. Every day that I work with women with AD/HD, I see creative, competent, talented women who turned down their dreams, thinking they just weren't smart enough to pull it off. Actually, they just didn't have the "organizational package," the skills that a good secretary could have covered for them.

The Assertion Blues

When we examined cultural messages, we saw the reasons that women have trouble with assertion. Now we see the effect of that as it impacts achievement for the woman with AD/HD. For instance, when they hear "no" to a request for accommodations, they sometimes tend to accept this without pushing the issue further. Sometimes women don't have the assertive language skills to turn a request into an assertive statement without becoming aggressive or retreating into passivity. They're not always comfortable or accustomed to stating their needs in a calm, non-defensive, non-apologetic way. In addition to these troubles with assertion, often these women haven't progressed far enough through the grief cycle or integrated the idea of AD/HD to the point that they own the idea of AD/HD in a deeply personal way that enables them to not apologize or over explain their needs.

When that identity is still new and belief in AD/HD is still shaky, it's hard to push through to be assertive, especially when questioning authority at school or at work. I repeatedly saw how long it took women with AD/HD to be able to ask for even simple, reasonable accommodations in college such as extra time, for note-takers, or for a non-distracting environment.

The single most common cause of failure in college among with students with AD/HD I have worked with is their unwillingness to ask for help because they are afraid to ask for special help, feel embarrassed, or feel as if this means they aren't really "cutting it." Because of my work with these women, I was able to understand the strength of these difficulties: the embarrassment they had to overcome and their perception that they'd be seen as trying to get away with something.

The Mask of Competency

A woman's need to keep up a mask of competency makes it difficult for her to expose vulnerabilities in order to get the help she might need to do her best work. If she's doing well, she often feels she is managing to fool people. When her difficulties aren't obvious to others, the last thing in the world she wants to do is announce that she has problems and needs some special help. She tries to hide her difficulties, often feeding into that tendency to overwork and creating a gulf between herself and other people. It feels so good to finally be seen as competent she doesn't feel she can risk setting limits when people ask even more of her. The problem with this is that people aren't going to say, "Oh, you're doing a great job! I'm not going to ask you to do more." What happens is that the more they do well, the more is asked of them. It's a double bind or Catch-22; the better they do, the more difficult the organizational demands become, and also the more difficult it is to keep up that front. If they set a limit on the amount of work they take on or talk about their difficulties that might wipe out the good work they have done. They often feel they would disappoint people who have good opinions of them and create a situation in which others would only see their limitations from then on.

It reminds them on some level of what they experienced as children, when it often seemed that the trouble they caused or the problems they had had wiped out other people's good feelings about them. They were such confusing children with such inconsistencies or sensitivities that they often frustrated those around them, especially those in authority. This explains why women are often willing to go to extremes in order to keep people from seeing those parts of them. Again, that often creates the very thing they were afraid of—not being able to keep up with the demands. Because they're not getting assistance or accommodations to help them maintain their success, they are eventually drained so much that either things are left undone or are done poorly—or they just simply leave.

Depressed Mood

By the time many women with AD/HD are adults they are often already depressed. Sometimes this depression is a coexisting, full-blown mood disorder of its own, which is not related to the AD/HD. On top of this, women also have a variety of hormonal changes related to PMS, pre-menopause, or menopause that intensify the feelings of depression and anxiety, even when they're on medication.

Women can experience a chronic, low-level depression as a result of the AD/HD: they are often coping without knowing what they're coping with, dealing with low self-esteem and feeling trapped, helpless, or bombarded. We will discuss four areas that affect the mood of AD/HD women, starting with the concepts of being *overwhelmed, overloaded, and overworked.* Then we will explore how being *non-assertive* and engaging in *negative self-talk* further the problem. Finally, we will also see how some AD/HD women can be *highly reactive with quickly changing moods.*

Overwhelmed

The word that I hear more often than any other word from women with AD/HD and disorganization is "overwhelmed." We've seen how the tasks that often fall to women are especially difficult for a person with AD/HD, bringing up feelings of failure, being overwhelmed, and not being able to complete a task. The tasks themselves bring about a certain level of chaos and confusion. This feeling of not having control is often a contributing factor to depression. A woman with AD/HD just doesn't have the kind of skills, structure, or equipment that would allow her to feel that sense of control. So it's not the same thing as when things get messy and out of hand for other people, as they might after a busy weekend. At some level, other women feel that they can come in, roll up their sleeves, and get everything cleaned up and back in order.

For the woman with AD/HD, though, there is more going on than that. First there is her perception that there are millions of separate items taunting her. In addition, there is often a huge backlog of disorder contributing to the feelings of being overwhelmed. Most importantly, she feels that she doesn't have the skill to easily, automatically, move in and get things back where they belong. This feeling of not having control, even when one has a strong motivation or desire, is a strong contributor to depressed feelings.

Overloaded from Not Saying No

Barbara, who had had successes in many areas throughout her life, "confessed" (as if to a crime) that she was unable to meet the demands of charitable and civic organizations who had solicited her volunteer assistance. She had actually said no to them. Other women in the group then admitted to her with relief that they, too, have "shamefully" considered lying about not being able to give time or else they have taken on these obligations for "good causes," which resulted in failure. These kinds of obligations seem to take on an aspect of religious devotion; failure to give selflessly to others almost carries the weight of a sin.

Another setup for depletion and overload for women is the difficult time they have in saying no to requests from other people. Women often feel that they have to take care of other people's needs. If other people's needs compete for attention with their own, they let go of their own. Because their lives are so overwhelming with so many competing demands from work, children, partners, and their environment, they often relinquish their personal nourishment, fun, career, or friends because it's the only area they feel they have enough control over to eliminate. Some women even try to cut down on sleep or skip meals because they're trying to find time any way they can in order to finish their work and meet the demands of other people. They cut out any path that leads to their own satisfaction or completion or gives them a sense of their own strength. As they cut themselves out in order to eliminate the sheer number of demands, they continue on a downhill spiral, leaving them more depleted, less nourished, and more overloaded.

They often think that they'll just wait until the demands stop; then they'll focus on themselves.

- *I'll wait until people at work stop giving me so much to do*

- *I'll wait until people at home stop asking for things*

This, of course, never happens. Instead, ironically, the more efficiently they meet other people's needs, the more demands increase. Because of that need for approval and the need to cover up areas of difficulty, women often escalate their need to perform, to keep up, to not disappoint anybody by letting them down. Instead of saying, "No, I can't handle this, this is my limit," they just hope that one day the demands will stop. However, the more that people at work, for instance, view them as successful and competent and the more is requested of them, the better it feels on some level. Because of this kind of reinforcement, these women try even harder to meet those demands, often feeling increasing pressure to perform, yet becoming more and more depleted. At the same time, they worry about disappointing people by turning down requests. "They'll know I've just been fooling them and they'll lose all their faith in me." So women keep on saying yes.

Overworked

Constant overwork and overload in order to prevent reminders of those painful messages of childhood failures is another setup for depression. These women will go to great lengths to prevent maligning messages or even hints that they're not competent.

- *You know you don't measure up*

- *Who are you kidding?*

They fear that someone will find them out and that the impostor will be discovered underneath their fragile sense of competency. To prevent hearing, "You're not good enough," they'll keep saying yes for even a morsel of good feedback. It's hard for them to believe that they still can be viewed as competent, successful, and well-respected and at the same time still set limits on the amount of work they do. Ironically, by overworking like this, eventually they are not able to keep up because they become depleted or overloaded. This creates a self-perpetuating cycle and a self-fulfilling prophecy of failure.

It's easy to see that living with AD/HD as a woman, especially before diagnosis, is a setup for being overwhelmed, depleted, and overloaded and for feeling low self-esteem, helplessness, and hopelessness. All this adds up to depression.

Negative Self-talk

Negative self-talk also contributes a great deal to the development of depression.

- *I'm no good*

- *What's the matter with me?*

- *I act like a two-year-old*

- *Why can't I act like a grown-up?*

- *Why can't I do these things that other people can do?*

Negative "I" messages such as these are the result of years of difficulty in various areas of life, which are confirmed by the maligning messages of others.

SELF-TALK

AD/HD Happens

BLUNDER
DISORGANIZE
SHUT DOWN

Negative Self-Talk

"I'm so stupid!"
"Forget all this garbage"
"It's just an excuse"
"What's the matter with me?"
"What a jerk!"
"I'm a mess"
"It's hopeless"

DEPRESSION

As you can see in the Self-talk illustration, after a steady diet of experiences like this, you can eventually feel depressed in addition to coping with AD/HD. Then it's even more difficult to move and get things done, which makes women characterize themselves even more negatively. All of the old negative messages from the family, even if they're no longer receiving them now, are locked inside. AD/HD adults tend to characterize themselves as the source of the problem, and when AD/HD symptoms cause problems, they say things like:

- I'm a jerk
- I'm so stupid
- I'm a slob
- I'm so irresponsible
- It's hopeless
- I don't deserve to be a mother
- My children would be better off with somebody else
- How stupid could I be?

Add to this negative talk the overwhelming tasks, the brain chemistry, overwork, exhaustion and this self-barrage, and you have the perfect prescription for depression. Later when we discuss counseling we'll see what happens when this self-talk becomes more positive.

Reactivity: The Pressure Points

Don asked his wife Susan if she would run to the store after work and pick up some shaving cream for him. Susan looked at him blankly. "I can't, honey. I just don't have enough time. I have so much to do!" "But it only takes five minutes," he replied. "What's the big deal?" "It's not a big deal to you maybe, but to me . . ." and then she burst into tears.

It's easy to understand, considering the kind of experiences that we've examined, why a woman would be reactive. I conceive of it as if these women start out each day with ninety percent of their coping vessel already filled. Combine this with chaos, disorganization, and the energy it takes to cope each day, and we can see why it wouldn't take much to put someone over the top. It might be confusing to a person whose request seems like a small task, but to the individual with AD/HD, it may seem equal to climbing Mt. Everest.

In the above story, Susan might be at the point at which she has no more room to incorporate one more task. And on top of that, as one woman said to her partner, "It seems like five minutes to you, but it might turn into more like two hours." This kind of task might entail forty-five minutes of trying to get out of the house because she doesn't know where the keys are or the money is. On the way out she may drop something and become further involved in the tangled web of AD/HD. People often describe this as "walking through molasses" or having their hands tied together. So with all the best intentions, Susan might react in anger, frustration, or tears to her partner's request. This kind of behavior makes her feel worse about herself. By screaming out in anger at someone she cares about who doesn't deserve it, she feels more immature, or like a failure or a bad partner. This adds to her low self-esteem and increases her vulnerability to depression.

Quickly Changing Moods

People with AD/HD experience quick drops in mood that seem to be easily triggered. I think part of this has to do with the discrepancies we've mentioned previously. Until her core feeling about herself is more stable, and she's able to embrace both her strengths and difficulties, a woman's mood may drop or rise depending on which one of those extremes are being pulled on that day. Great success—she feels high in mood. Visible failure a few hours later or even the same day—she drops to a low level. In addition, a woman like this might be exquisitely sensitive; something irritating in the environment may throw her out of kilter and her whole body may go into a state of mini-panic. If she is concentrating intently and the phone rings, it feels as if everything is wiped out of her brain, as if the computer screen has crashed. Obviously, her mood goes down.

When a woman starts to embrace all of herself and her self-picture becomes more steady, she doesn't flip-flop back and forth so much between, *"Now I'm smart; now I'm dumb; now I'm good; now I'm bad."* Eventually, these kinds of emotional reversals diminish and the sense of self remains more constant. Then she will be able to look at the difficulties on one side and the strengths on the other and understand that they are all part of her.

"So tired, tired of waiting . . ."

Women often feel that they have to wait until their lives are in control before they start to focus on themselves. They want to wait until their lives are in balance before they allow themselves to move in a nourishing, replenishing, satisfying direction. As we saw earlier, they're so used to coping that they consider themselves a success when they are merely able to survive. They consider themselves doing well when they're not severely depressed. They're like those frogs that we talked about. They have no idea of how much emotional support they deserve or how much physical support they can dare ask for. They question, *"How much is too needy? When is someone going to figure out it's not worth the effort and leave me?"* They "keep on keeping on," spending more time and energy, draining their resources, and overworking in order to do things that leave them depleted. In this way, they sometimes create the very situation they've been trying to prevent.

As a result of being drained and depressed, women can push people away more than if they just admitted the truth and worked with their partner to get help for their original deficits. Instead, by not eating or sleeping, by overworking, becoming depressed, reactive, and overloaded, they wind up with the relationship difficulties they were trying to avoid. It's akin to money going out with nothing coming in, never balancing the accounts, and running a big deficit. Eventually it catches up; you're overdrawn and emotionally in debt.

Summary

Underachievement and depression are two painful results of AD/HD. Especially if undiagnosed, women with AD/HD will have a very good chance of not reaching their potential. They can likely get stuck in low and mid-level jobs that require them to use their lesser-developed skills rather than their strengths or their abilities to see the big picture. Along with the difficulty of saying no due to the cultural messages she has received, this stops her from getting the help she needs to focus on her strengths.

Being overwhelmed, overloaded, and overworked, being non-assertive, engaging in negative self-talk, and being highly reactive with quickly changing moods can all leave women locked in a state of depression. Guilt prevents them from enjoying life until their work is done. Since their work is never done, this also often prevents them from enjoying life. When they must fight to hold it all together and hide their struggle from others, they find themselves with an inner sense of chaos that makes them feel very vulnerable. Even when they feel "all right" for the moment, they never experience a sense of peace and relaxation because they have such a tenuous hold on organizational balance. This reminds me of people who say that they are "one paycheck away from being homeless." They know that if something goes wrong with their car or if a child gets sick, they'll lose their fragile grip on life. It's with the same sense of insecurity and with the same anticipation of disaster that people with AD/HD often approach everyday life. Even when things are okay for the moment, they know it would take very little to upset their delicate balance. In the next chapter, we will look at another area that is impacted by secondary effects: relationships.

CHAPTER NINE

A Third Secondary Effect

Relationships and Self Protection

V̶anessa, a beautiful, young woman in her twenties, had known from her childhood that she had AD/HD but never took it seriously or got treatment until she became my client. Over the years, she watched as her friends graduated from universities and started building their lives and careers. She knew that she was just as smart as they were but had been unable to achieve in school or to get her emotional reactivity under control in order to consider the possibility that college was an option. Up until then, whenever she encountered someone from high school who had graduated from college, she lied about her own college graduation, naming some prestigious school. The original AD/HD difficulties that had led her away from the college path were compounding rapidly. Each time she lied, she increased her feelings of shame and lowered her self-esteem. Her difficulties now were not just about AD/HD but also about lying, the anxiety of hiding, and her subsequent avoidance of people because she feared being found out, which in turn compounded her feelings of isolation. The relatively simple original difficulties of AD/HD led to such pain of underachievement that these other secondary effects compounded the difficulties, weaving the web until it became even more tangled.

The Tangled Web We Weave

A woman who grows up with AD/HD often makes a series of small, subtle decisions that leave her on the outside, apart from others. This moving away, conscious or not, compounds the original AD/HD difficulties, which then take on a life of their own, complete with emotional meanings that trigger an entire fabric of new difficulties.

The fact is that many people with AD/HD (especially without diagnosis and treatment) move away from relationships for one reason or another. Many feel like outsiders throughout childhood, teen years, and their twenties and then by mid-life they are not close to anyone; they feel isolated. We're going to look at some of the reasons why a person might continue in this unsatisfying way, often unconsciously, for self-protective reasons.

In Chapter 3, we looked at some of the ways women with AD/HD may choose particular kinds of intimate partners without realizing why. In this chapter and the next, we will look at how a lifetime of living with AD/HD often affects other kinds of relationships such as acquaintances, friends, extended family, and colleagues. The focus of this chapter will be on the need to self-protect and the focus of the next chapter is the tendency to disconnect. There you will find a new *friendship* inventory to help you explore your friendship barriers and discover how secondary effects from AD/HD may be at the root of these, along with some guidance on how to reverse this process.

First we will explore how as a result of her early wounds as well as her primary difficulties the woman with AD/HD often uses the legitimate need to *self-protect* in a way that is more defensive than healthy. The sources of self-protection will include the *fear of being unmasked, the pain of being misunderstood, and the tendency to misinterpret,* which often leads her to create the very situations she has been trying to prevent.

Self-Protecting

We all need to protect ourselves, but we have to find healthy ways to do it, not ways that create more isolation, depletion, and cutoffs. Without working through some of these issues, the only means left to us are automatic self-protective devices that distance us from others. Often women haltingly take one step out of that defensive posture, put their hand out, get too close to the fire and shrink back instinctively. It takes a while to desensitize and to keep moving forward instead of moving back into the closet. As we discussed in Chapter 7 one of the main reasons women with AD/HD can have these difficulties with relationships is that the emotional legacy of shame and guilt, which causes her to move away from people. She feels a need to protect herself, both from bombarding stimulation as well as from feeling wounds to her vulnerable self-image that she has developed. She does this through hiding and separating from relationships.

Because of this she may push people away instead of setting limits that actually would allow her to grow closer to people, a goal which is often her true desire. These feelings may have become so intertwined with the sense of self that it becomes very difficult (although essential) to sort them out and untangle them.

Fear of Being Unmasked

When an AD/HD symptom threatens to appear or does occur, it can send a woman into a mini state of panic. She'll be discovered. Her cover will be blown! It's like being a spy in a foreign country. She's constantly wondering with each particular symptom such as blurting out or forgetting, if this is the clue that's going to give her away. Will it erase her reputation for competence and with it any goodwill and approval that she's worked so hard to achieve? Will this be the moment when she's finally going to disappoint someone and they will uncover her mask?

Feeling Misunderstood

When these women feel they are misunderstood or are seen as odd, those old wounds of not fitting in and resulting need for self-protection are activated. This further moves them away from people. The amount of energy she needs to invest in organizing and getting herself together makes it difficult to keep up with the ordinary social and recreational events that other people do. Women with AD/HD feel such an energy drain just trying to keep their lives together. Because they feel so different from others, even if they do begin to form a relationship, they soon begin to feel misunderstood.

A client of mine, Joan, started to form a friendship at work with another woman. She was feeling good about this because one of her goals with AD/HD was to try not to isolate herself but to make more friends and have a good time. After a weekend filled just trying to keep her life together, she was exhausted. Even though she hadn't done anything out of the ordinary, she felt as overwhelmed as another woman might have felt after a full weekend of special events and activities. She told her friend at work on Monday, "I'm really tired." When the friend inquired, "Oh, what did you do? Must have been a great big weekend!" all she could think of was that she had gone out to dinner and the movies with her husband on Saturday night. The friend laughed and said, "How could you be so tired? You didn't do much!"

If someone else were being teased for being unable to keep up the pace, she might have shrugged it off, but it felt like ridicule for this woman, and it triggered old wounds. Gradually, she began to move away from this relationship. She did not know how to explain why she was so different in her energy levels and capacities, especially since they both had high-level jobs in which they functioned equally. Often a woman feels that if she "comes out" and is open about her difficulties that it may shatter her fragile sense of competence, so she continues to hide, spending inordinate amounts of time and energy compensating, covering up, and feeling like an impostor.

Other Communication Struggles that Make You Feel Misunderstood

Sometimes you will feel misunderstood because the primary AD/HD difficulties are still areas of struggle and make it more difficult to communicate or make yourself understood. When this happens and you aren't taken seriously or listened to, your wounds are activated again. Two of these communication struggles are discussed below: small talk and regulating your speech.

Small Talk

Women with AD/HD often move away from relationships in the initial stages of forming friendships because of their *difficulty in making small talk* or difficulty with finding the words that they want to say when they want to say them. *Sometimes it is as difficult to find the words in your messy mind as it is to find a paper on your messy desk.* Kate Kelly and Peggy Ramundo (1995, pg. 66) call this a "reaction time irregularity." They go on to point out that a person with this difficulty might look rude or disinterested when they actually may be having "trouble retrieving things from memory in a demand situation".

In addition, AD/HD individuals have difficulty regulating their speech. They may interrupt, blurt out, or shut down. They may talk too fast or jump from topic to topic in a way that is difficult for others to understand or follow their thought process.

There is a cultural expectation for a woman to make small talk; it's the way that women start to make friendships and test the waters, a vehicle to reveal oneself. The woman with AD/HD does not want to be found lacking, though, so her natural instincts lead her to protect herself in defensive ways. Sometimes she avoids these situations, where she feels unable to participate in discussions about current or cultural events. This cuts off opportunities to get to know people. The feeling of not being able to reveal herself makes it even more difficult to move into a deeper relationship.

Being Misunderstood Because You Are Not Explaining Yourself

A woman who has AD/HD (inattentive type) has a real need sometimes for a time out away from other people to recharge and recover. Because of her feelings of vulnerability and her difficulty explaining her differences, she may move away from people without an explanation instead of talking about her special needs, which may actually leave her feeling closer to another person. As Hope Langner, therapist, coach, and specialist in women with AD/HD said (2000) *"It's difficult to always have to say the hard thing out-loud."* (p. 5).

This is again an area where women have to learn to understand the difference between healthy self-protection and defensive behavior that pushes people away. They should plan what they are going to do when they have an "AD/HD attack," when they get overloaded. Without this plan, women often walk away, tune out, withdraw or abruptly say no because they don't know how to talk about what is going on, and they feel embarrassed about being different.

Patty "overloaded" each Sunday when she and her husband went to the traditional family brunch and spent the entire afternoon with her husband's large extended family. This included several sets of brothers and sisters and many children of various ages and several family pets. The teenagers played music, the children played video games, the men and women discussed politics, and the women prepared and served food and cleaned up. There was a football game perpetually on television. Even though Patty liked most of her relatives, she found these Sundays a strain. Keeping up small talk, as well as hiding her ignorance about the current political situation, combined with the incredibly distracting and overwhelming noise level left her on the brink of tears after about an hour.

In addition, her sisters-in-law always discussed the latest fashions and engaged her in talk about these things, which left her feeling badly about her lack of "feminine know-how." An hour after breakfast, she would slink away, either into a back room where she hoped she wouldn't be missed for a while, or if it was nice weather, go for a long walk and try to regain some sense of balance. She became increasingly self-conscious, though, about appearing standoffish and became more and more convinced that they considered her weird or an outsider.

So her original need for reduced stimulation took on a life of its own, creating more negative feelings about herself and perhaps negative feelings about her behavior from her family. Patty needed to be able to describe her needs in these situations and find a way to take care of herself while still staying connected to people who were significant in her life.

Healthy self-protection is vital, and it needs to be built into your life. The balance to work toward is not to clam up, tune out, or leave the room, but to protect yourself, without apologizing, putting yourself down, or moving away from other people.

Misinterpretation (Creating the Problem You Were Trying to Prevent)

Misinterpreting others is the next big area that causes problems in relationships. Without checking out people's reactions, we often misinterpret the way that people react to AD/HD symptoms; this causes us to behave in ways that actually do push people away. The Secondary Effects Chart shows that these are self-perpetuating cycles, actually creating the problem we're trying to avoid. In these cases, instead of getting closer to people as a woman actually desires, her defensive

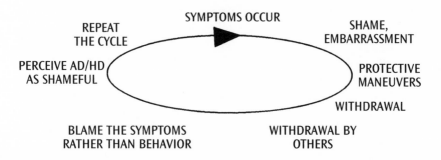

SECONDARY EFFECTS

SYMPTOMS OCCUR

REPEAT THE CYCLE

SHAME, EMBARRASSMENT

PERCEIVE AD/HD AS SHAMEFUL

PROTECTIVE MANEUVERS

WITHDRAWAL

BLAME THE SYMPTOMS RATHER THAN BEHAVIOR

WITHDRAWAL BY OTHERS

actions sometimes move her away instead, which once realized only lead to more shame or embarrassment. Her behavior can become quite baffling to others. *This behavior pushes people away; other people react to your behavior, not your need for "time out."* In the above example Patti's lack of explanation for her actions left her feeling misunderstood but it also led her eventually to misinterpret her family's responses to her behavior. They reacted, but it wasn't because she had a need to have some alone time. It was because she walked away constantly without explanation. She compounded her original problems.

Julia, a bright, young woman in a small management agency, felt she had difficulty getting her ideas out clearly in small groups. She would either talk too fast or not be able to contribute appropriately to the discussion. She became focused on the idea that one supervisor in particular thought, that Julia didn't measure up. Julia started to avoid people who were at these meetings (and specifically this supervisor). Julia started feeling more and more convinced that they didn't like her at this company because of her difficulty in expressing ideas in meetings.

When Julia started to examine this situation in counseling and began to understand what she might be doing to create it, she saw that this other woman was probably reacting to Julia's avoidance of her. When she lost some of her defensiveness about this, Julia was able to see that her behavior was pushing people away, rather than her AD/HD symptoms, which in this case really hadn't affected their opinion of her capabilities. They thought she was bright. Because of her past experiences, she had over-focused on this as a reason why others wouldn't like her. It was actually her behavior unrelated to AD/HD that was causing her relationship problems.

My Story

I worked at a large counseling agency with a lot of demands for completing forms and filling out paperwork. I was so sensitive about my handwriting because of all the years in school of getting papers back with big red marks on them, that I lived in fear of checking my "In Basket" every day to get back my forms after they were processed by a clerical staff person. I had been what I called "clerically abused" at another agency in which one member of the clerical staff put me down, complained about me, and was very upset with my performance. She called me sloppy and careless. At that agency, my forms would come back to me with words like, "I can't read this! Careless errors!" with those big red marks again.

Many years later at this new agency with a really nice clerical staff, I expected the same thing to happen. I approached each day with a great deal of anxiety, as if I were still in the seventh grade and going to get my work returned to me with red ink scrawled across the forms saying, "This is a mess! This could have been done by a second grader! Be more careful!!" Even though I am not naturally prone to paranoia, no matter how good my work actually was, I became convinced the clerical staff talked about me and didn't like me because I had messy handwriting, (which is ridiculous if you look at it objectively). But all those years of experience were working on me unconsciously. Instead of going to them and talking about it (they really were lovely people) I started to avoid them. Eventually, they probably did think I was not a friendly person. So perhaps at some point, I was reacting correctly to the fact that they weren't friendly to me. Whatever the reality of the situation was, I had created a very different scenario due to my past experiences

Eventually, when I understood my behavior and understood my difficulties, I was able to talk about it. Not only did this harmful cycle of emotions get broken, I actually received more help with my work because I was able to talk about the difficulty that I was having. The secrecy and shame attached to the original problems take on a life of their own. It's very important for women with AD/HD to understand how shame, guilt, and a desire for self-protection can color your perceptions and create interpersonal difficulties, as well as prevent you from getting needed assistance.

Summary

In this chapter, we have looked at self-protection as a way that living with AD/HD impacts your relationships. When a woman with AD/HD gets treatment and her inner feelings change about AD/HD, it becomes easier to talk about difficulties. She then begins to accept that she won't always be understood but she can continue in relationships anyway. At some point she needs to separate out those who are not supportive and not pursue those relationships, as well as understand that other people can provide nourishment and relationship benefits even if they don't understand her perfectly. Women with AD/HD can still get what they need from relationships without expecting perfect acceptance and understanding from others and without moving away from important relationships by defending themselves in unhealthy ways.

In the next chapter, we will look at disconnecting in relationships and you will get a chance to take an inventory of the effects AD/HD may be having on your relationships, especially your friendships and with your extended family. You will discover small steps you can take to maintain relationships and reconnect with people with whom you may have lost contact.

CHAPTER TEN

Are You Friendship Challenged?

Getting Back on the Road to Relationships

In the last chapter, we looked at self-protection in relationships as a secondary effect of living with AD/HD. Another reason that women move gradually away from relationships is that they simply, as one woman put it, "disconnect." Friendships, connection, and closeness are emotionally important to most women. What I discovered from years of working with women with AD/HD is that their special challenges, both primary symptoms and secondary effects, create barriers to forming and maintaining these connections. This brings with it a special kind of pain. These women want to show what's in their heart, to give and connect yet when they find it difficult or when they act counter to their true desires and feelings about other people, their self-image is affected. They begin to question their own character. They say things like the following:

- *"I must have a rock and not a heart"*
- *"I must be a bad, selfish person"*
- *"People don't know my heart"*

Building and maintaining friendships requires a whole host of extra responsibilities and consistent connections. This runs counter to the executive functioning (EF) problems of many of these women and leads them to feel overwhelmed. Relationships simply bring too many things to do and to consider, adding to stress and feelings of being overwhelmed. Women feel, at some level, that developing more relationships or even a few relationships to a deeper point will put them over the top. When this happens, they often begin to avoid others, withdraw and then feel lonely and isolated.

As Time Goes By

In addition to beginning and maintaining relationships, many women have let established relationships slip away. Small occasions and important events with other people are missed: there are an increasing number of missed thank-you notes, missed birthdays, or invitations that are not reciprocated. The connections just aren't kept up, and eventually they're gone. They then anticipate scolding, rejection, or negative reactions when they think about trying to reconnect or rectify a situation, so they tend to avoid them altogether. While this may be true for everyone to some extent, women with AD/HD with particular histories or wounds are especially sensitive to and avoidant of this kind of potentially critical feedback further increasing the negative cycle.

This is because being good at relationships goes to the core of their identity as women. Men are more often easily forgiven for these relational lapses since it's not so much a part of our culturally established gender role expectations. Because they don't expect it of themselves, they don't attach shame, guilt, and feelings of failure to it when they let relationships lapse. The challenge and the goal is to find a way to stay connected without becoming overwhelmed.

Disconnecting

Phone and email are a special focus in this chapter because they are considered vital connections to build or maintain relationships for many women. These have never really been examined from an AD/HD perspective, but problems with these forms of communication contribute to these relationship issues for women with whom I have worked. Sometimes they are even more challenging than face-to-face communication and can add still another layer of fear and negative expectations that sometimes rise to almost phobic proportions. In addition to losing out on ways to stay connected, women who don't like to talk on the phone also feel badly because once again they do not enjoy something they perceive most other women enjoying.

In this chapter, which is divided into four parts, we will begin to understand the reasons for the avoidant behavior and isolation of women with AD/HD. We will look at simple strategies to stay connected or reconnect without becoming overwhelmed when trying to develop or maintain friendships.

- **Part One:** This section will examine how executive functioning problems play a role in these difficulties

- **Part Two:** This section will examine the emotional overlay of life with AD/HD and how this further interferes with friendship

- **Part Three:** This section gives simple, small steps to work your way back to the road to relationships

- **Part Four:** This section will help you to take own inventory of how your relationships may be affected by AD/HD and then make a plan for yourself

Part One:
EXECUTIVE FUNCTIONING AND ITS ROLE IN RELATIONSHIPS

As mentioned before, Tom Brown, Ph.D., talks about several components of executive functioning that are affected in individuals with AD/HD. The four below form the basis for the problems involved in relationship building. As you will see, they are all closely intertwined.

Activation

If you have problems with activation, you find it difficult and exhausting to organize yourself to move toward a goal or to initiate a project. It is easy to see how this could impact starting or maintaining relationships.

Quick Loss of Energy

You may start out with the best intentions about a friendship building activity and even make an elaborate plan but then lose energy by the time you move toward a particular action. Countless women I work with have big hearts and big plans, especially when friends or extended family are stressed or in crisis, but run out of cognitive energy when it comes to carrying out the plan. For instance, they often think about dropping off a present or dinner for someone in need, visiting someone in the hospital, sending get well cards, writing a note of condolence, or making a big deal of a happy occasion. When women with AD/HD drop the ball at times like this, it is particularly damaging to their sense of themselves as caring people.

Becoming Distracted

This looks very much like the above example, but in this case, you are bombarded by so many other thoughts and demands that you are distracted from your intent to call or have someone over. This might start off as foremost on your mind, but you become distracted to the point that the idea is lost somewhere in your mind, much like an important piece of paper lost among many other papers on a top of your desk.

Memory Issues

You may think a great deal about a particular person you want to communicate with, respond to, or stay in touch with, especially if you have just seen her or become aware of a situation that needs attention. Ellen Littman, Ph.D. (2002), describes what happens next.

"When a woman with AD/HD is spending time with a good friend, she is there one-hundred percent (100%) – enthusiastic, involved, witty, and passionate; many friends find the interaction exciting and rewarding. The woman with AD/HD revels in the highly stimulating delight of feeling connected and accepted. Yet when the friend is no longer present, the woman with AD/HD cannot always hold onto the intensity of that emotional experience, or even to its memory. In her friend's absence, a woman with AD/HD often becomes immersed in urgent-seeming issues, which all but obliterate thoughts of her friend. Moved to a back burner, the friend, however treasured, is in danger of falling off the psychic radar screen." (pg. 60).

Disorganization

Sometimes your brain is activated, you keep up the energy, you go to make the call or write the email, and then you can't find the number or address! The cognitive window begins to close, a tidal wave of other events and thoughts sweeps over you, the moment is gone, the call is left unmade, and the impulse is buried.

Cognitive Confusion and Difficulty

Problems with sequencing, planning, prioritizing, and selecting what to focus on from all those possibilities swirling past you are ways that cognitive challenges interfere with these kinds of activities. In addition, struggles with dividing your attention between all the competing details and figuring out how to get the information you need to finish carrying out a plan can also stop you in your tracks.

Feeling Overwhelmed

Women with AD/HD are overwhelmed by the amount of voice-mail or email they may need to answer or to keep track of. They feel they have too much to do already, and they just don't want more input. All or nothing thinking sets in, and they keep waiting until they have enough time to respond, but a big enough chunk of time never comes.

Problems with Expression

As was mentioned in the last chapter, you may have what Kelly and Ramundo call a "reaction time irregularity" that may interfere with communication and make small talk difficult. Talking on the phone or communicating through email, two vital methods for connection and relationship building that do not involve eye-to-eye contact, are often even more challenging. When it comes to the phone, the lack of nonverbal cues used in face-to-face communication such as eye contact, facial expressions, and gestures can make talking on the phone challenging, especially when it comes to figuring out whose turn it is to speak

Many women with AD/HD enjoy emailing instead because it is not verbal. It allows them to control the pace and avoid on the spot demands that may spotlight their language difficulties. For other women who have difficulties with written communication, however, this presents a situation in which they feel self-conscious. Then there are the women with AD/HD who are *tech phobic* and confused and afraid about computers, particularly the whole *online thing*.

Part Two:
THE EMOTIONAL OVERLAY

As if these kinds of challenges were not enough, the emotional overlay of relationships makes the whole thing even more daunting. In this section, we will look at fears that may be resulting in continued avoidance, leading you away from connection.

Fear of Feeling Overwhelmed

This is not just about feeling overwhelmed but it is about the actual fear of opening yourself up to taking on more when you are already drowning. For example, you may feel that you cannot spare time on relationships because it will take time away from getting organized. You may feel that you cannot "play" until your work is done.

Fear of a Negative Response

You may feel afraid that you will read scolding messages on your emails or hear reprimands on your voice mail saying, "Why didn't you return my call?" You may feel afraid that when you actually do return a call that you will hear a negative tone of rejection, criticism, or disappointment.

Fear of Not Knowing What to Say

Sometimes years of feeling incompetent or stupid, especially feeling as if people can't really make sense of what you are trying express, may result in "*phone-phobia*," a fear of talking on the phone, which often results in shame and guilt because of this avoidance. When too much time has gone by, and you are too embarrassed, you may instead opt to never to see that person again. This is very common among my women clients.

Fear of Not Being Able to Protect Yourself

One reason you may be afraid to talk on the phone or commit to a date is that you may be afraid that you will feel trapped. This may be coupled with the fear that you won't be able to set limits on your time or say no to requests that may leave you overcommitted.

Fear of Differences

You may avoid situations in which you might feel in danger of exposing your deficits or differences. You can cover up for a short time sometimes if you work things out carefully, but with extended stays, you know there is a greater likelihood that more of your "weird things" or deficits will be exposed and along with them the reopening of painful wounds. You may also feel that such a situation is calling for you to perform in ways that everyone else does effortlessly but that you have trouble with and have no way of hiding. You may feel that you have no way to explain your differences or special needs.

Fear of Feeling the Pain of Underachievement and Failure

If you feel the pain of underachievement, you may have a difficult time being with others of similar ability or education who have achieved what they may have originally hoped for. Instead of using these encounters to discover clues as to what you want or to ask for guidance, you wind up withdrawing and becoming more isolated and depressed. Consequently, you are less likely to know what they want. One bright woman with AD/HD diagnosed later in life described the pain of her underachievement by quoting Marlon Brando from *On the Waterfront* when he said, "I could have been a contender." Her pain was reactivated by the potential friendship with women whom she perceived had achieved more than she had, and so she withdrew.

Part Three:
BACK ON THE ROAD TO RELATIONSHIPS

This section offers a number of simple, small steps to take to begin to confront the barriers to relationships presented in parts one and two. The first step is awareness and coming to an understanding of your primary emotional barriers. It will take a long time for you to be able to identify when you are stuck and to know what kind of obstacle you are confronting. Then you can begin to think of ways to slowly break the cycle. You will notice that the following suggestions are very simple.

Don't fool yourself into thinking you will make huge changes quickly. It is like starting a diet or exercise program. If you undertake too much too fast, you may start out strong, but old feelings and habits will eventually reemerge. Remember, when you are trying to form new patterns of behavior, the slower you go, the longer you will last. Slow, steady awareness and small steps will help you confront these complex inner conditions. In the next part of this chapter, you will take your own inventory and choose a first step to getting back on the *road to relationships*. But first, we will look at the EF, primary AD/HD difficulties and the emotional overlay that we examined above with corresponding suggestions.

Steps to Help with Activation

Activation means organizing or initiating your brain to begin an activity. *Medication* is often an effective intervention for those who have serious problems with activation. Many women report just being awake and alert all day as a huge improvement in this area. They feel a tremendous difference in their ability to counteract "*the paralysis of will*" that leaves many bright women sitting for hours, remote in hand, aimlessly changing channels with a million intentions and good thoughts trapped inside their head not being translated to action.

Another strategy that helps with activation is to *make an appointment way in advance* with someone. Put it down in your calendar so far in the future that you don't feel threatened about it. Then one day . . . there it is. Spread this out with a few people over a course of months, and you will begin to put some structure into your relational life. Instead of having to select this activity on a particular day when it is competing and with all the other things pressing in on you, you will have already pre-selected it. You can also do this with holidays and initiating invites, as well. Get something on the calendar a year early for a particularly big event. That way you will schedule around it instead of fitting it in with whatever else is going on at that time in your life when it "pops up" unexpectedly.

Steps to Help with Loss of Energy

Watch out for *plans when they get too elaborate* and require too many intricate kinds of action. These may cause you to get sidetracked and to lose energy. Try something like this instead. Keep the elaborate plan . . . enjoy writing it down or mapping it out in great detail or with great vision but then break it into smaller steps. *Think of it as lots of little great plans instead of one big grand one.* So for instance . . .

If you make the call, then you can bake the cookies. If you bake the cookies, maybe then you can make a beautiful package to deliver it in. If you deliver it, maybe you can allow yourself to write a song to accompany it. But first just look up the person's address!

So many beautiful and thoughtful plans don't get carried out because you are trying to complete them all. Act by taking the first small step and then go from there. If you don't have ten hours to complete it, let yourself spend one minute on the first step so that you will feel you at least made some contact. The longer you wait, the harder it will be to do anything. So remember:

- *Think small to start*

- *All or nothing thinking usually comes out on the side of nothing at all*

Steps to Help with Memory Issues

As we discussed earlier, many people just fall off your radar screen. *Why not make big list of all the people in your life you want to remember?* This goes beyond a list of people's birthdays. I'm talking about *just remembering their existence* on a frequent basis. Brainstorm all the people you want to remember who are important to you in some way and put the list up on a bulletin board in front of you. This way you can glance up from your computer or your desk and remember to call just to check in. That's the hard part, to check in when there isn't anything triggering you, like an event or invite. I thought of this when I saw the movie *50 First Dates*. At the end of the movie, Drew Barrymore's character solves her memory problems that have been interfering with her relationship by viewing a video tape every morning of who she is and who the important people in her life are! I thought that was great idea!

Steps to Help with Disorganization

I could tell you to get a Personal Digital Assistant (PDA) or some strategy like that, but women with AD/HD often find that such strategies fail. You need to take emergency measures so that even if you never get organized, you won't let it interfere with your friendships. I suggest that you follow the *10 minute rule—don't spend more than 10 minutes* looking for numbers, directions, etc. Often women will do anything not have to ask for this information again and instead spend hours looking through piles trying to avoid admitting they have misplaced something. Sometimes, of course, you just don't have the information, in which case, you need to find ways to *prevent* this from happening. If you tell people you will get back to them, it is a good idea to ask them to contact you by a certain date if they haven't heard from you—just in case! Some women leave the message, "Please don't assume I have your number" on their voice mail and ask callers to leave it each time. Of course, I love email because once I have gotten an email from someone I can usually find it again to respond. I always have it in there somewhere!

Steps to Help with Feeling Overwhelmed

Since many AD/HD women feel overwhelmed when it comes to friendships and relationships, especially when it involves entertaining for special events and holidays, a number of these suggestions will focus on that.

Do It Your Own Way at Holidays

- You don't have do things the same way as everyone else

- You don't have to put on a huge traditional event

- You don't have to entertain on the holiday itself

Often there are days around a holiday when you can entertain less formally. Bring in Chinese for the Super Bowl instead of having Christmas dinner at your house. Meet out at restaurant or at a park. It doesn't have to be fancy or expensive. You supply the house; they bring the food or vice-versa. You can arrange to drop in or have them drop by for short visits. Invite people for off times such as tea, dessert, or late afternoon lemonade on the porch. And don't forget, you can go on a nice vacation sometimes instead of being with your family. If single, go alone, with friends, or with extended family. They might want to skip all the stress, too.

Reciprocating in Different Ways

Just because someone had you over to their house for a formal event doesn't mean that you have to reciprocate in exactly the same way. The point is to show them that you want to continue the relationship and that you care about them and appreciate their efforts. Giving of yourself doesn't mean anything if you are not giving your true self. For instance, some people give elaborate homemade gifts, some give expensive store bought ones, and others make donations to their favorite charity in your name. They are all expressions of caring and giving and all are authentic for those people. I heard a line somewhere recently that expresses this well. *"If two people in a relationship are exactly alike, then one of them is unnecessary!"* We enrich each other by our differences. If you are comfortable with yourself, other people will be comfortable with you. They will enjoy doing something different and being opened up to a different world.

Two for Tea

This involves taking time for someone without it taking a toll on you. I remember a special time during a winter holiday season that made me see holidays and relationships from another perspective. Instead of a huge holiday event, I got together one afternoon in a cozy tearoom with a friend I hadn't seen in a long time. It was probably more intimate and meaningful for both of us, filled with warmth and love and laughter instead of a rushed day of stress. Most importantly, we could both actually focus on what was really important— each other and our relationship.

I have come to believe that one way around the conflict of feeling overwhelmed but wanting to connect at special times is to start to think about the real meaning, the real purpose of these occasions, which is to build connection and closeness and to give pleasure to someone else. If you think like this, you can start to move away from of these "shoulds" and "have to's" that keep women locked in self-defeating patterns.

Steps to Help with Problems of Expression

Expression has to do with trusting yourself to express your ideas and to respond clearly. *Plan your long or stressful calls or confrontations around medication cycles* so that it will be easier to communicate and less of a strain. If you need to communicate something important that may require facts to back you up or support to help you remember your key points, it's ok to *write it out first*. Prepare so that you can feel confident. If you need to wait until it's your turn to respond on the phone, take notes so that you won't forget what you wanted to say. That way you won't have to interrupt to prevent yourself from forgetting.

Steps to Help with Fears

Fear of Feeling Overwhelmed

Women are afraid to take time away from what they need to do or from getting organized. Think about these quick ways to check in and touch base. *One Liners:* Leave a quick message on email or voice mail. You can call when you think no one is home just so that they will get your message when they return and know you were thinking of them. These might include messages like, "Thinking of you," "Miss you," or "Hi. Call me."

- *Watch Your Window Closing:* Develop sensitivity to when your window of attention is closing. You can feel when someone or an idea is slipping away and that soon you will be buried or distracted with other mental notes. Just like you can learn to feel when your medication is wearing off, you can begin to notice when that window is closing and either quickly write yourself a big note or better yet make these kind of quick calls.

- *Life Lines:* Get a friendship niche; in other words, one thing you know how to do quickly and easily. I have found my friendship niche—"Say it with flowers." I have memorized one very important number: 1-800-flowers. It can be expensive, but I have found that flowers or gifts you can send from these kinds of online sites or catalogs can go a long way in communicating caring, keeping up that connection, and making an impact.

Fear of a Negative Response

If you are afraid of being reprimanded for waiting too long to call and that is keeping you from reconnecting, you have to find a way to *test the emotional waters.*

You may need to break the ice by having someone else call up and setting up a get together for several people. Or you may have someone open the letter or email you are afraid to open or listen to the voice mail message and have them scan it first to see if the true force of your negative expectations are accurate or not. These measures may seem extreme, but it is better than to go on avoiding. Usually the reality of your expectations will not be as bad as you think. You may just need to have someone with you for support while you open up or listen to the message.

You may email or leave a message when you think people you are feeling uncertain about won't be home. This way you can get a message back from them so you can get a feel for how they are going to respond to your overture before you actually talk to them. Like I said earlier, these get to be phobias, and you need to desensitize yourself slowly as you continue to approach the feared situations.

When you do actually talk to the person, *avoid over apologizing* or putting yourself down. And don't try and make up for all the relationship difficulties you think you have caused in the past. You can simply say, "I've missed you" in an email or voice message and go on from there. Sometimes there will actually be someone who will want you to go to extremes to pay for perceived insults; then you will have to decide if the relationship is worth pursuing. At this point, though, we are just talking about getting past the first hurdle of reconnecting.

Remember, it is *better late than never.* This is especially true for women with AD/HD who feel that it's too late when they haven't responded in a timely way to an important occasion. Especially when there has been a death of a friend or family member, your attention will be greatly appreciated after the people who were there early on are no longer there.

Fear of Not Being Able to Protect Yourself

This has to do with setting limits and boundaries to make you feel safe in relationships. Decide what you can give happily so that you can connect with others as well as protect yourself. (Solden, 2002, pg. 195) If you sometimes feel trapped when talking on the phone, try setting limits as follows: "I can only talk for a minute, but I wanted to get a call in to say a quick hello."

Saying No to Draining Things and Yes to Support

It may make you uncomfortable for awhile to say *no*, but again, if you think of saying no as a way to protect relationships by not over committing and then breaking promises, you will be acting in service of the relationship.

Learning to say yes to good offers of love and nourishment is equally important. Also learn to say yes to yourself to get support if you want to undertake something elaborate or something that is within your range of deficits. Remember, you want to create good experiences and enjoy your friends and family, not put on a show that is actually creating negative feelings.

Sometimes a fear of conflict might make you hold back. *Medication* can provide a cushion or barrier so that your feelings aren't so raw. This can help you state your needs more easily. Remember, you can't attain perfect understanding from each relationship. There may be parts of you they can't really understand, but in basically healthy relationships, that's something to *accept and to expect.* If you are having trouble with this area, you may want to look at previous chapter on healthy self-protection.

Fear of Differences

A fear of differences often arises out of a history of feeling misunderstood and having experienced painful emotional wounding from others who did not understand your AD/HD. But instead of hiding or pretending when you don't know how to explain your differences or needs in a situation, you will be better off if you can find ways to communicate about it. Remember *you are always communicating* even if you aren't talking about things, so you want to make sure you are communicating what you really want to be saying instead of letting your actions be misinterpreted.

If you know what may be problematic at a particular function, *strategize in advance.* Think about what you would like to contribute and how you can find an alternative to isolating yourself or disappearing. Remember to describe what you need objectively instead of characterizing yourself negatively. You might say, "I am not good at chopping vegetables. How about if I set the table instead?" rather than, "I'm completely incompetent."

Fear of Feeling Pain of Underachievement

Use the pain that may surface with others around this issue as a guide to what you want may want to pursue. Ask for mentoring. If you are feeling depressed, you may want to seek out professional help, a support group, or career counseling.

Part Four:
FRIENDS AND FAMILY INVENTORY

Fearful Forms of Communication

Directions: Avoiding certain forms of communication can interfere with the development or maintenance of friendships or lead to disconnection from those you care about. Check those activities below that you avoid and then write comments to yourself about these situations on a separate sheet of paper, naming specific people, situations, and behaviors that come to mind.

Telephone

_____ Answering calls

_____ Making calls

_____ Returning calls

_____ Listening to messages

Email

_____ Writing messages

_____ Reading messages

_____ Responding to messages

Situations that Call for a Response

_____ Acknowledging a friend or family member's loss

_____ Acknowledging a friend or family member's illness

_____ Acknowledging a friend or family member's special occasion

Invitations

_____ Initiating or sending invitations

_____ Accepting or declining invitations

_____ Reciprocating invitations

Emotional Reasons for These Behaviors

Directions: Identify which fears, feelings, thoughts, or self-talk you have that may be leading you away from connection or resulting in continued avoidance. Check all those that apply to you and then write about any specific situations that you are aware of being sure to include details.

_____ Fear of feeling overwhelmed

_____ Fear of losing time needed to get organized

_____ Fear of a negative response or reprimands

_____ Feelings of guilt or shame

_____ Fear of not knowing what to say, sounding stupid, or being judged

_____ Fear of not being able to protect myself or to set limits

_____ Fear of differences or being misunderstood

_____ Hiding problems

_____ Fear of feeling pain of underachievement and failure

_____ Feeling depressed

_____ Others: _____

Taking the Next Step

Directions: Think of or write about a specific friend that you have had difficulty initiating or maintaining a relationship with or with whom you have had difficulty reconnecting.

Name a strategy that you could begin, for example, the ones discussed in this chapter or your own.

_____

The first step to take is:

_____

What is smallest step yet meaningful heartfelt way to reconnect?

The only goal is to take the smallest step to touch base with those from whom you are disconnected.

Summary

Women with AD/HD want to connect but because of their difficulties with executive functioning, they often develop emotional barriers. The combination of cognitive struggles and emotional barriers or the intersection of these makes them avoid relationships even more which decreases the likelihood of starting or maintaining relationships or of reconnecting after a break in the connection. Many fears, negative expectations, and much pain surround these areas. They key for these women to take stock of their barriers and make a plan to slowly start getting back on the road to relationships.

PART III

EMERGING

CHAPTER ELEVEN

Finding Your Way

Self-Assessment and Paths to Diagnosis

Self-Screening

First Steps

What happens when a woman is having difficulties and doesn't know if it is AD/HD or something else? The first step is to read a lot of current information on AD/HD and take a variety of self-assessment or screening checklists. Below is my assessment with an explanation of how and why I developed it.

Up until the time I first wrote this book, one of the difficulties had been the lack of a self-assessment tool designed specifically for women. Although women share many primary and secondary symptoms of AD/HD with men, they do have some significant issues in regard to AD/HD that differ. Many women screen themselves out early on, even when they start to have an inkling that some of these characteristics describe them. When they look at various diagnostic descriptions, they often feel that even though they saw a few words, a few lines, or even a chapter that might apply to them, the majority of material is not "them." They then fall back to their previous mindset that they are just being lazy or disorganized, which often leads to depression. This is especially true for women *without* hyperactivity (or what we now call inattentive type AD/HD) Picasso's image of a sleeping woman represents the way a woman without hyperactivity may look and feel as contrasted to a more hyperactive, and consequently more easily identifiable, AD/HD individual.

When I first wrote this book, the concept of AD/HD in adults, let alone women, was still a relatively new phenomenon. It had only recently started to come into the mainstream of diagnostic possibilities for mental health professionals. With the publication of many new books on adults with AD/HD, as well as the conferences, newsletters, and support groups that popped up throughout the United States and around the world, word began to spread that this condition really exists and that it may account for the difficulties of countless adults.

I designed my self-screening tool specifically for women because it is critically important for women who think they may have this disorder to be as educated as possible. Just as it is important to be an educated consumer when purchasing a major item like a house, car, boat, or computer, today it is equally imperative to be an educated consumer when it comes to mental health care, especially when you are dealing with something that is new or unfamiliar to the public, as well as to many professionals.

I wrote this checklist as an alternative to the more traditional ones since women's cultural tasks and roles are different from men's. This is not a substitute for all the other kinds of screening and diagnostic tools but extra information and a new way to look at this from a woman's perspective. I changed the name in this revision from assessment to screening because it is really designed as an initial screening rather than a full assessment as to whether or not you have AD/HD.

Screening Tool

Every woman has the kinds of feelings or problems listed in this checklist at some time or another in her life. The important question is if you have them more severely than the average person. Have they been present for most of your life? Do you feel these particular symptoms are the major reason you may be having difficulty in your achievement level, self-esteem, relationships, and moods? If your overwhelming reaction to this list is a big "Yes!" you might want to consider a professional consultation and full AD/HD assessment.

Solden Self-Screening for Women with Attention Deficit Disorder

© copyright 1995 Sari Solden
(not to be reprinted without permission)

Directions: Check the boxes next to items that apply.

Stimulation Filtering System

- Do you feel bombarded in department stores or grocery stores?

- Do you feel overloaded and exhausted after a day at the office?

- Do you feel overloaded from the noise and activity at parties?

- Do you often shut down in the middle of the day, feeling assaulted?

- Is it impossible for you to shut out nearby sounds and distractions that don't bother others?

Time, Money, Stuff (TMS)

- Is time, money, paper or "stuff" dominating your life and impacting your ability to achieve your goals?

- Are bills and important papers and forms piling up unattended?

- Are you spending a majority of your time coping, looking for things, catching up, or covering up?

- Have you never learned to balance your checkbook?

- Is your car constantly filled with all sorts of stuff?

- Do you feel that you can't clean up without a tremendous amount of effort?

- Do you often feel life racing out of control or that it's impossible to meet your daily demands?

- Do you have trouble meeting deadlines, planning, and prioritizing tasks?

- Do people frequently get annoyed with you for being late or forgetting appointments?

- Is packing for trips a nightmare?

- Despite your best efforts, is it impossible for you to maintain systems?

- Do you spend much of your energy on organization to the exclusion of many other things you'd like to do?

- Are you too embarrassed to have someone come to your house to clean because they would see your mess?

- Are you too embarrassed to hire someone to help keep you organized because you think you're beyond help?

- Do you start each day determined to get organized?

Relationships

- Do you avoid people because of all the clutter in your life or your disorganization?

- Have you stopped having people over to your house because of your shame at the mess?

- Have you been thought of as selfish because you don't write thank-you notes or send birthday cards?

- Do others ever call you a slob or spacey?

- Do you feel like you are "passing for normal?"

- Do you feel like an impostor?

- Do you often go blank in conversations?

- Is small talk difficult for you?

- Are there times when you can't stop talking?

- Are there times when you can't help yourself from interrupting others even though you know you shouldn't?

- Do you have difficulty discussing world events?

- Have you had difficulties with sexual relationships because you can't concentrate enough?

- Have you often formed relationships with people who function as caretakers?

- Do you have special fears of abandonment or winding up alone because you don't think you could meet the demands of daily life by yourself?

- Do you hesitate to get close to intimate partners for fear that you couldn't manage the demands of marriage and children?

Emotions

- Can a request for "one more thing" put you emotionally "over the top?"

- Do you often feel overloaded or depleted?

- Do you feel depressed because you can't get everything done in your life?

- Have you felt this way for a long time? Since childhood?

- Do you find that you can't maintain a balanced life and meet the demands on you?

- Do you engage in negative self-talk about your disorganization or forgetfulness?

- Do you feel you are irresponsible?

- Do you worry excessively or have an inner sense that things are going to fall apart?

- If someone disturbs one of your systems, do you have a strong angry reaction?

- If the phone rings while you are concentrating, are you thrown into a state of "mini- panic?"

- Can you be distracted from one mood to another easily?

- Do you feel you are on a treadmill that you'll never get off?

Staying Alert, Energy Levels, and Activity Level

- Do you drink an excessive amount of coffee or cola every day?

- Have you abused stimulants to stay focused such as cocaine, alcohol, or marijuana?

- Do you feel like a couch potato or a tornado, at either end of a disregulated activity spectrum?
- Do you feel as if you are in a fog?
- Is your motor always running?
- Do you feel that your mind is hyperactive, always thinking of new ideas?
- Is it very difficult for you to sit still or feel relaxed for long periods of time at meetings or lectures?

Ideas and Synthesizing

- Do you feel that you have many more ideas than other people?
- Do you feel that you can't synthesize, organize, or act on your ideas in an orderly way?
- Do you have difficulty prioritizing?
- Do you have difficulty reading and remembering basic facts?
- At the end of the day, have you collected a multitude of notes scribbled on random pieces of paper?

Achievement

- Have you watched others of equal IQ and education pass you by?
- Are you starting to feel despair of ever fulfilling your potential and meeting your goals?
- Are you clueless as to how others lead a consistent, regular life?
- Are you unable to figure out how to focus on your abilities because you're already drowning in demands?
- Do you find it very difficult to meet the demands of an 8-5 job?

History

- Were you called a daydreamer as a child?
- Were you called messy, spacey, lazy, selfish, or oversensitive?
- Were you ever diagnosed as having learning disabilities?
- Were you clumsy, bumping into things a lot?

- Were you either extremely shy or extremely social and talkative as a child?

- Were some of your grades in school way out of sync with the other grades?

- Did you have problems organizing your locker, drawers, closet, or room?

- Were you promiscuous as a teenager?

- Did you change schools or colleges more than average?

- Did you change majors several times?

- Have you had more changes than average in your life?

- Do you change jobs frequently?

- Have you changed life paths frequently or had more and different jobs than other people?

Women's Issues

- Do you have difficulty keeping track of your jewelry, makeup, clothing, and accessories?

- Is it very difficult for you to shop in department stores?

- Do you have difficulties with impulsive or compulsive shopping?

- Do you find it overwhelming to help your children organize their school and social life?

- Are you unable to provide the structure required, especially if your children have AD/HD?

- Do you find yourself using food or sex compulsively as a way to focus or self- soothe?

- Do you find yourself shifting from one activity to another when you are trying to do household tasks without accomplishing much?

If you answered yes strongly to many of these questions, or if even a few of these are causing you great difficulty in your life, I would encourage you to pursue the question of whether you have AD/HD.

After Self-screening: Now What?

If after you go through a preliminary self-assessment, do some reading about AD/HD, perhaps go to some lectures and/or go online to complete some initial self-assessment checklists you still feel that AD/HD comes closest to describing your difficulties, then it is worth pursuing a professional evaluation. Remember that you can have all the symptoms on any checklist or description and even have had them chronically and severely and still not have AD/HD. Your symptoms could be due to depression, anxiety, or other interpersonal difficulties aside from the AD/HD and must be evaluated in the context of a fuller diagnostic picture with a professional who is experienced with adult AD/HD. (See Chapter 12 for more information on diagnostic challenges). If you are having difficulties that don't seem to fit AD/HD but are still disturbing to you, I urge you to seek professional help anyway. The mental health professional that you choose, however, must understand the subtleties of AD/HD, especially for women who may have had their symptoms masked for many years. It is not uncommon to get misdiagnosed because AD/HD is similar to so many other disorders. It also may happen that your symptoms are dismissed because they are not seen as rising to the level of a diagnosis. Because of this you will need professional and experienced assessment and diagnosis that includes a diagnosis for AD/HD and for other difficulties that might be impacting you, as well.

Paths to Diagnosis

Short Circuiting the Process

I have found that people often get diagnosed with AD/HD in a way that is not particularly helpful especially in the long term. For example, someone could just read something about AD/HD, immediately go to a psychiatrist, get a prescription, go home, and that's it. Or someone may go right in for a full battery of tests with a psychologist who says, "Yes, you have AD/HD," get medication and go home with no explanation, no clear steps to take, or no referrals for counseling or support—no guidance. In these situations, at least the person would know if he or she had AD/HD. Some people will go on to read a lot more about it, get involved with others who have AD/HD, and develop a network of support.

For most adults, though, that won't be enough. If they get the diagnosis and medication too quickly or if the process is too brief, and they just go off on their own, they won't become involved with other people and continue to become educated about their AD/HD. They won't have the necessary time to absorb and integrate this new kind of identity. They won't have someone to work with on restructuring their lives and confronting the difficult situations that come up when they try to make the necessary changes. Ultimately, they often feel disappointed.

Let's look at the steps you might go through to get a correct diagnosis using a process that is most helpful.

Which Professional Should You Start With?

If you're already seeing a mental health professional talk to him or her about your reactions to your reading and the self-assessments you might have taken. If your mental health professional has the expertise, he or she may be able to assess you or recommend another mental health professional who specializes in AD/HD. Your mental health professional may send you to a psychologist for a complete neuropsychological evaluation or to a psychiatrist for a diagnosis and medication without this kind of extensive testing.

In other cases, you may start out discussing your feelings about AD/HD with your family doctor or a psychiatrist. Other mental health professionals or organizations in your area, or doctors who work with children with AD/HD may be able to give you direction, as well.

You may also want to try and get referrals from local AD/HD support groups, national associations or the Internet.

The Quality of the Experience

There are a variety of approaches, tools, and professionals that can be involved or useful in this process. The experience and thoroughness of the professional with whom you are working is critical, throughout the process, as well as at the moment of diagnosis. I have seen people get complete work-ups yet have a destructive experience and/or a misdiagnosis, and I have also seen professionals who are sensitive, thorough, and experienced not use any specific tools and do a great job of sorting through the issues. You must have the feeling that the process is thorough and specific to you with lots of opportunity for you to explain the details of your unique inner experience from your childhood all the way through your adulthood. You are a complex human being and not just another case of AD/HD. You must feel that the professional is looking for what is *there*, not just AD/HD and not just emotional causes for your symptoms.

If you can't find someone who understands what you are describing, go somewhere else. It's important to be open-minded and listen to what they have to say about the other possible causes of your difficulties but also trust yourself. Many professionals don't have the experience or willingness yet to see AD/HD in women. Find a professional that you can trust and work with in a partnership as you both try to understand your challenges.

Before You Go to a Professional

Before you go to a professional for discussion of your symptoms or assessment, write things down that seem to relate to you as you read or highlight them, for example:

- Think back from your childhood all the way through to the present and jot down difficulties you may have experienced. Look at the questions on the self-screening tool above and expand and explain any of these that are particularly relevant to your own experiences. You may go into more detail for yourself than you may have time to convey to the person you are going to see but doing this will help you remember details that you can convey during your interview.

- Think about any unusual inconsistencies in school, job changes, or social relationships, or perhaps a time when you may have experimented with substances. Think especially about times you may have used stimulants such as caffeine, *No-Doz*, or diet pills in college, or other things like cocaine or tobacco that helped you focus. People sometimes remember unusual experiences of being able to focus when they happened to be taking a medication for something else such as an antihistamine.

- Especially think about the organization of your daily life so you can give the person you are explaining things to a real feeling or flavor for what happens during the course of a typical day that is out of the normal range in terms of frequency and difficulty, for example, you might describe your morning routine or your work situation, whatever is really causing you severe problems during the course of a day or a week.

- Look at the times when things were going well and try to figure out what kind of support you had then which helped your life to work. Try to remember when things might have stopped working well such as when you might have hit a level of demands in your life that caused you not to be able to function as well.

- Talk to your family. If your parents and brothers or sisters are available, talk to them about what they remember about your childhood. Try and pick a family member who will be supportive, not critical, and ask him or her about problems in school either with behavior and relationships or reading and writing. Did any teachers report any concerns? Do they have any report cards with teachers' comments on them? Did you have unusual problems organizing your belongings? Does anyone else in the family have problems with attention or distractibility?

- If you had any unusual problems, when did they begin? Was there anything else significant going on in the family at the time?

Your First Visit with a Professional

Take your notes with you and don't be afraid to use them. You don't want to work with someone who is overwhelmed by all of this or with your style of communicating. The last thing you need is more shame. On the other hand, there is a limit to how much reading or information a professional can take in and use, especially right there in a session when she wants to be talking to you and not reading your notes. You may want to send these notes in advance or leave a copy of them rather than asking someone to read them all right there at the meeting.

Potential Aspects of the Evaluation Process

The Interview

Before the actual evaluation begins, you need to have an explanation regarding what to expect and how this will be helpful to you. It's important for the professional to spend a lot of time with you to separate out the psychological from the neurological symptoms. As Thomas Brown, Ph.D. from Yale University (1993) emphasizes, assessing what we now call inattentive AD/HD requires extremely careful listening and questioning during the interview. He states that identifying the cognitive symptoms of AD/HD when there is no hyperactivity present requires much more subtle measures than "the simple observations or reports of overt behavior, which can identify hyperactive-impulsive types of ADD." This is critical because much of what happens for women with AD/HD, especially inattentive type, is not easily observable from the outside. This can lead to the misdiagnosis we look at more in depth in next chapter.

Different Assessment Tools

Thomas Brown, Ph.D., has an assessment tool called the *Brown Attention Deficit Disorder Scales* (BADDS) (1998). This helpful tool can be used by a professional when conducting a structured interview as a way to explore your experiences and give you a chance to explain your responses, not just as a quick checklist. Most adults will experience all sorts of nuances and this can be used as a way to explore many areas of executive functioning in depth. (See Chapter 5 for more on executive functioning). Even if you use a take-home checklist to fill out and return, it should be discussed, not just left to stand on its own.

Testing

Neuropsychological Evaluation

This kind of extensive testing can be used in addition to the interview, checklists, and/or computerized tests. Done by a neuropsychologist or psychologist trained in this kind of evaluation, this can help explain the ways in which your brain functions well and which areas it has more difficulty. It may reveal gaps in your abilities that may explain your difficulties, or it may reveal problems in a few areas that might be causing you real problems in your everyday life, for instance with memory or sequencing.

Benefits of a Comprehensive Evaluation

An experienced evaluator can use a variety of tools, a structured interview, a complete neuropsychological evaluation, or all of them to make the diagnosis. Many adults have a strong history of AD/HD without many other complicating factors. In these cases, after a complete interview and history, the diagnosis can be relatively clear to a professional experienced with adult AD/HD, especially if he or she is also clearly able to rule out other co-existing disorders. Overall, my experience has been that women benefit from following the more comprehensive path as long as it is with an experienced and sensitive professional, even though it may be more expensive and time-consuming.

Even after this initial assessment period, an extensive interview, history, and checklists, a professional may still be unclear that AD/HD is the cause or only cause of someone's difficulties. This could be because of childhood histories or current coexisting difficulties that impact the diagnostic picture. Specific learning disabilities may also need to be sorted out. You might have other neurological conditions, mood disorders, or personality difficulties clouding the issue. In these cases, there are a lot of good reasons to go for a more in-depth, full battery of neuropsychological testing, which can provide a great deal of valuable information.

The more comprehensive evaluation and explanation by a sensitive professional can help individuals understand that they have AD/HD and start to integrate that idea in a deeper way. The tests can also help family members to understand and accept the diagnosis more easily because they can often see the difficulties and gaps in black and white. These tests and this process is useful to break through denial.

Another very important reason to go through a thorough testing process is that it is required in order to get certification for legal accommodations at school or at work. Sometimes you can also get extended time on professional exams.

Another reason to get full testing is personal knowledge. Some people, even if they know they have AD/HD, want to better understand their neuropsychological profile. They want to know their strengths and weaknesses in particular areas. It is always helpful to know more about yourself.

Downsides of a Comprehensive Evaluation

Neuropsychological testing is expensive, and there is no absolute yes or no answer as to whether or not someone has AD/HD. As Drs. Hallowell and Ratey point out in *Driven to Distraction*, the test results may not accurately reflect a person's daily functioning because often the testing conditions provide the motivation and stimulation that a person with AD/HD needs in order to pay attention. Sometimes then he or she will do much better on these tests than real-life difficulties would suggest.

Another downside to this kind of comprehensive testing is evaluation done by someone only looking for and believing in psychological reasons for your symptoms. This can be a devastating and dismissive experience.

Testing is not necessarily for everyone, especially as a way to begin. Timing is critical in the context of the entire AD/HD treatment plan. I personally feel that the approach and route appropriate for each person needs to be determined on an individual basis. Many people cannot afford neuropsychological testing even if they need help very badly. If these people can be accurately diagnosed without testing they should be treated and carefully followed. Others may have a very clear history with no complicating factors and can be diagnosed from checklists and interviews. They may not need information for school or careers or for the purpose of self-acceptance. They may want to go ahead with the confirmation of a diagnosis and treatment from a psychiatrist and with treatment from a mental health professional, coach, or group or with their own ongoing investigation of AD/HD resources. There are many areas in which it is not easy to be tested by someone experienced in the diagnosis of adults with AD/HD or the wait may be very long for a person who is eager to get started with medication.

The Reporting Session

After your first one or two sessions of testing, you will meet with either the person who did the tests or a supervising psychologist who will give you feedback. This "reporting session" is critical because diagnosis is the start of treatment. "Hope begins with the diagnosis" (Hallowell and Ratey, in *Driven to Distraction*, pg. 216). Quite often with a diagnosis, a woman with AD/HD will feel relieved and be on her way to understanding. A whole range of feelings will accompany diagnosis. In my opinion, the best chance of success in treatment will occur if these feelings are explored with a caring mental health professional who can discuss your problems, explain your feelings, and answer the myriad of questions that will accompany your diagnosis and beginning of your treatment. This is a critical juncture in your life, and you don't want it to be done in a quick, clinical manner.

Although the testing may be thorough, too often I've seen test results that aren't thoroughly reviewed with the client and carefully and sensitively explained. They should illuminate your strong areas as well as your difficulties and review what can be done to help, what's effective, what kind of strategies you can use, and where to go from here. You need to get a solid verbal and written explanation of the results, including referrals and/or suggestions. Be sure that the practitioner has been clear about what it means and what the next steps are.

You may want to take a tape recorder to this session or take notes in order to remember what is said. If someone balks at this, you should question whether or not they understand the memory challenges involved in AD/HD. You may also want to bring a supportive person with you to help remember what is said because you might mishear things since you are in a vulnerable space. I had a client mishear, misremember, or misinterpret part of her report because it brought up the negative way she had come to view her symptoms. The report had explained in one place that she used "inefficient memory strategies" because of her AD/HD, but all she remembered was that she thought the conclusion of the report was that she was "*deficient*." Other women have been told that the evaluation showed they were actually gifted in many ways, but they came away from the reporting session hyper-focused on the lower scores in other areas that validated the problems they were experiencing.

Make this experience work because you may get what feels like a lot of confusing information, and you'll want to be able to go home and process it afterwards. Ask for an explanation of your strengths as well as your challenges. You don't want to feel as though you are a part of a mill in which you are whisked in and out. "Go get some medication, thank you, good-bye, and have a nice life." This *is* for life and is the beginning of a long, slow process, which should be approached in a very human way. You have the right to ask for that and to find someone with whom you feel comfortable.

When you are on the path to diagnosis, if you feel like you're being dismissed, told that you don't really know what you're feeling, or that this couldn't really apply to you, and you still think you have AD/HD, ask the professional to explain her position. If you think that AD/HD could still be the source of your difficulties, continue to look for someone else who might give you a second opinion. On the other hand, don't ignore the fact that you may have a different disorder that may look like AD/HD that needs treatment.

Summary

This way of looking at people and especially women is still relativity new. We used to think that cognitive challenges were always based in emotional or family issues. We never understood that people have different *brain-prints*, just like fingerprints. People are just beginning to recognize how much we're influenced by our brain chemistry, and our brain wiring. Everyone is different; everyone has variations. All the different chemical transactions that go on in our minds—our behavior and emotions—are reactions to our brain chemistry. Now we're seeing that cognitive differences and subtle variations may account for our difficulties.

Even though it is starting to become accepted, there's still a tremendous disbelief and lack of knowledge about AD/HD in adults, particularly women, and especially for those women who have never been hyperactive. That is why it's so important to go thorough a complete process of evaluation. This can be done in different ways, but it should begin with a self- assessment through checklists and reading, including the one here geared to women. Then prepare for a meeting with an experienced professional so you can give him or her a thorough understanding of what you are calling AD/HD—make it a personal look at your particular challenges. After the testing or interview, make sure you have a good understanding of your challenges and that you come away with a plan, feeling hopeful. If you are discouraged or confused, go back and ask for a second opinion. In the next chapter, we will look in depth at why and in what ways women are sometimes misdiagnosed.

CHAPTER TWELVE

Cases of Mistaken Identity

Diagnostic Difficulties for Women

Women with AD/HD often feel that despite years of trying to keep their heads above water that they are sinking deeper and deeper and are feeling more trapped and helpless. Many women with undiagnosed AD/HD are unable to explain or have anyone else help them understand their experience. It may be incomprehensible for others to believe that a seemingly successful woman, or a woman who has never been hyperactive, may have AD/HD. Instead, she may be written off as having typical "female emotional problems" or serious psychological disturbances. The greater her outward signs of success, the more baffling it is to those around her. And if she has been visibly struggling, it just reconfirms other people's opinions that she is indeed weak, incompetent, or helpless.

In the last chapter, we looked at the process of getting diagnosed. Now we will look a little more closely at how the diagnostic process can be hampered when AD/HD symptoms are confused with other conditions.

Preview of This Chapter

First we will look at how histories that don't include hyperactivity combined with the ways women compensate for their difficulties can blur the diagnostic picture. Then we will look at ways that misdiagnosis commonly occurs. It is important as you read to remember that the goal is not just to get a diagnosis of AD/HD but, to get *correct* diagnosis and treatment!

135

Why A Woman's AD/HD May Get Misdiagnosed or Missed Altogether

She Doesn't "Look" Chaotic

The inner sense of chaos experienced by so many women with undiagnosed AD/HD can be hard for others to see. Sometimes other people don't believe them even when these women try to reach out and explain. Quite often because women with AD/HD have achievements in other areas, they're told they are overreacting or overly sensitive. As I've emphasized repeatedly, it's the discrepancy between these kinds of difficulties and the achievement in other areas that makes it hard for someone who is not aware of AD/HD to understand how her troubles could be related to something cognitive or attention related rather than something psychological or emotionally driven.

Many Mental Health Professionals Aren't Trained to Identify AD/HD

When women do decide to go for professional help, they might choose a mental health professional who doesn't understand this disorder as it often appears in women. A woman might talk about the same general things that other clients do, about relationships or feeling depressed, but underlying everything is the intense feeling of not being able to solve her real life problems. She might describe the difficulties in maintaining order in her daily life over and over again as she talks about her inability to make decisions, her disorganization, lack of routines, and her feelings of being overwhelmed and out of control. A mental health professional not used to seeing AD/HD in adults might seen these issues as related to "family dynamics," causing her to act out at home, or she may be termed as "passive-aggressive" toward her husband. An initial inquiry into AD/HD might be too quickly dismissed because of her lack of a stereotypical history.

Perhaps a mental health professional will see it as a more severe, psychological disorder such as depression, not realizing that battling the AD/HD may have caused this secondary condition of depression. The cause and effect can be confused. I have seen many women who have been in therapy for years with other mental health professionals working on some valid family and secondary psychological problems but never working on their basic underlying problem—the AD/HD. She might be seen as denying her depression or her real feelings. This, coupled with her tendency to not be assertive with authority figures, might make her accept a mental health professional's opinions, feeding into her already insecure feelings.

Individuals and professionals today are much more aware of adult AD/HD than ten years ago when I wrote the first edition of this book and diagnoses are easier to come by. But even with the increased media and professional attention on adult AD/HD, women, especially those with inattentive type AD/HD, still often have difficulty getting diagnosed.

A History Lesson

When a woman goes to a counselor, psychologist, or psychiatrist to get help, one of the first things a mental health professional will probably do is ask for a complete childhood history of problems, as well as her present life difficulties. Yet the histories of women, particularly those without hyperactivity, don't always conform to what is considered a typical AD/HD history. From the complete story that she relates, the mental health professional eventually makes a diagnosis. In many cases, a woman's history and current story don't *seem* to "add up" to AD/HD.

Childhood Histories without Hyperactivity

If you went to a mental health professional complaining of depression or being overwhelmed or overloaded, and there's absolutely no childhood history of hyperactivity, it could make it difficult to get a diagnosis of AD/HD. You may, in fact, have the opposite history. You may not have moved much at all or have had difficulty in moving directly from an impulse to an action. There might be great discrepancies in your energy levels. You might not be hyperactive on the outside, but you may feel an internal restlessness that you don't display.

Childhood Protective Factors

A diagnosis of AD/HD requires that the symptoms be severe and of a chronic nature. Mental health professionals look for how chronic or long term a problem has been. If they don't see this or if the problem looks like it has happened recently, then they might not feel that AD/HD is the problem.

Many women have had what I call "protective factors" in their childhood such as structured parents or high IQ, which can lead a professional into thinking there wasn't or isn't a problem. The problem was there, however, it just hadn't surfaced yet because these factors were "protecting" the individual from obvious outward signs of AD/HD.

There are many circumstances in a person's life that can delay the full impact (severity) of AD/HD symptoms until later when organizational demands and complexities increase. Many women grow up in structured environments and don't "hit a wall" until college, marriage, work, or children. They may not find out until later in life that they are unable to achieve or function in the same way as others of the same educational or ability level.

Other "protective factors" such as being highly intelligent or talented in one area can also be misleading to a mental health professional. If you are bright, your intelligence may have covered your organizational or attentional weaknesses, and you could have come out looking like an average student instead of a very bright one with AD/HD. Or if you were very talented in one area, that may have focused you to the point that your difficulties weren't noticed as much.

Compensation Blurs the Picture

The various ways of compensating that women develop often without realizing it blur the picture making it even more difficult to recognize the AD/HD in a woman. They may have achieved much in their professional life and/or have successfully managed a family. Their life works as long as they maintain their compensations, but this is often a fragile balance. Beneath the mask of well-compensated adults, you may see women who hold things together in an unhealthy way or with a great deal of anxiety. In other words, they've paid a price. Eventually, when the stress of the process by which they cope becomes too hard, they might finally hit a wall. They may be getting through their daily lives, but the pressure of doing the little routine things is intense. They may end up seeing a mental health professional for depression or anxiety.

Some of the ways these women cope and compensate include the following:

- Self-medicating

- Over-controlling

- Over-organizing

- Under-achieving

- Under-producing (financially)

- "Assisted living"

So while these women might not present as underachievers, they can still have AD/HD. It's hard for a professional to diagnose AD/HD in these women who present well to the world or to believe the severe, daily difficulties these women describe. *For example, a nurse was tested and found to have AD/HD, but the psychologist felt that this woman didn't need medication because she had a job in which she was getting good evaluations. Her career provided a very stimulating environment in which she could move around a great deal. The mental health professional thought that this was perfect for a person with AD/HD. What this diagnostician didn't see was the overwhelming demands this nurse felt in what she perceived to be a chaotic environment. Even though she was doing well, the process was unsatisfying to her, highly anxiety provoking, and both emotionally and physically draining. When she was treated with medication and made some adjustments in her workday, she felt great relief.*

Sometimes a woman with AD/HD may have found a good fit at work and be highly successful by getting support to fill in her gaps. Again this would be make some professionals hesitate to consider a diagnosis of AD/HD even though she may be floundering at home.

Self-medicating

Some women seem to manage well, but when the mental health professional inquires further it is discovered that they have been trying to "fix" their own brain chemistry by self-medicating. They might be drinking excessive amounts of caffeinated coffee or colas in an attempt to stay alert, awake, and focused. It may turn out that they've been using other substances that act as stimulants such as nicotine, diet pills, antihistamines, or even cocaine.

Instead or in addition to self-medicating with stimulants, they might be self-medicating with pain medications, alcohol, marijuana, or food. These substances are often taken at night to sleep in order to counteract the stimulants taken earlier in the day to stay awake. This kind of self-medication may appear as a substance abuse problem to a mental health professional, which it may be by then. The important point to remember is that the self-medication allows AD/HD individuals to achieve at a "normal" level, thereby masking the true level of difficulty caused by the AD/HD. This is obviously not a healthy cycle, and despite the positive short-term benefits, there are many negative long-term effects.

Over-controlling

One way some women mask their AD/HD symptoms is to anchor their lives with extensive systems and controls. They may seriously limit the amount of activities in their lives in order to keep things under control. They may function like blind people who would be totally thrown off if someone interfered with their systems by moving something in their environment. If their compensations weren't carried out or if their systems were disturbed in some way, more of their true difficulties would emerge. This fear that they would "lose it" if something was disturbed leaves them only able to function when they are being overly controlling of their environment.

Over-organizing

If a professional asked such a woman about the level of disorganization in her life, she might honestly respond, "I'm very organized. I'm never late. In fact, I'm always early. I never forget appointments, and my house is very tidy. I have a place for everything." Based on these responses, it would be difficult to see her as having AD/HD or difficulties with shifting attention or impulsivity. But, *and this is the key*, if the professional looks more closely at her daily life, she or he may begin to understand that the woman's whole life may be centered around organizing and that she may feel that if she doesn't do this, everything will fall apart. This woman is *over-organizing*.

Just saying that you are organized doesn't mean you don't have AD/HD. You might be focusing on organization to the exclusion of everything else. This could become obsessive, agonizing about the placement of every one of your possessions. Or you might stay up to all hours of the night preparing carefully for the next day's ordinary routine in order to successfully be on time and fully prepared. Unfortunately, this is a difficult way to live, often at the expense of your family or other areas in your life. Again, the important diagnostic distinction is to determine the amount of time and energy it takes to stay organized compared to people who don't have these difficulties with disorganization.

Under-achieving

Some of the sexual bias that still exists in regard to women might make a professional predisposed to judge a fairly successful woman as having achieved a great deal when, in fact, she may be severely underachieving. Her level of ability may be far greater than she has been able to display because of her life long difficulties. As she was growing up, the cultural or family stereotypes of gender expectations may also have minimized concerns regarding her life choices and levels of achievement. If she now voices disappointment about her accomplishments, especially if she has achieved what most people think is a fair amount of success for a woman, she may be seen as overly ambitious, aggressive, or perfectionistic. *A highly intelligent woman can continually have her AD/HD misdiagnosed or missed altogether and continue to harbor the painful sense that she is seriously underachieving without understanding why.*

Under-producing

Half the Job: Half the Money

As Stephen Copps, M.D. writes (2000, pg. 1) *"often the person with ADD feels he's twice as smart, works twice as hard an makes half as much money."*

A woman named Joan came to see me. It had been hard for her to get diagnosed because it wasn't obvious that her life had been completely dictated by her undiagnosed AD/HD. First, she had to leave the large corporation where she had started her career because of the fast pace and demanding schedule. Eventually she went to a mid-size company and then to a small one. Finally, she was unable to take the kind of constraints or demands of working for someone else, so she started her own business, which she ran out of a home office. She was doing well. She was organized and completed her projects. What she didn't do was make as much money as other people of her own abil-ity level. Because she would become disturbed and actually non-functional if anyone touched or moved anything in her well-designed environment, she found herself unable to take advantage of office help, which could have helped her to increase her work load. Her AD/HD had dictated the terms of her employment to the point that she had become a serious financial under-producer.

Assisted Living

Another reason it can be difficult to get a diagnosis of AD/HD, especially for a woman, may be that she has a relationship with a "caretaker." A caretaker is someone who naturally and willingly fills in the gaps for an AD/HD person and takes care of the details of daily life, thereby preventing the full impact of her condition from becom-ing visible. Obviously if the relationship ends, such a system falls apart. When her newly emerging disorganization appears at the same time as her depression and anxiety over the lost relationship, the AD/HD might still be missed.

Cases of Mistaken Identity

Now let's look at situations that can result in specific kinds of misdiagnoses. The following information is not a substitute for pro-fessional and expert diagnostic procedures but is provided to make you aware of and alert to the possibilities and complexities involved. In addition, be aware that there are overlaps between these categories and that there are an infinite number of possible situations any one individual may be facing.

1. Cause or Effect

Sometimes if you have two disorders, AD/HD and something else, the other problem will get diagnosed instead of the AD/HD because it's easier to see or because someone is not looking for AD/HD as one of the possibilities because of the things we discussed above. Sometimes coping with undiagnosed AD/HD actually results in another condition such as depression. If you treat the AD/HD, the other condition might disappear. Of course, you may need treatment for both. Here are two essential questions to always ask:

- Do you have _____ *and* AD/HD but only the _____ is seen?

- Has the AD/HD *produced* the _____?

If so, unless and until the AD/HD is treated, the treatment for the other condition will not be completely successful. For example, we will fill in the blanks with these conditions:

- Depression
- Anxiety disorders
- Substance abuse

Depression

- Do you have *depression and* AD/HD but only the *depression* is seen?

- Has the AD/HD *produced* the depression?

Depression is probably the most common disorder that can mask AD/HD in women. A woman may have distinct periods of "major depression" in which she may feel hopeless and lose interest and pleasure in her activities, but frequently women experience less intense, low-level feelings of depression that are often the result of struggling for a lifetime with undiagnosed and untreated AD/HD. It is understandable to see how women can burnout if they have been carrying this unknown "problem" with them their whole lives. Unless the AD/HD is treated, the treatment for depression will not be completely successful. If the AD/HD is treated, the depression might disappear. Of course, a woman may need treatment for both.

Anxiety Disorders

- Do you have *anxiety and* AD/HD but only the *anxiety* is seen?

Has the AD/HD *produced* the anxiety?

Like depression, it is easy to feel anxious when one has AD/HD, especially when it is undiagnosed and untreated. Living a lifetime feeling insecure that things are going to fall apart can take an emotional toll and produce symptoms of anxiety. Unless the AD/HD is treated, the treatment for anxiety will not be completely successful. If the AD/HD is treated, the anxiety might disappear. Of course, a woman may need treatment for both.

Substance Abuse

- Do you have *substance abuse and* AD/HD but only the *substance abuse* is seen?

- Has the AD/HD *produced* the substance abuse?

When AD/HD goes undiagnosed and untreated, it can contribute to substance abuse because women may self-medicate in order to focus. Many times in this situation, however, the primary underlying AD/HD will be missed in diagnosis and only the substance abuse will be addressed. People who have abused substances in order to "fix" their unknown AD/HD are in great need of proper medication. Unfortunately, these are the very people many doctors hesitate to prescribe for, fearing they will become addicted to or abuse the medication. While this is a legitimate concern and needs to be approached cautiously, many experts maintain that when the right medication is prescribed and monitored correctly, these people are greatly helped, and, in fact, do not abuse it. Unless the AD/HD is treated, the treatment for substance abuse will not be completely successful. If the AD/HD is treated, the substance abuse might disappear. Of course, a woman may need treatment for both.

2. Look Alikes

AD/HD can look like other disorders, and there are two ways misdiagnosis can occur in these cases. One, the AD/HD can be mistaken for another condition. This is similar to the *cause or effect* we just discussed, but in this case the AD/HD just looks like another disorder. The other disorder is *not* present as it was in the above discussion. Here is the essential question in these cases:

- Have you been mistakenly diagnosed or are you mistakenly being treated for *another disorder* which *looks like* AD/HD while your AD/HD, the *real* problem, goes undiagnosed and untreated?

For example, here's how you can fill in the blanks with a particular condition: Have you been mistakenly diagnosed with depression which looks like inattentive AD/HD while your AD/HD, your actual problem, remains undiagnosed and untreated?

The other way for misdiagnosis to occur between look alikes is for the AD/HD to get diagnosed but the other condition to be missed.

For instance, if you have menopausal symptoms, is it AD/HD, menopause, or both? What follows are just some of the conditions that may be diagnosed incorrectly when your AD/HD remains undiagnosed and untreated. In all these cases the two conditions that look alike can both actually exist; you don't want to identify the AD/HD and leave the other one unidentified either.

Anxiety Disorders

Obsessive Compulsive Disorder (OCD)

One kind of anxiety disorder is called Obsessive Compulsive Disorder or OCD. Obsessions refer to thoughts and compulsions refer to behavior. Typical compulsions make a person feel that he or she must perform certain acts over and over again such as excessively washing his or her hands. Obsessions are non-productive, unwelcome, repetitive thoughts that are out of control. These thoughts or behaviors take on a life of their own, producing negative consequences in one's life that take up a great deal of time.

Women with AD/HD may *seem* to have this disorder when instead they have developed compensations that look like compulsions or obsessions as a way of coping with their AD/HD, memory problems, sequencing, or executive functioning problems. Behaviors such as spending exorbitant amounts of time making lists or compulsively organizing one's surroundings are examples of how someone with AD/HD may be trying to compensate for her inner chaos. To a mental health professional, compensations for AD/HD can sound a lot like OCD, especially when a client relates her struggles of constantly trying to remember what has to be done and mentally organizing lists of things to do.

If these are compensations, it's possible that the OCD-like symptoms may be reduced when the AD/HD is treated. Remember though that these compensations may take on a life of their own; women may hold onto them for dear life as a way to keep their world together, especially before treatment for AD/HD. They feel if they let down their guard for even a moment, all will be lost. The compensatory behaviors originally helpful for AD/HD difficulties can eventually take up as much time and have as much of a negative impact in one's life as the original symptoms they were attempting to control.

Social Phobias and Feelings of Panic

There are several reasons that a woman may display symptoms of social phobias, or panic disorders, that really stem from undiagnosed and untreated AD/HD. One reason that a woman may avoid social situations is that she never knows if and when her brain will work efficiently or whether or not she will know what to say in a particular group setting. Some women with AD/HD are extremely sensitive to stimulation and often experience sensory overload in social settings. In general, they may withdraw because they feel the need to protect themselves from the bombardment of extra obligations and the stimulation that comes as a result of relationships.

For years Donna thought that she was having panic attacks in malls before she was diagnosed with AD/HD. When a woman has a panic attack, she often feels as if she is going to die or as if she is having a heart attack. Donna had had long-term psychoanalytic treatment for this that focused on analyzing her separation issues from early childhood. When she was diagnosed with AD/HD and began to view this from an AD/HD perspective, she began to understand why she felt over-stimulated and overwhelmed in malls due to the bright lights, strong smells, and loud sounds. Armed with this explanation, she began to relax. Her treatment for AD/HD alleviated much of the discomfort in these situations.

On the other hand, a woman may develop psychological reactions that take on a life of their own because of the many years of being exposed to these situations and the way she comes to view herself and her symptoms. She may feel she has disappointed people by not keeping up her end of social expectations, which then sets her up for expectations of negative reactions from others such as being scolded or shamed. Another reason women with AD/HD may avoid relationships is because of the sense of shame they have about the way they live or because their hair, clothes, jewelry, or other "womanly" things aren't "up to snuff." I've had clients turn down good job opportunities that involved socializing just because it was too demanding to figure out what to wear. In these situations it is not just AD/HD alone that causes the problems but it may be actual social phobias that have developed, as well.

Generalized Anxiety Disorder (GAD)

Women with Generalized Anxiety Disorder worry excessively about a great many things and may or may not have racing thoughts.

Women with AD/HD commonly describe what feels like a million unfiltered thoughts bombarding them, swirling around in their heads. As one AD/HD woman said, thousands of thoughts are speeding past so quickly that she can't grasp them, leaving her internal world disorganized and chaotic. This experience can sound a great deal like generalized anxiety disorder in which an individual is worrying about all the bad things that might happen, frequently replaying scenes from the past that caused them humiliation. A woman with AD/HD may report racing, confusing, unending thoughts, but it might not be this same kind of worry. It is more about not being able to catch them and organize them into a manageable form. If the AD/HD is correctly diagnosed and treated, these symptoms can be reduced, but if women are misdiagnosed as having generalized anxiety disorders when their problems are really AD/HD, the treatment will not be as effective. Since women with AD/HD are aware of so many things to do all at once, many of which they have trouble figuring out how to do, this can of course produce tremendous anxiety, as well. They may require treatment for both their anxiety and their AD/HD.

Depression

In our earlier discussion of depression in *Cause or Effect*, depression was a real issue to be diagnosed and treated even though the AD/HD was left unidentified. In a look alike case, the depression would be mistaken for inattentive AD/HD. When a woman complains of difficulty concentrating, being disorganized, lethargic, or even restless and agitated, these can all be symptoms of depression, as well as AD/HD, inattentive type. As a woman with AD/HD put it so well when describing whether she felt she was depressed or AD/HD, she said, "I can't sustain a depression!" I thought that was a very exact distinction she was making. Since AD/HD is a problem with maintenance, she felt she couldn't even maintain a depression.

Of course, it is very common for a woman to also be depressed by the time she has lived all her life undiagnosed with AD/HD. She may have come to view herself as a failure and to experience the pain of underachievement and problems with relationships that may leave her feeling isolated. In these cases, she may also need to be treated for depression, as well as AD/HD. She could also just be biologically predisposed to depression in addition to the AD/HD.

Adjustment Reactions

Sometimes something less serious is diagnosed instead of the AD/HD, such as an adjustment reaction. When you think back to the atypical history sometimes presented by women with AD/HD, it's easy to understand how a professional might view a problem originating in the present that triggers her AD/HD challenges to surface and present a roadblock in a given situation. This frequently happens to young women with AD/HD when they go to college, get married, have children, or start a new, challenging level of work.

Let's say you are a newly married, young woman in your twenties, undiagnosed with AD/HD. You go to a mental health professional because you find yourself completely disorganized and unable to keep up with the demands of your new life. As a child, you led a protected, structured life. Your mother kept a highly organized house, and the Catholic school you attended also kept you very organized and structured. Your new level of disorganization might appear to be the result of your new marriage. In actuality, the protective factors of your life prevented the AD/HD from becoming an obvious part of your history. You may get a diagnosis of Adjustment Reaction with Anxiety (as a result of the new marriage), and the AD/HD may remain undiagnosed. Of course, you may have both conditions and may need counseling for help with the adjustment to marriage, as well.

Personality Disorders

The language used by a woman with AD/HD to describe her feelings, stress, and daily challenges, as well as the possible emotional, excited, expansive way in which she conveys these experiences, can sound like more serious psychological disorders to mental health professionals not familiar with AD/HD in women. What looks like self-centeredness, self-focus, or preoccupation could just be difficulty blocking out one's thoughts and needs or difficulty in meeting the demands of life. Forgetting appointments or birthdays, in other words things that are important to other people, can be interpreted as being self-absorbed, selfish, narcissistic, or passive aggressive rather than AD/HD. Typically, a mental health professional will try to discover the underlying meaning of the forgetting and the inattention rather than look for cognitive difficulties.

Women who are experiencing intense struggles in their daily lives with their AD/HD and who express it with strong affect might be seen as histrionic, dramatic, or perhaps just exaggerating their difficulties. If a woman is reporting high achievement in some areas of her life but has severe difficulties that she needs help with in daily routine activities that might be misinterpreted as dependent.

People with AD/HD sometimes describe a feeling of fragmentation, falling apart, or not being able to hold things together. In addition, a woman with AD/HD may report instability in her mood, relationships, job, or basic identity. If a mental health professional doesn't understand that this can be a *cognitive* state, not just an *emotional* state, she might be diagnosed with a severe personality disorder instead of AD/HD.

Once more, of course, it is important to say that because of the difficulty of living undiagnosed with AD/HD, or for completely separate reasons, a woman could have AD/HD and one of these other difficulties or not have AD/HD at all. It is important when you go to get diagnosed that you don't see someone who exclusively gives AD/HD diagnoses but someone who tries to distinguish cognitive factors versus true psychological causes for symptoms.

Abusive or Chaotic Childhoods

One of the most difficult circumstances to separate out from AD/HD during the diagnostic process is when a woman has grown up with a history of abuse. Women from both groups have difficulty clearly remembering their childhood. Any of the following types of abuse could result in AD/HD-like symptoms: sexual abuse, physical abuse, emotional abuse, or verbal abuse. A woman may also have had a chaotic childhood environment that could result in AD/HD like symptoms, for example, if her parents abused drugs or alcohol. With the diagnostic criteria requiring a chronic nature and severity, women with both AD/HD and abusive, chaotic childhoods report *chronic* and *severe* problems throughout their lives, especially in the areas of concentration and distractibility. Sometimes a woman may get a diagnosis of AD/HD but these other underlying childhood wounds or a condition like Post Traumatic Stress Disorder (PTSD) go unaddressed. Alternately, the symptoms of hyper-vigilance or distractibility as a result of childhood factors might not be diagnosed as a separate condition but are used to rule out the AD/HD as the cause of the symptoms.

Physical Conditions or Illnesses

Sometimes only AD/HD is treated whereas there may be a number of other physical conditions or illnesses impacting a woman's behavior. It is not uncommon for mental health professionals or doctors to discount reports of moodiness, distractibility, and concentration variability to "plain old, female sensitivity" or to psychological factors and not catch the underlying hormonal imbalances or AD/HD. (Hormonal fluctuations and their effects in relation to AD/HD will be covered more in depth in Chapter 15: Special Women's Issues). Throughout a woman's hormonal cycles, many symptoms of AD/HD can be exacerbated causing her to lose the compensations she may have been using for years, even though the symptoms she is experiencing at that time may, in fact, be PMS, perimenopause or menopause and not AD/HD.

In addition to hormonal changes, there is a wide range of physical conditions that need to be sorted out and eliminated before jumping to the conclusion that a woman has AD/HD. There may have been an early head injury or more recent injury or illness that might account for AD/HD-like behaviors that haven't been a chronic condition. A woman may simply be experiencing the usual loss of memory that comes with aging, or it could be Alzheimer's if symptoms occur later in life. That's why the long -term factor has to be thoroughly investigated. On the other hand, many women who are undiagnosed AD/HD and beginning perimenopause become frightened that they are at the beginning stages of Alzheimer's when in fact they are just hitting a wall caused by the combination of these two events. This calls for expert diagnosis and may require a team approach combining the psychiatrist or psychologist with the woman's doctor who is treating her hormonal shifts.

There may be other circumstances such as thyroid conditions, Chronic Fatigue Immune Deficiency Syndrome (CFIDS), or hypoglycemic conditions that need to be sorted out, as well.

Narcolepsy, a sleep disorder, can look very much like un-aroused AD/HD, according to Edna Copeland. Ph.D., (1995) They may not meet the full criteria but often struggle to stay awake during boring tasks or tasks like reading that require concentration. Other sleep disorders like sleep apnea can cause some of the same symptoms as inattentive AD/HD. All of these physical conditions need to be considered when making a diagnosis when the symptoms look like those of AD/HD. These must be looked at carefully to distinguish and treat.

This is why an entire health profile of the person has to be studied before any diagnosis is reached.

Learning Disabilities (LD)

Learning disabilities can mimic or accompany AD/HD. Learning disabilities are distinguished from AD/HD in that learning disabilities are permanent impairments in specific processes whereas AD/HD is a neurochemical disorder. Because of its "chemical" nature, AD/HD can be treated with medication whereas learning disabilities cannot. They can only be compensated for and accommodated. In many situations, individuals have both AD/HD and learning disabilities even if the learning disabilities go undetected. There are many important questions one has to ask in trying to differentiate between a learning disability and AD/HD. Why can't someone pay attention? Is it because they are highly distractible, or do they have an auditory processing problem? Why don't they read? Is it because they can't concentrate or get bored or because they have trouble distinguishing words? Why is someone's handwriting illegible? Is it because their writing cannot keep up with their rapid thoughts or because they can't form the letters properly? If a woman is being treated for AD/HD, and it's not helping significantly, she may have to look further for possible learning disabilities. AD/HD medication will not address a learning disability.

Creativity, Life Style Choices, and Independent Thinkers

On a last note, it is important to remember that sometimes a person who is highly creative, energetic and busy can display AD/HD symptoms when they don't have AD/HD. It's important that people who may have some organizational difficulties or other AD/HD-like symptoms don't get diagnosed with having a disorder when there is none. A woman could be very creative, making her way of life look similar to AD/HD. A woman could be very messy with her things all over the place, but this could be part of a visual life style, a "right-brain" way of seeing things. She should only be treated for it if it is a problem for her or a significant problem for those close to her. If the person can function fine, if she can find her possessions, if she is enjoying this exciting, creative kind of life, then there is no problem. If she is thriving, feeling good, having meaningful relationships, and is financially in control, then there is no problem. She should not be diagnosed by how she looks on the outside alone.

Summary

Many women with AD/HD have been coping and compensating so well for so long that it may be hard to see their struggle under the surface. Mediating circumstances such as family support, structure, or high IQ coupled with a lack of hyperactivity can easily cloud the picture of the chronic nature and severity that is required for diagnosis; and in this all-too-common scenario, the woman's inquiry into AD/HD might be quickly dismissed.

A professional could misinterpret the confusing picture that a woman with AD/HD may present. She may complain for years of low-level depression, low self-esteem, or feeling out of control and overwhelmed. She may be over-pathologized by a mental health professional who may be predisposed to see her as chronically depressed, dependent, hysterical, narcissistic or passive aggressive, depending on how she presents herself.

It is a mistake to insist that you don't have other difficulties and assume that every problem you may have is AD/HD, but *in the absence of severe mental illness or other neurological problems, in the absence of other great stressors, family problems or other things that would account for severe difficulties with disorganization, you must keep going in pursuit of a correct diagnosis. If you feel, in spite of other achievements or abilities, even after therapy, that you're coming up against these problems over and over again, continue to pursue the correct diagnosis. If you're spending your life looking for things, if you're overwhelmed, out of control, buried with paperwork or details, unable to take care of routine household tasks, you might be on the right track if you are considering AD/HD as an explanation.* In the next chapter, we will look at the first stages of treatment.

CHAPTER THIRTEEN

Solden's "MESST" Model of Treatment

Medication, Education, Strategies, Support, and Therapy

Let's begin with the diagram, "All Roads Lead to Success," an over view of treatment that we're going to follow throughout the rest of the book. When I say "treatment," I mean getting better, whatever that means to you. Treatment does not have to mean individual psy-

ALL ROADS LEAD TO SUCCESS

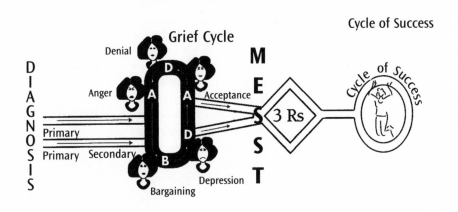

Cycle of Success

Some take the high road and some take the low road, but you have to stay on some road to lead to success.

chotherapy each week but depending on your particular history and present situation might indicate a combination of medication, coaching, support, or counseling. Each individual on the road to successfully living with AD/HD might take a different route; depending on your history, you might meet with fewer or more roadblocks or detours on the way. The important thing is to always get back on the road and continue onward. At the end of the journey, though, do not expect to find yourself to be a different person but more of who you really are. For the trip to be successful, you will need fuel (medication) and good company (you can't do it alone, and you can't do it with "toxic" help). You will also need a map to know where you're going, what signposts to look out for along the way and how to tell if you've arrived. Most important, you must be sure you are headed where you really want to go. (Solden, 2002).

AFTER THE DIAGNOSIS:
AN OVERVIEW OF THE PROCESS

The moment of diagnosis, when explained by an experienced and sensitive professional, often brings a feeling of great relief and hope. At some point after a diagnosis most people will seek some type of help. This is either with some type of professional or through association with others along with a program of self-care.

Sometime you may be searching for help with your primary symptoms of AD/HD such as distractibility or impulsivity, for instance, a woman may feel that she can't get her life on track or that her home life and/or work life are too difficult and time-consuming. For others, it may be secondary symptoms such as depression or anxiety that cause them to look for answers. In these cases, women may experience difficulties with mood, self-esteem, relationships or achievement that have developed as a result of living with undiagnosed AD/HD. Usually, it is a combination of primary and secondary symptoms that will prompt someone to seek out help.

As you follow along with the treatment diagram, you can see that after receiving a diagnosis, gaining an initial understanding and beginning to seek help, you start a process called the grief cycle, which consists of the five stages described below. The last stage of this process, and the ultimate goal, is acceptance. It takes a long time to truly get there. To help move you through the stages of the grief cycle and toward acceptance, I will suggest and describe tools, as well as areas of change (The *MESST* Model and the 3 R's) to help facilitate this. These will be described a little later in the chapter. As you see, the successful outcome of going through the grief cycle is that you begin a whole new cycle of success. Let's look at these a little bit more closely now.

The Grief Cycle

The concept of the grief cycle was originally conceived by Elizabeth Kubler-Ross to describe how people confront and come to terms with terminal illness. It has since been applied to any major life change. Dr. Lynn Weiss, in *Attention Deficit Disorder in Adult*, as well as Kate Kelly and Peggy Ramundo in *You Mean I'm Not Lazy, Stupid or Crazy?!* (1995) have applied the grief cycle to the process of accepting AD/HD. I have my own description of what I have seen happen as people go through this cycle in one form or another. There might be an obvious working through of the cycle, or the process might be more subtle and less linear, but eventually all people diagnosed with AD/HD must work their way through all the stages if they are to move forward in their lives. It takes much longer to reach acceptance than is commonly thought. What looks like acceptance early on is often resignation, or as I call it in my book *Journeys through ADDulthood*, (2002, pg. 20), "pseudo-acceptance."

Here are some descriptions of the feelings and challenges that go along with the grief cycle.

The Grief Cycle . . .

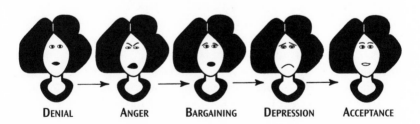

DENIAL   ANGER   BARGAINING   DEPRESSION   ACCEPTANCE

. . . becomes a new cycle of
SUCCESS!

Denial

After the period of relief that can accompany diagnosis, you might enter a state of denial. At first, you might either deny the reality of AD/HD, or accept it superficially, but continue to question if it really applies to you. Even if you say that you have AD/HD, you may not yet have integrated it in any kind of deep or meaningful way that will help you adjust. Even after diagnosis, when your AD/HD symptoms emerge, you may fall back into an "I'm stupid or irresponsible" stance. Even if you give lip service to the idea of AD/HD, it may take you awhile to integrate it into your perception of yourself.

As with any new life-altering event, label, or change of self-view, the person diagnosed with AD/HD often goes through an initial period of shock. This shock can persist for a long time, unless they've had a lot of time to investigate AD/HD before diagnosis. If the individual has been reading, integrating and thinking about AD/HD, applying the information to herself, and has become convinced that AD/HD is her problem before diagnosis, then, of course, she may have already worked through some of these feelings. If, however, the first mention of AD/HD is followed too quickly by diagnosis and medication, the person might believe that they are moving effectively through the grief cycle, but they might have to go back through the cycle again in more depth.

Another way that people deny their AD/HD in this first stage of the grief cycle is to deny the impact it has had in their lives and that it's going to continue to have in their lives, and especially the changes that they will have to make. This happens most frequently as a result of a quick diagnosis followed by medication prescribed without any in-depth education or follow-up counseling. A person in this situation won't have an understanding that this condition or treatment involves more than just taking medication. Also, if they do not fully appreciate the reality of AD/HD, they will not be able to understand the potential strengths that can accompany AD/HD and learn to capitalize on them. Skimming the surface of the grief cycle prevents a woman from immersing herself in a process that can be an exciting and fulfilling challenge.

Anger

After a woman understands that she does have something called AD/HD and has had it for a long time, she begins to look back and see how deeply it has affected every area of her life. At this point she will often move into the next stage—anger. She often feels anger at lost opportunities, looking back at the paths that she didn't take. She focuses on the point at which things started to go off course and begins to feel anger at a system that let her down as a child. She may feel anger her family who didn't help her or teachers who misunderstood her or people who blamed her. Or she may just feel angry in general that this is happening to her and that life has been so hard even though she has been unable to understand why or how to fix it. It is helpful for an individual to see that anger is a natural part of the grief cycle and that it is important and necessary to go through it in order to move beyond it and continue in a positive direction.

Bargaining

When a woman understands that she has AD/HD, she is naturally encouraged and excited to learn that she can take medication that will help. She may say, "Okay, I have AD/HD, but I'll just take my medication, and I'll be all right." Unfortunately, medication for AD/HD is sometimes discussed as if it were a magic pill. Medication is a cornerstone of treatment, as we will see, and is often essential, but it is not magic or perfect and not sufficient as treatment. Because the benefits of medication don't always match a person's expectations, disappointment and discouragement often set in.

Depression

When the medication doesn't cure everything, even if women with AD/HD feel better and many areas of their life are greatly improved, they still have many of the same difficulties. Thus begins the next stage in the cycle—depression. They're caught in between two worlds: they want to forget about AD/HD and go back to the way it was—but they can't. Even if the system wasn't working very well, at least it was familiar. They've seen other people with AD/HD, and by now they know that there's a long road ahead of them, but the process seems like too much to deal with. Often they are not yet getting enough of the support needed to make necessary changes. As a result, they may feel isolated and lonely, which also contributes to feeling depressed.

As a result of the new focus they achieve through their medication, people are able to see their lives much more clearly. They might not have had the energy before to face or to deal with problems in a relationship that may have been buried for years. It is natural at this point to feel the loss of dreams, hopes, and opportunities.

As defeated as a woman may feel in this stage, in truth, all the feelings described above may be signals that can point to the way out of depression. For instance, they may be messages to her that she needs support in order to continue to move through the cycle.

The emotions a woman feels as she works her way through this cycle are all natural and necessary. It means that she is integrating the idea of AD/HD, getting to know herself, and understanding her past in a way that will lead to a more satisfying way of life.

Acceptance

With the right kind of support, counseling, and education and with the passage of time, people move to a new level—acceptance. Sometimes they repeat the other phases again and again without reaching acceptance. Sometimes women move to acceptance and then repeat another entire cycle. One of my clients, a year after diagnosis and an initial acceptance of it, continued to have bouts of returning to the view of the AD/HD as bad character on her part and continued to berate herself with each emergence of AD/HD symptoms. As time went on, though, these periods occurred more frequently, more intensely, and lasted for a much briefer time.

However the process goes, at some point, if women continue to work at it, they will integrate the idea of themselves as a person with AD/HD in a deeper way. At that point, they stop thinking of AD/HD as a matter of willpower or moral failure.

At the stage of acceptance, they are able to start sorting out their primary AD/HD symptoms in a less reactive way. They learn that although they can manage their AD/HD symptoms, they will still occur. They learn to recognize their responses to the AD/HD and begin to change them so that they don't make things worse for themselves.

Eventually they learn to be desensitized to other people's judgments and start to externalize or get rid of this deep sense of shame and secrecy. They might still feel this shame, but it's outside them now. At this point, AD/HD adults stop apologizing or attacking; they feel they are more in control and state clearly what they need.

It is in the acceptance phase that they shift to focus on their strengths. No longer feeling the need to hide, they are able to ask for more help. Once they begin to be proactive, they develop a new sense of self-esteem, have less depression, and find more hope. They start exploring options and renegotiating roles and relationships to make their lives more satisfying. When the new cycle of acceptance is initiated, it takes on a life of its own. This is what I call the Cycle of Success. (As discussed in Chapter 23)

Solden's *MESST* Model

THE "MESST" MODEL

Medication   Often the cornerstone of treatment, a beginning

Education   Learn as much as possible; lectures, books, newsletters, organizations

Strategy   Intervention must match level of organizational deficit

Support   Emotional; identify with others
Physical; negotiate tasks

Therapy   Individual, couple or group
Communication skills, working through shame
Secondary effects; depression, self-esteem/relationships

© Sari Solden, MS 1994

The following combination of tools and interventions will help you as you progress through the grief cycle and manage your primary AD/HD symptoms. I use the acronym "MESST" as a desensitizing tool and as a convenient way for me to remember the basic elements of treatment. As you see in the diagram, the treatment consists of integrating various elements. Each element will be covered in more depth over the next few chapters but the following provides an overview of important elements of treatment. The term treatment here is broadly defined to mean how you need to treat yourself as you progress toward acceptance and then continue on to live a satisfying life.

A woman with AD/HD can follow this model on her own, but eventually she will need to enlarge her support system to include other people in a variety of ways. Medication should always be accompanied by an emphasis on the whole life of an individual with AD/HD and some options for continuing counseling or support. She may attend support groups, join AD/HD organizations or employ the support of coaches, family members or a counselor to facilitate this process.

Medication: This is often the cornerstone of treatment.

Education: This involves learning as much as possible about AD/HD and especially about your own brain and how it works. I encourage you to attend lectures and conferences, read books, go online, and join organizations.

Strategies: Strategies are modifications to your environment that provide structure and keep you on track. These include internal cognitive shifts in perspective and attitude such as giving yourself permission to get help, which enable you to act on external lifestyle modifications to promote, organize, or boost cognitive energy. Lifestyle changes can include implementing the use of low-tech strategies such as old-fashioned beepers and buzzers or planners or higher-tech strategies such as PDAs or computer organizing software.

Support: Through this you gain identification and emotional support from others who understand as well as physical support in your deficit areas and develop a philosophy of interdependence. Remember—the level of intervention must match your level and type of organizational deficit. This also includes professional coaching.

Therapy (counseling with a mental health professional) This can consist of individual, couple, or group work. Some of the issues addressed may include communication skills, working through shame, overcoming negative expectations, and learning to make good choices. Depression, relationship issues and underachievement are other common issues that can be explored, as well as learning to set boundaries and state needs.

The tools of the *MESST* model will make it easier for you to progress in the following three critical areas and continue to integrate what you discover about yourself, your strengths as well as your difficulties. I refer to these as the three "R's."

1. Restructuring your life

2. Renegotiating your relationships

3. Redefining your self-image

These are the subjects of Chapters 19-23 and are the pillars needed to build and modify your inner and outer life as you continue on your journey of learning to live a meaningful and satisfying life at home and at work even though you still struggle with the challenges of AD/HD.

Restructuring your life means making the changes that allow you to live more in accordance with your strengths and to get the support that you need to help with your difficulties. In order to do this, you usually need to renegotiate the relationships with the people in your life both at home, at work, and in your personal life. This is not easy to do and it requires stating needs and setting limits. In order to do this, ultimately, you will need to work on redefining for yourself what it means to be a successful woman. All the roles and rules you have internalized have to be re-examined. This requires that you reach the kind of acceptance we talked about in the discussion of the grief cycle. The goal for you, and what is critical in order to restructure your life, is to truly enjoy the kind of woman you are even if you don't fit a traditional mold.

Now that you have had an overview of treatment, we will look at the first step of the MESST model in the next chapter and highlight some of the important information about medication. In the chapter following that one, we will look at other related physical issues for women that may be affecting you or your treatment. In Chapters 16 and 17 we will continue with the middle sections of the treatment model, education, strategies, and support and complete the last phase of the *MESST* model, therapy (counseling), in Chapter 18.

CHAPTER FOURTEEN

The Beginning of the "MESST"

Medication

Running on Empty

Something interesting happened as I was rewriting this chapter on medications. I ran out of medication! I had dropped off my prescription to be filled and was intending to pick it up the next day. The next day came and with it a severe winter storm leaving me stranded at home to write all day without my medication. This experience brought home the point very clearly that medication is not a luxury for me. This was not fun! I did not have the necessary cognitive energy to do this task.

Not in Kansas Anymore

When the snow lifted and I was able to get my medication, I felt like the tin man in the Wizard of Oz in need of oil to begin moving again. Then as I began to write, my mind was much more fluid. I had the cognitive fuel to function. My brain was the same brain it was the day before, I had the same interest, motivation, ideas, and abilities, but without the medication, I just didn't have the fuel to access those parts of me and use them. Even a luxury car like a Rolls Royce isn't going anywhere without fuel.

In the same way, medication for individuals with AD/HD is often the fuel that allows the brain to function smoothly and work to its potential.

Overview

This edition updates the changes in medication since the original printing of *Women with AD/HD* in 1995. These are just brief summaries of the basics and not intended to be comprehensive, as that is beyond the scope of this kind of book. Please check the resources at the end of the book for more places to investigate current and complete information. Also, to keep abreast of the most current research and information on medications, go to the Internet, your physicians, or your AD/HD organizations.

The rest of the chapter covers symptoms and how the medications improve them, an overview of the most common medications used for AD/HD, as well as medications used to target other symptoms that often accompany it or develop as a result of living with AD/HD. In addition to the physical effects you may experience from taking the medications, I will talk about the common emotional reactions women have to the changes brought about by taking medication. In this way you will know what to look for and what to look out for when you begin a new medication.

My Take on Taking Medication

AD/HD is a neurobiological condition. It is critical to look at the psychology that develops as a reaction to living with your particular brain, but medication is the foundation to give you the energy to make the other necessary changes. It is often the cornerstone of treatment on which all the other strategies can be built. The correct medication can give you the focus to be able to strategize effectively, engage support, and to stay on track in order to make your life work again.

It is important to remember that if you try medication or use it for a while you may not always need to use it forever. Some people may use it to give their brain a jump start in order to begin to make better choices, to find a better fit for their work, to set up and use strategies and to find support.

A Balanced Approach?

At the same time I was struggling to write without medication, my editor questioned me about whether I was giving a *balanced* approach to the idea of taking medication. I thought this over and wondered if I were writing about wearing glasses or taking insulin whether I would have to give a balanced approach to those treatments as well. Every medical treatment has risks and must not be abused or overused. Antibiotics have great benefits but shouldn't be overused. Aspirin has great benefits when needed but also many potential negative side effects. All medication, including those for AD/HD must be carefully monitored. It's important to remember that when we talk about medication for AD/HD, I am assuming proper diagnosis, differential diagnosis, expert medication consultation, and ongoing monitoring.

The Decision Making Process

Even though the correct medication can provide a foundation, it is rarely taken lightly or for fun or just to enhance performance that is already good. It is hard work to tell your story over and over to try and explain the subtleties of your inner experience and explain the difficulties with daily life that might not match the official diagnostic criteria perfectly. It is especially burdensome for women to try and convince a professional that their difficulties are severe, especially if they have never had hyperactivity, and especially if they have a good education or other outward signs of competence that make people question their struggles.

No individual with AD/HD I have met says, "Great, I really want to take medication that affects my brain on a regular basis." Most people have fears and concerns about safety, long-term effects, side effects and fears about what it will do to them or how it will change them. However, even with all that, most people who get diagnosed with AD/HD as adults have been coping with so many difficult symptoms for so long that at some point they go ahead and try medication with tremendous hope of finding relief. Some find it immediately and dramatically. Others persevere in spite of less than perfect results. It is often difficult to find the right dose and the right medication, but they keep trying, because as some women have said to me, the possibility that they will be able to be awake and alert all day is worth it. These are things that others take for granted! People with AD/HD have great strengths, but they also have great struggles, and the hope and possibility that they will begin to be able to express what they have inside of them and to connect in new ways to people they want to be close to are benefits important enough for them to accept potential downsides.

What if You Can't Take Medication or Don't Want to

Even though medication is often effective, some people do not feel comfortable taking it for a variety of reasons. Some do not like taking any medication at all, and others are unable to find a medication regimen that works without side effects. Others still are unable to take medication for AD/HD for other medical reasons. I want to emphasize that although it is often more difficult to cope with the symptoms without medication, I have seen many people struggle and work through the difficulties by focusing on their strengths, using support, structure, exercise, meditation, good nutrition, and dietary supplements, or whatever else works for them, to help their brain function more efficiently. Doctors Hallowell and Ratey in *Delivered from Distraction* have a lot to say on this in Chapter 25. For instance, they talk about how nutritional remedies can help. They suggest adding Omega-3 fatty acids to the diet for general health, citing fish oil as the best source. (I discuss more lifestyle changes in Chapter 16). Without the benefit of medication, it also becomes even more important to gain education about your brain, to affiliate and identify with other people who have similar challenges, and especially for women, to learn to set limits and boundaries and ask for what they need.

What Kinds of Doctors Prescribe AD/HD Medication

When adults first began to get treated for AD/HD, they were mostly prescribed short-acting Ritalin. Over roughly the last ten years, many more stimulants, as well as other medications that can be combined with stimulants, were developed and used to pinpoint more accurately and treat more effectively the combinations of difficulties that adults with AD/HD often face. With this new array of medications came new kinds of psychiatrists who specialize in psychopharmacology. They are experts in using medication to treat mental health challenges that originate in the brain. It is often surprising to clients that their therapy is commonly handled by a different mental health professional than a psychiatrist and that the psychiatric appointment is often just a brief medication check up. This has developed as we have come to better understood how much of our challenges are a result of brain chemicals, not just our experiences. We now know that counseling combined with medication is often the most effective treatment to address a wide variety of challenges, including AD/HD.

Before You Go to the Doctor

Although the first line medications are still stimulants, the range of possibilities has increased to give us many more choices of delivery systems and combinations.

I suggest that before you start on a medication, you take the time to read enough about it to ask informed questions during your "meds" consultation. The more you know before you talk to the doctor, the more assertive you can be if you feel your concerns aren't being adequately addressed. Having medication "thrown at you" isn't going to be very helpful, and you need a doctor who can support and help you through this important process. You may have conflicts about taking medication. You definitely need to feel comfortable with the concept and the process before you start.

Working with Your Doctor Who Is Working with Your Brain

If you have a doctor with a wide repertoire of choices and a willingness to work with you as a partner, it may take longer to find the right combination because there are so many possibilities to tweak and adjust but the possibility of finding the right combination for you is increased greatly. In the end, you must remain the expert on your own brain. Be willing to listen to the expertise and guidance of your doctor, but also be willing to draw a line and express yourself when your experience is telling you something isn't working right. Some doctors are conservative and like to go slowly and tweak carefully whereas others are more experimental and aggressive. You need to find the kind of doctor and approach you are comfortable with. The important thing is to have good communication with your doctor, so that he or she can monitor your responses and adjust and fine-tune your medication.

Why Do All the Experts Have Different Approaches?

Hallowell and Ratey have said that there is no "cookbook recipe" to find the exact medication for the right person at the right time.

I use the analogy that just as artists use different palettes that produce different combinations of colors, all resulting in unique works of art, so too, do experts with medications use different approaches and combinations of medicines for particular individuals and situations.

Where to Find the Right Doctor for You

It might take some perseverance to find the right doctor. More doctors now are aware of AD/HD and comfortable with it, so you might start your search with your family physician. If your child has AD/HD and has a psychiatrist who prescribes medication, he or she may be able to diagnose and treat you as well or refer you to a colleague. If the professional who diagnoses you is not a physician, such as a psychologist or therapist, he or she should be able to refer you to a prescribing physician if you want to pursue medication consultation. Networking at your local AD/HD support group is also a good way to find an experienced general practitioner or psychiatrist who is experienced in treating adults with AD/HD in your area.

Overview of Medications Used for Adults with AD/HD

Stigma, Suspicion, and Safety

The stigma of using medication for AD/HD has improved a great deal since I got my first prescriptions for Ritalin over ten years ago and was met with great suspicion each time I went to fill a prescription. When I had to call pharmacies to see if they carried a particular dose or kind of medication, they refused to give me information over the phone because they thought I was "casing" the pharmacy to burglarize it for narcotics. It was a very humiliating experience that I hope that does not still happen to anyone in this country today. Among people who need medication for AD/HD, it is more common that they have anxieties and concerns about starting medication rather than a desire to abuse it.

In this section, I will give you an overview of some of the different kinds of medications often used for adults with AD/HD. First I will discuss the medications used to target the AD/HD symptoms, and then I will discuss other medications that target other accompanying difficulties.

What Are the Goals of Using AD/HD Medication?

Some of the goals of using AD/HD medications are to help the patient do the following:

- Stay consistently awake and alert

- Maintain steady energy for projects

- Maintain focus and decrease distractibility

- Decrease impulsivity

- Make activity levels more moderate: reduce hyperactivity or increase activation

- Filter out or reduce excess internal and external stimulation and overload

The process of paying attention involves several varied and complex stages of self-regulation and requires a kind of cognitive flexibility. This means an individual can do the following:

- Choose what to attend to at any given moment. (This means the ability to filter out thousands of bits of stimuli and to zoom in on that which is important and move into the background and blur the focus on that which is not important)

- Sustain attention to chosen stimuli

- Shift attention to a higher priority when necessary

- Develop strategies to maintain different types of attention

Paying attention also requires inhibiting certain responses when making the above choices. This involves inhibiting the following:

- Acting until information has been processed

- Speaking out one's thoughts (This involves internalizing speech or "talking inside your head" without actually speaking one's thoughts out loud unless that is the desired thing to do!)

How Medications Work for AD/HD

The above complexities of attention are commonly linked to the inefficient or inconsistent transmission of information in the brain through chemical brain messengers called neurotransmitters (NTs).

You can refer back to this in the pocket guide which you read earlier. But to review, neurotransmitters send information between the millions of nerve cells in the brain.

The medications for AD/HD are chemical compounds used to bring about a desired change in the balance in the brain. Medications used for AD/HD help the two most common neurotransmitters usually associated with AD/HD, Dopamine (DA) and Norepinephrine (NE), function more effectively. Medication works on these neurotransmitters by making them more available where they are needed, thus "smoothing out" the transmission of information in the brain and consequently reducing some of the most troublesome AD/HD symptoms. The NTs regulate different aspects of mood, cognition, and behavior. Imbalances in Norepinephrine have been associated with low energy, lethargy, and decreased alertness. Lower amounts of Dopamine are linked to a decrease in pleasure, motivation, attention, and cognitive processing speed. Stimulants make your brain able to use Dopamine (DA) and Norepinephrine (NE) longer and more efficiently.

Types of Medications Used for Adults with AD/HD

Stimulants

How Stimulants Work in the Brain

Stimulants make your brain able to use Dopamine (DA) and Norepinephrine (NE) longer and more efficiently.

Benefits of Stimulants

Stimulant medications are still considered the first choice in medication management for AD/HD and have been proven in multiple studies to be the safest, most effective treatment contrary to much of the media perception and representation. When prescribed for adults with AD/HD, these medications can help increase alertness and focus and help regulate activity levels. They also can help reduce an individual's reactivity and distractibility. They may increase the ability to filter out stimuli that are not important or relevant to the task at hand and may decrease the impulsivity and other characteristics often associated with AD/HD. They are effective for about 80 percent of the people who take them. Since they do not need time to build up for effectiveness, patients have some control over their use. They can start and stop stimulants easily or use them as needed since they do not stay in the blood system.

For women with AD/HD on these kinds of meds, there are often sexual and intimacy benefits, as well. Women with AD/HD who are not on medication are often distractible during sex, thinking about what they need to do; this is not out of lack of involvement or lack of feelings toward the partner but merely the inability to focus that much attention. This can result in difficulties with orgasm, but stimulant medication can help focus her on sex rather than on the shopping list! So a woman's ability to focus, relax, and enjoy intimacy is enhanced just through the normal treatment of AD/HD with stimulants.

Types of Stimulants

What follows is a brief description of some commonly used kinds of medications. Remember that for each of these, the dosages prescribed, the side effects, and the positive effects will vary greatly from person to person.

Ritalin (and its many forms)

Ritalin in its various forms is still the most commonly used stimulant medication and the one most often tried first. It is a short-acting medication with an immediate release. It has an approximate peak effectiveness time of two to four hours. It is available in generic form, too, but may actually have a different chemical base for administration. Some individuals have reported a difference in absorption and effect. Ritalin is also available in a variety of long-acting extended or sustained release forms with many different names for instance Ritalin LA (long acting).

Side Effects

Patients need to watch for what is called a "rebound" effect when it wears off. This causes some people to feel irritable and jittery or to have headaches. If you are aware of this, you can learn to take the medication at the point before it begins to wear off or recognizing the beginning of this feeling can remind you it is time to take your next dose. This rebound effect can vary from a little annoying to very bothersome. There are new possibilities of taking Ritalin in combination with other kinds of medications to smooth out these effects or the possibility of taking longer acting compounds to minimize these problems. In addition to the rebound effect, common complaints include appetite suppression and sleep disturbance.

Dosing

The dose is variable and is not dependent on your weight, so don't compare your dose with someone else's. It has a highly individualized effect.

Time-release

All forms of Ritalin have different means of releasing the medication and length of time of effectiveness. With the long-acting forms, there is a different amount of medication released at different times of the day often remaining effective for six to eight hours instead of the usual four.

Concerta

Concerta is another form of long-acting Methylphenidate (Ritalin). The unique difference between Concerta and other long-acting forms is in the delivery system. It was developed to provide a smoother, more consistent delivery of medication over a 12-hour period.

Focalin

Focalin is a modified version of Ritalin and contains only the most active component of Ritalin. Because of this special formulation, the usual dose of Focalin is half the amount of the Ritalin dose

Dexedrine

Dexedrine, another kind of stimulant, is available in an immediate release (IR) form with an approximate optimal blood level of two to four hours as well as a spansule, which is a slow-release (SR) form. The SR form gives the same amount of medication, such as 5, 10, or 15 mg. but spreads it out further, up to a six-hour period. This results in a lower dosage given over a longer period of time.

Adderall and Adderall XR (extended release)

Another common stimulant prescribed in both these forms is Adderall. Initially, it was thought that regular Adderall would have a more sustained effect, but upon further investigation it was found to last from three to six hours in most people. Since that time, Adderall XR has been developed, using the same medication contained in small "beads" inside a capsule that can provide approximately ten to twelve hours of consistent medication level.

Non-Stimulant Medication Sometimes Used for AD/HD Symptoms

Below are a few non-stimulant medications sometimes used to target the symptoms of AD/HD in adults.

Straterra

This medication, whose brand name is Atomoxetine, had been widely used in Europe for its antidepressant effects. It is the now the first non-stimulant medication that has been tested in children, adolescents, and adults for the purpose of treating AD/HD. It is usually prescribed to be taken once or twice a day in order to provide full-day management of symptoms.

What Does Straterra Do in the Brain?

It works by using a different method than stimulants to prevent the "reuptake" or recycling of Norepinephrine in the brain so that more is available for a longer period of time. Straterra been reported to result in fluctuating effects on AD/HD symptom control within the first few days, but may take two to six weeks to reach and maintain a consistent blood level for the best results to be achieved.

Benefits of Straterra

The effects produced by this kind of medication may be different than those of the stimulants, so it may help particular people who have not had their symptoms targeted with the stimulants as well as they had hoped. On the other hand, it may not affect the areas you need help in. You need to observe and watch for which symptoms it effects in different situations and monitor closely.

Because Strattera is not a stimulant, it may have advantages for those not wanting or able to take a stimulant for health reasons such as high blood pressure or heart problems. Also, because it is not considered a controlled substance, those with substance abuse concerns, those prescribing for them, and those in recovery programs might find this an appealing alternative to stimulants.

I do not want to imply at all that there is a high risk of abuse of prescribed stimulants for the general population of adults with AD/HD or even automatically for those with substance abuse histories. Research shows that many adults with AD/HD who use and abuse substances do it in an effort to self-medicate because they were not properly diagnosed and treated in the first place. Diagnosis, proper treatment, and monitoring eliminate much of the need for abuse for many of these individuals. But for those with an eating disorder, serious substance abuse histories, or current abuse, it is important to be very careful and to consider alternatives to stimulants.

As Hallowell and Ratey say in *Delivered from Distraction*, "Stimulants are not addicting or habit forming if taken properly. On the other hand, if you grind them up and snort them or inject them, as some people do, then they are dangerous." (pg. 18).

Wellbutrin

This is an atypical antidepressant. The effect on AD/HD symptoms is not considered to be as useful as the effect of stimulants and may take several weeks to develop. It has been described as having an effect similar to the combination of a less potent stimulant and an antidepressant. It has a higher potential than other antidepressants for triggering seizures, especially at higher doses.

What Does it Do in the Brain?

It is thought to be a weak reuptake inhibitor of Dopamine, Serotonin, and Norepinephrine.

Benefits of Wellbutrin

For individuals who also deal with significant clinical depression, this may prove useful and is sometimes used in combination with stimulant medications. It can also be useful for those not able to take a stimulant for AD/HD symptoms. This medication is also sold as Zyban and is used for smoking cessation.

Modafinil (brand name Provigil)

Modafinil is a memory improving and mood brightening medication that reportedly enhances wakefulness and vigilance. Modafinil is less likely to cause jitteriness, anxiety, or excess locomotor activity for some people than traditional stimulants.

What Does It Do In the Brain?

Its pharmacological profile is notably different from the other stimulants described. Promotes wakefulness without generalized central nervous system stimulation. It focuses its action in the wake/ sleep center of the brain.

Benefits of Modafinil

Current research suggests Modafinil is safe, effective, well tolerated, and long-acting. Modafinil is proving clinically useful in the treatment of narcolepsy and is beginning to be used with patients with AD/HD, especially those who struggle with daytime sleepiness, which many women with AD/HD report. This medication has not been approved for use specifically for AD/HD but for many women with these symptoms it may be an effective treatment.

Other Medications That Target Accompanying Conditions

There are many other medications used to address other symptoms and conditions that affect those with AD/HD. These are beyond the scope of this book but may very well be suggested by your doctor. Take time to read about and research any medications suggested. For our purposes here, I will focus on a commonly prescribed kind of antidepressant for women struggling with depression or a variety of anxiety symptoms.

Antidepressants: SSRI (Selective Serotonin Reuptake Inhibitors)

Inefficiencies or insufficiencies in another chemical neurotransmitter, serotonin, are associated with depression and obsessive compulsive behaviors: Zoloft, Celexa, Luvox, Paxil, Prozac and Lexapro are some of the most common *SSRIs*.

What Do They Do in the Brain?

SSRIs slow the reuptake of the chemical serotonin and as a result make more of it available longer.

Benefits of SSRIs

Five Reasons an SSRI Anti-depressant may be prescribed along with AD/HD Medication

1. Women often feel chronically depressed as a result of coping with undiagnosed AD/HD all their lives. In many cases, once a woman is on the proper dose of stimulant medication, her depressive symptoms will often be alleviated along with the AD/HD symptoms. If not, her doctor may use this kind of medication to treat her depression in order to address her AD/HD. Therefore an antidepressant combined with a stimulant is often effective.

2. Often women with AD/HD are prescribed this kind of medication for the symptoms of hormonal fluctuations such as PMS or menopause. See details in the next chapter. These kinds of medications are also often used to treat the anxiety and social anxiety that result from living with AD/HD, as well as compulsiveness such as obsessive list making associated with trying to cope with and compensate for the AD/HD. Sorting out true obsessive/compulsive disorder from AD/HD compensations or from impulsivity can be difficult.

   According to Hallowell and Ratey in *Driven to Distraction*, behaviors that are referred to as compulsive, like shopping and overspending, are often impulsive behaviors for someone with AD/HD rather than truly compulsive. These impulsive behaviors can cause serious problems but might be helped more through treatment for AD/HD, whereas true compulsions are helped more by SSRIs. SSRIs, such as Luvox, makes more serotonin available thereby often reducing obsessive symptoms. Often medical treatment for AD/HD will let them "relax their hold," as the medication will to some degree make up what they had been compensating for. (As discussed in Ch 12: Diagnostic Difficulties)

3. These kinds of medications can also be used to help smooth out the effect of the stimulants, by helping to ease the rebound effect or jitteriness that sometimes accompanies the use of stimulants for some individuals. An experienced doctor will know how to balance these to find the right combination for you.

4. Women with eating disorders are often helped by these kinds of medications, as well. (More on eating disorders in Chapter 15).

Your Experience of Being on Medications

Dosing and Side Effects

Dosing of stimulants usually starts low and goes up until you seem to be getting the maximum benefit without side effects. When you have a change or symptom that you do not want as a result of taking the medications, this may be a side effect of how the chemical compound works. It is not very common, but sometimes people experience a racing heart or jitteriness, agitation or exhaustion when the stimulants are wearing off. Insomnia and tics may happen with some stimulants. If the stimulants are otherwise helpful, this is often corrected by reducing the dose, or adding another medication to help minimize such effects. Other side effects of SSRIs can include dry mouth, loss of libido, gastronomical upset and weight gain for women.

For many people taking medications, there may be mild side effects or none whereas others may have more annoying or intolerable side effects. Often people stop the medication though it might be possible to work with their physician to find a way to decrease these side effects by adjusting the dosage used, taking the medications with food for some types of meds, or changing the time of day, number of times a day, or possibly varying the medication from short acting to long acting, to name a few. It's also important to stay with a trial of medication long enough to find out what is the correct optimal dose without it causing side effects.

How to Monitor the Effectiveness of Your Medication

People often experience a dramatic, positive response to the prescribed medication—sometimes within a few hours. They feel awake and alert for the first time in their lives. They're coming out of their fog.

On the other hand, they may not feel dramatically different. They may have to look back over a course of several months to see that their lives have improved in significant ways. For instance, they may have accomplished more, stayed on track, or seen improvement in their relationships. Some people may need input from others to check on their improvement.

It is often helpful when you begin a new medication to keep a diary and observe yourself so that you can really understand how a particular medication, dose, or schedule affects you. Target one or two specific situations to start that have presented great challenges for a long time and note the differences you feel now that you are on medication. Sometimes that will help you determine the effectiveness of a certain medication and enable you to give your doctor important feedback. Here are some sample areas to observe:

- Is the medication helping you in social situations?

- Is it helping with reading?

- Is it decreasing your emotional reactivity?

- Have your relationships improved?

- Is it easier to organize or do paper work?

Medication can have great effects on every area of your life. It is not simply a matter of taking a pill in order to be able to study. The surprising thing is that medication helps women not just with school or work or organizing but can also allows them to be able to stay with a conversation and to interact and connect with people in a new way. It can help reduce their anxiety and help them stop responding to each new distracting or interesting idea that arises.

Since medication has a brain-organizing effect, I personally usually recommend that an individual take it all or most of the time instead of for specific tasks, especially for those with low activation because they may never get up to do something without first using the medication!

Range of Feelings You May Experience When Using Medications

There can be a wide range of feelings associated with medication. Even if you saw a psychiatrist for medication in the beginning, it is valuable to talk to a counselor to track and work through the effects of the medication and ask questions about what's normal and what can be expected. You may have to work out feelings of being disappointed, wondering "Is this all I can expect?" or "What should I be able to expect, and what do I need to do now in addition to the medication?" At some point it's not unusual to become disappointed in the effect your medication is having. Some people feel very excited at the beginning like when getting a new toy. Of course, most people continue to experience great help from the medications, but at the beginning, the exhilaration from each new experience is often mood elevating as well. One woman told me she felt tremendous excitement because she never thought that drawers actually worked before! Now she said she understands how to fold clothes, put them away, and actually close the drawers.

Successful treatment with medication does not mean that a woman will like everything she is now aware of. As a therapist I know that medication can prompt lots of changes in relationships. Even a positive change can be difficult.

Summary

It's clear from this long discussion that I feel medication can be extremely helpful for the symptoms of AD/HD, as well as other associated conditions with which women struggle. The use of medication for those diagnosed correctly is part of an entire treatment plan but is not a substitute for finding a good fit at work or at school. It is not for the purpose of changing a person into something else or someone else but rather as an aid for finding one's self and being able to manifest what is inside.

For the first time, you might understand and experience the experience of other people who aren't bombarded or overloaded on a regular basis. It has been compared to the difference between vision and seeing. With AD/HD, you might be able to see, but it is cloudy and foggy. Medication can provide real vision.

Medication can also help make the transmission of information through the brain messengers more efficient and to help block out some of the overwhelming stimuli coming in. It can give you sustained energy, help you stay awake, be focused and alert and cut down on emotional reactivity, thereby enhancing your relationships and overall success. It can provide a cushion so you don't feel as sensitive, open, and raw. Women are sometimes amazed at their experience with medication, especially at first. They can go into a super-sized store, a clothing store, or the grocery store for the first time without become completely overwhelmed and shutting down. It's these daily moments that are great triumphs for women.

It is important to remember that the positive changes that you make now that you are on medication are changes *you* are making, steps *you* are taking, now that you have the right fuel. It is sometimes easy to give all the credit to the medication instead of giving yourself credit for all your hard work. You must do this in order to start developing your own sense of confidence so *you* can continue into the future with increased positive expectations.

Let's go back to the analogy that we used at the beginning of this section: once you have the proper medication (fuel), you still need to keep your vehicle oiled, tuned up, and drive it properly. We will look at this over the next few chapters. In the next chapter, more physical issues related to AD/HD and women will be addressed.

See the resource section at the end of the book for more on this subject.

CHAPTER FIFTEEN

"Let's Get Physical"

Women's Treatment Issues

There are a number of other special physical issues that impact women, their treatment, and coping skills besides the previously mentioned medication. Over the years, many women throughout the country have asked me questions concerning AD/HD and special woman's issues such as PMS, menopause, and pregnancy. When I first wrote this book there was little information available on these connections. Over the course of the last ten years, however, there has been much more focus on these connections as many more women have been diagnosed, treated, and studied. They have let their voices be heard, and they have shared their experiences. In addition to the whole range of hormonal shifts, this chapter will also briefly cover pregnancy, eating disorders, and addictions as they relate to women and AD/HD.

The Cycle of Changes

Females go through a wide range of hormonal changes in the journey from girlhood to womanhood. Just before puberty, a girl begins to experience the physical and emotional changes related to her monthly fluctuations in estrogen. During the time just prior to ovulation, the estrogen level has gradually risen to its highest level during the month. Following ovulation and prior to menstruation, estrogen drops rapidly. During times of low estrogen production, women often experience fluctuations in mood and sleep patterns, increased anxiety, depression, decreased interest in activities, difficulty concentrating, poor memory, and other cognitive deficiencies. After the onset of menstruation, estrogen again begins to be produced, and the cycle starts over. This leads to the typical emotional and physical changes, which for *many* women are so severe that they feel anywhere from mildly to severely impaired both emotionally and physically by Premenstrual Syndrome or PMS.

As women enter the perimenopausal phase, they experience symptoms of estrogen deficits that may occur over a period of time or may be a rapid transition. Along with the changes in cognition may come hot flashes (flushing of the skin during sudden plummets in estrogen level), increased irritability, increased feelings of anxiety and/or depression, and for many women, the onset of severe problems getting to sleep and staying asleep. As estrogen falls, dopamine, norepinephrine, *and* serotonin levels drop until a woman reaches the completion of menopause and ovulation/menstruation has completely ceased.

Women, Hormones, and AD/HD

Hormonal fluctuations may impact responses to medications requiring more complicated treatment and also may challenge an already overtaxed system. Low estrogen states can lead to symptoms similar to AD/HD such as poor concentration, inadequate memory, and cognitive dysfunction. As one of the leaders in the discussion of women, hormones, and AD/HD, Dr. Patricia Quinn, in *Gender Issues and AD/HD* (2002, pg. 195) says:

"Women with AD/HD by definition may already have disorders in the serotonin, norepinephrine and/ or dopamine neurotransmitter systems. It is now known that estrogen increases the concentration of these neurotransmitters at the neuronal synapse and that during low estrogen states, symptoms emerge that indicate further impairment in functioning."

With this in mind, let's look at the variety of ways that hormonal changes can impact a woman's symptoms of AD/HD throughout her life.

PMS

Many women with AD/HD who also experience PMS have told me that their AD/HD symptoms become more severe before their periods, even when they are on stimulant medication that is effective during the rest of the month. It is now understood that estrogen stimulates a significant amount of dopamine production within certain parts of the brain that helps to regulate the efficient transmission of information within the brain and body. Remember, it's the insufficient and inefficient supply of dopamine that causes many of the most troublesome AD/HD symptoms. If estrogen stimulates the production of dopamine, a monthly drop in estrogen will certainly aggravate the symptoms of AD/HD. During the time of the month when this neurotransmitter causes PMS symptoms, it also throws off the delicate balance between the other neurotransmitters, consequently changing the effect of the medication. Therefore, in addition to stimulant medication, women may also sometimes need *another* medication at certain times of the month to help the neurotransmitter affecting the PMS, thus allowing the stimulants to do their job (Nadeau, *ADDA*, 1995). These are often the medications that affect serotonin such as SSRIs discussed in the previous chapter. In their book *Answers to Distraction*, Hallowell and Ratey report that many of their female patients feel that birth control pills have a stabilizing effect on their hormones thereby eliminating the problems of PMS and the consequent increase in AD/HD symptoms.

In addition to addressing this medically, it can also be helpful emotionally to know that this time of the month is going to be challenging despite their best efforts. As a result of understanding this, they can do two things. One is to adjust their self-talk when their difficulties and AD/HD symptoms increase so they don't berate themselves, worsening their feelings of depression, or increase their anxiety by fears that they are losing their ability to control their AD/HD. The second thing they need to do, whenever possible, is to decrease the amount of stimulation and stress during this critical period and to increase the amount of support and structure. They also need to take extra care to get an adequate amount of sleep, proper nutrition as well as plenty of exercise and relaxation.

Perimenopause and Menopause

The impact of hormonal fluctuations on AD/HD also holds true for both perimenopausal (the gradually decreasing estrogen levels that happen during the 5-15 years prior to menopause), and, of course, for women entering the menopausal phase. The increase and change in severity of the AD/HD symptoms may be further complicated by the severe physical symptoms of breast tenderness, abdominal bloating, back pain, joint pain, overall water retention, weight gain and severe fatigue.

Many menopausal women are now being diagnosed with AD/HD for the first time because previously developed coping skills that hid the symptoms are compromised once the estrogen changes exacerbate the symptoms. Women starting menopause have voiced their concerns to me about the cumulative effect on their physical and mental health from the stress produced by these two conditions. Just like women with PMS, the tremendous hormonal changes at this time of life can throw off what had been previously effective treatment for AD/HD. In addition, the normal effects of aging can also contribute to decreased cognitive abilities and memory, thereby interfering with compensations they may have relied on for many years. The losses and stresses that all women face during this period, combined with the exacerbation of AD/HD symptoms due to hormonal changes, can create quite a crisis. In the book she co-edited and published with Kathleen Nadeau, Ph.D., *Understanding Women with ADD*, Dr. Patricia Quinn says that the symptoms of aging added to the AD/HD symptoms *"may tip them [women] over the edge as their barely manageable lives become unmanageable."* (2002, p. 97).

Like anyone else going through menopause or becoming diagnosed with AD/HD for the first time, these women benefit tremendously from counseling, education, and support, as well as medical intervention. Since menopause creates some of the same symptoms as AD/HD such as ". . . increased distractibility, gloomy mood, irritability, restlessness, extreme fatigue, and even memory problems" (Hallowell & Ratey, *Answers To Distraction*, pg.140), I would encourage women with AD/HD experiencing menopausal symptoms to talk to their gynecologists about their AD/HD symptoms and conversely to talk about their menopausal symptoms with their doctors who prescribe their AD/HD medications. Women and their physicians are starting to understand the possible need for adjustments in the stimulant dosage and the anti-depressant dosage for women experiencing these problems.

Hormone Replacement Therapy for Perimenopausal and Menopausal Symptoms

Recently there has been great discussion and debate on the safety of hormone replacement therapy, which has made this an even more difficult decision and issue for women with AD/HD. Some studies have shown that hormone therapy may resolve the increases in symptoms, but other studies have had conflicting results regarding the long-term consequences. One recent study indicated that long-term estrogen therapy actually demonstrated an increased risk of cardiovascular disease such as heart disease and blood vessel disease that could lead to high blood pressure and/or stroke.

Herbal Therapies for Perimenopausal and Menopausal Symptoms

There are also numerous herbal products on the market that sell themselves as natural solutions to menopausal symptoms. These include such things as black cohosh, evening primrose oil, several soy based products, and many others. Remember that herbal remedies, although natural, can have negative interactions with prescribed medications, as well as severe side effects. Qualified naturopaths or herbalists will always recommend that you carefully study any product that you are ingesting for medical outcome, and that, at a minimum, you discuss any potential interactions with other medications with a knowledgeable pharmacist. Some women choose to take hormone therapy whereas others do not, but an adjustment in other AD/HD and mood related medications may be required in either case. Finding a healthy balance that works for you is key. The best advice is to do your own research and then discuss your individual situation with your doctors to balance the risk and the benefits. There are also other sources of information listed at the end of the chapter that could be quite useful.

Pregnancy

Many issues come up for women who have been diagnosed with AD/HD around the choice of pregnancy. One great area of concern to women with AD/HD, especially those who have experienced the benefits and relief of medication, is the prospect of undergoing the strain of pregnancy and nursing without medication. As a general principle, women should avoid taking any medication during pregnancy, so this has to be carefully discussed with a doctor to weigh the risks and benefits.

As described in the section above, women with AD/HD have increased symptoms when they are in lower estrogen states, however, during pregnancy, women actually have higher estrogen levels so they often report better functioning. This should be hopeful news to women who are afraid to become pregnant because they will need to go off their medication during that time.

Despite great fears that they shouldn't have children, that they won't be good parents and despite the stress of coping with their challenges, every single day women with AD/HD get up and do the many things that a great parent does for a child. Often the intensity of how a woman who has AD/HD experiences life and her emotions brings much spontaneity, joy, and surprise to their families!

Eating Disorders

Food is often associated with being comforted, filling "empty feelings inside," and giving an individual a sense of control over something when it seems as if nothing else in life can be controlled. It is not difficult to see how this pattern could develop in a women coping with the overwhelming symptoms of life with AD/HD. These attempts at gaining a feeling of control, however, leads to their own severe consequences such as anorexia (not eating enough), binge eating (overeating as an addiction), and/or bulimia (binging and then vomiting). For bulimic women, they binge to "fill up" or cover up shame and pain and then purge to get rid of the increased shame and possible weight gain from having binged. This addiction always adds to the shame cycle; it never resolves it. It is vital for women who experience these additional challenges to treat both their AD/HD and these other issues, as neglecting to address either will prevent success of either treatment.

In *Answers to Distraction*, Drs. Hallowell and Ratey report connections between AD/HD and eating disorders and suggest that perhaps the high stimulation provided by starvation is a form of self-medication for those who struggle with focus. They say that some research indicates stimulants can be effective in these cases if the woman with an eating disorder is actually trying to fix an underlying attention deficit disorder.

Of course, anyone with the symptoms of an eating disorder should see a physician or a mental health professional. These are serious conditions that need professional attention. As was mentioned earlier, SSRI anti-depressant medication is also used in the treatment of women with eating disorders. In Chapter 20 of *Gender Issues and AD/HD* (Nadeau and Quinn, Ed., 2002), John Fleming, Ph.D. and

Lance Levy, M.B. emphasize that prescribing a stimulant medication to a woman with AD/HD who also has an eating disorder needs to be carefully considered by an expert and that it should never be given in place of ongoing monitoring and behavioral intervention. They also make the point though that while this group of women may have a higher potential for abuse, any treatment with stimulants should be monitored so they are not used for appetite suppression. Treating the AD/HD may also help improve executive functioning that could improve control of eating behavior and reduce impulsivity.

I agree with these authors that it is important to help women with AD/HD who are self-medicating in this way to look for stimulation of a healthy kind and to help them find ways to use their leisure time in more valuable ways, in other words, to help them "fill up" their emptiness in a healthier way.

Levy and Fleming also make the point that AD/HD may contribute to eating disorders because of the complexity involved with the routines of meal planning, shopping, preparation, and even remembering to eat. They suggest that part of any intervention for women with AD/HD should involve looking at the impact of diet and offer help in meal planning, shopping and preparation in order to make it more routine.

Substance Abuse and Addictions

In order to self-medicate, many people with AD/HD use food, as well as caffeine or nicotine to help them focus or relax. In her new book, *When Too Much Isn't Enough*, Wendy Richardson, MFT, talks about other "substances" used to self-medicate such as Internet use, overworking, shopping, or gambling. Additionally, some people abuse substances like alcohol, cocaine, marijuana, or prescription medication to change their uncomfortable inner cognitive state. In some cases, adults with AD/HD become addicted to these substances and need to be treated for substance abuse and begin a program of recovery before many professionals will treat them for AD/HD. However, in some cases, if the excessive use of substances is primarily driven by this need to self-medicate, beginning a program of proper medication will often eliminate the craving for these substances. This needs to be assessed carefully in the context of the relationship with a mental health professional experienced in the area of substance abuse. For some it may be appropriate to carefully treat the AD/HD with stimulants or other medications used for the treatment of AD/HD while maintaining treatment and recovery from chemical dependency.

Addiction and AD/HD specialist Wendy Richardson, MFT, (2002) talks about the special needs of women with AD/HD in recovery from addiction. She points out that the goal for them is to learn to lead a balanced life and to break the pattern of self-medicating used to reduce feelings of shame and guilt present for women with AD/HD.

Summary

Women with AD/HD have special hormonal challenges and fluctuations that impact the treatment of AD/HD and their ability to cope with it. This often requires changes in or new medications or other interventions such as rebalancing the activities in their lives. It is especially important for women to understand what is happening at these times so that they can alter their self-talk and have explanations for these changes. In addition, eating can become problematic for women with AD/HD. Some of their cultural responsibilities are impacted by the AD/HD and so can cause disruptions in their regular routines. The medical treatment of eating disorders and other addictions coupled with AD/HD is complex and must be handled with healthy respect by a team of professionals who thoroughly understand AD/HD as well as the other conditions or addictions they are treating. They must at least be open to the need to treat the underlying AD/HD as a possible contributing factor to the other conditions.

There are many other conditions that women with AD/HD have sited as impacting them. To learn more about women and AD/HD and topics such as Chronic Fatigue Syndrome Fibromyalgia and PTSD, you may want to look at the Resource section for women in the back of the book.

CHAPTER SIXTEEN

The Middle of the "MESST"

Education and Strategies

In Chapter 13 we gave an overview of the *MESST* and in Chapters 14 and 15, we discussed the *beginning* of the *MESST* medication and other physical issues that affect treatment for women with AD/HD. Now we get to the *middle* of the *MESST* model in which we look at two other critical elements, *education* and *strategies*, (including life style changes) which need to follow or accompany medication. For those not taking medication, this become even more critical. In the next two chapters, we will talk about support (including coaching) and therapy.

Education

The next element or stepping stone in the *MESST* Model is education. In addition to the women's issues that we talked about in the last chapter, it is important to generally learn as much as you can about AD/HD and specifically learn about your own brain by observing and noticing what works. There are two aspects to education about AD/HD. One is the informational aspect and the other is the emotional benefit. Gathering information provides you the opportunity to learn about structures, strategies, and medication, and learning about the emotional side helps you manage your AD/HD by moving you through the grief cycle so that you will be able to integrate AD/HD as deeply as you can into your self-image. It helps you internalize the AD/HD so that you can accept it as part of who you are and how your brain works. Books, websites, conference, groups, lectures, magazines, and newsletters have all proliferated since the time this book was originally published. There is a wealth of information out there and by learning and becoming involved you get not only an intellectual understanding but an aide to emotional healing, as well. Here's an example of how the informational and the emotional sides of education about AD/HD work together.

Just a few months after I was diagnosed, I subscribed to a newsletter that was active at the time. After a while, I got a notice that it was time to renew my subscription. Instead of telling me to do so in a straightforward manner like any other newsletter, I read, "I know how hard it is to find a stamp, and it might take hours to find an envelope, put it together, and mail it, but it's very important to re-subscribe." That made a deep impression on me—I "got it." These people really knew who I was and understood the difficulty of something so seemingly simple.

Gathering Information

I recommend that you take advantage of whatever is available in your area as well as investigate the list of resources at the end of the book. Join organizations such as ADDA (National Association for Adults with Attention Deficit Disorder) and CHADD (Children and Adults with ADD) and find local support networks that help adults. Associating with other adults with AD/HD, either in person or through reading their stories will help you to learn about other people's experiences. People often meet for the first time at national conferences after having gotten to know each other for a long time with online discussion groups.

Emotional Education

Of course, all of the above ultimately have an impact on you emotionally. Here are some of the most important emotional benefits of gathering information.

Breaking the Isolation

Education goes a long way toward breaking the isolation that adults with AD/HD often feel when they have no idea that their symptoms are a real condition. The effect on your self-image of learning there are millions of other adults like you who are coping in a positive way and living successful lives cannot be underestimated. Education will give you the advantage of hearing these subjects talked about for the first time. You're not just getting information, you're learning about other people's experiences. Knowing that others have gone through similar experiences has a soothing, healing effect.

Education also goes a long way toward relieving anxiety and self-doubt, because as I said before, it takes a long time for people to consistently believe that they have AD/HD in the beginning. It is good to get this idea reinforced from those who are positive about it, who are coping and living well with it.

A conference is a tremendous experience for people with AD/HD who might only have read about it before or attended some local groups. This can be a good way to take the first step in alleviating some of the old feelings of shame, guilt, and isolation. As I described in Chapter 1, to see hundreds of people in the same place for several days who are not hiding any more, who are not in the closet any more, who are talking about all the things that they have experienced, meeting them live, getting to like them, and getting to know them, is very exciting.

Strategies

Strategies help you modify and structure your environment to be more effective and to be a better fit for your brain. There are endless variations of strategies. Some work for a while and what works for others may not work for you. Try not to judge yourself by the perfection of these approaches. Remain flexible. This is the area you have trouble with, so it is not as easy as deciding to "just do it." You are *strategizing* about how to help your *problem with strategizing*! Expect this may be an area of frustration at times and that a strategy may be very successful for a while and then need adjustment. Stay open and experimental. Just keep trying. Use your abundant creativity and a keep sense of fun about it. I think of strategies the same way I look at medications, they may work for a while but then may need monitoring and readjustment. That is to be expected and not viewed as failure or with discouragement.

My purpose here is to give you a few new ways of thinking about strategies. For a more in-depth look at strategies, see the end of the book for all the great resources out there that are specifically designed to help you in this area.

First, we will look at four different types of strategies:

1. **No Tech** (paper, etc)

2. **A Touch of Tech** (electronic or digital)

3. **Personal** (life style and cognitive changes)

4. **Interpersonal** (other people helping you). Even though using professional supports such as organizers, coaches, and therapists is an interpersonal strategy, I have put this discussion of professional help in the next two chapters, which deal with support and therapy.

After we look at these four ways of thinking about strategies, we will look at the potential pitfalls and benefits of a few different well-known approaches. I include this to emphasize the general principal that when thinking about strategies—one size does not fit all! Then we will look at other approaches and different ways to think about strategies that broadens the discussion from simple tips to life style changes and internal modifications. At the end of the chapter, you can go further in devising your own strategies by using the strategy grid to think up your own approaches to your specific challenges. To get you started, other suggestions precede the grid.

"TMS" and the Four
Different Types of Strategies

Strategies often are focused on what I call "TMS." As I described in Chapter 5, this refers to problems women have with *Time, Money, and Stuff* (TMS). I use this play on words alluding to the all too familiar "PMS" to remind women that the problems of AD/HD are also about body chemistry and not character flaws. First I will give you a few examples of applying strategies to TMS to start you off. These are just a few of endless variations.

Time

No Tech: A low-tech approach to keeping track of appointments is to try a new kind of calendar. Some women go through many different types until they find a system that works or they make up their own. As for keeping track of time, the fanciest, gold-plated, elaborate

systems aren't always the best for someone with AD/HD. For example, an old-fashioned kitchen timer is a low-tech approach to keep
track of time. Just set it for when you have to leave or when you need
a reminder to alert you to what you need to do next.

A Touch of Tech: It is much more common now than it was when
I first wrote this book for adults with AD/HD to use PDAs (personal
data assistant) or Palm Pilots to keep track of appointments. You can
also preset alarms on them to remind you of appointments that day
or in weeks to come. This works great for some while others would
never consider this kind of non-paper approach. And, of course, be
sure you don't lose your PDA with all your info on it!

Personal: In terms of personal strategies to deal with time,
broader life style changes such as exercise or better nutrition and
sleep can modify your inner environment and make it easier for you
to be alert and on time. An example of an inner modification would
be to give yourself permission to schedule fewer activities in a given
time frame, give yourself more down time to refocus and remain calm
as you transition, or plan to arrive very early for appointments with
small, portable projects to do while you wait such as knitting or reading or making lists!

Interpersonal: This type of strategy might involve the use of an
informal coach, or buddy, perhaps on a daily basis at first, to help you
manage your time, plan your route for the day, or stay on track with
projects. (Professional coaching will be covered in the next chapter).

Money

No Tech: This type of approach might include cutting up your
credit cards

A Touch of Tech: This type of strategy might be to use online
banking to pay bills and keep track of your accounts

Personal: This type of strategy might include taking a course in
money management

Interpersonal: This approach might mean sitting down with a
partner, friend, or assistant once a month at a predetermined time to
pay the bills

Stuff

This is a *big* issue for women with AD/HD. Many of the tasks involved with organizing and making decisions about everybody's "stuff" falls to women. Figuring out where to put the stuff and then remembering where you have put things, (all the papers, clothes, notes, lists, birthday cards, letters, bills, etc) requires a lot of coordinating, sequencing, integrating, prioritizing, and tracking.

No Tech: This approach might include putting your keys in the same place every day.

A Touch of Tech: This approach might be the use of an online organizing website such as the popular www.flylady.net. This is a delightful place where the fly lady has a suggestion for every aspect of managing your life, clutter, money and time and sends you daily emails to support you and help you make step-by-step progress. Some women swear by it!

Personal: Such a strategy might involve a cognitive shift that allows you to get extra help for some tasks. As we will discuss in the section on support, sometimes the best strategy is to get someone to help you or to do tasks for you! In *Delivered from Distraction*, Ned Hallowell offers us a new perspective in Chapter 22 when he tells us, "You just have to get *well enough* organized." This means don't spend all your time organizing for its' own sake. Use your time developing your strengths and just get as organized as you need to be in the service of this.

Interpersonal: This approach might include a session with an organizer who can help you to set up your environment in a way that works for you so that you can better use and maintain it. Professional organizers are discussed in the next chapter on support

One Size Does *Not* Fit All!

The underlying message here is that what works for others may not work for you. Some seemingly straightforward approaches are often complicated by the AD/HD itself as an individual attempts to compensate for difficulties. Sometimes solutions become part of the problem! In the examples below, I will talk about two common strategies and show how some people run into trouble with them and how the same strategy can work wonders for others.

Post-its and Lists: Devils or Angels?

Remember, ordinary organizational advice and strategies and solutions may not work for you. For example, sometimes advice to make lists or use post its can go too far with the amount of ideas one person with AD/HD can generate. "Post-it thinking" is not always sufficient if you have serious organizational deficits. You might wind up looking like the woman in the Post-It-HELL illustration.

Reminders and prompts *can* be wonderful for those with executive function problems. For me it was a great pleasure when I was a houseguest of a well-known AD/HD coach. It was like having a big sister watching over me, walking me through the day. I was amazed at how relaxed I felt. There were unexpected large notes or signs everywhere, anticipating what I, or someone like me, might forget to do. There were gentle, and some not so gentle, reminders such as:

- IF YOU OPEN THE DOOR, CLOSE IT

- IF YOU LIFT THE TOILET SEAT, PUT IT DOWN AFTER

- IF YOU OPEN THIS DRAWER, CLOSE IT

Even deep inside the refrigerator where I thought I could take a little break and go unnoticed: IF YOU TAKE THE LAST CAN OF SODA, REPLACE IT! If this works for you and your family, something like this could be a great strategy, or, of course, it could drive your family crazy!

In addition to notes, lists are great, again, unless they go too far and take on a life of their own. In Chapter 12, I talk about how some people begin compensating for memory and executive functioning problems with lists that become a bigger problem than the original symptom, taking up more and more time, making someone a slave to the list rather than using it as a tool. I recently learned of a man with AD/HD who took this to the extreme and made daily lists up to 20 pages in five- point font, single spaced. It's hard to know how or when to stop, especially if you have some compulsivity thrown in with your trouble with categorization. You can wind up with long lists of unrelated items.

On the other hand, lists can be wonderful tools for those with these challenges. The message is that one size does not fit all. I recommend lists for clients who struggle with remembering things they need to do every day. If you struggle with remembering things you need to do every day, these can be like little cheat sheets so you don't have to think it all through each day, for example:

- How to clean up the kitchen step-by-step

- What to put in kids' lunches

- What to do every morning before leaving the house

- What to do every night before bed

Also post directions by the computer or on the many TV remotes, anything with directions that are hard to remember that repeatedly stop you in your tracks or requires that you continually asking someone for help. Adults often feel stupid or incompetent asking for these types of directions so they resist this idea.

The question you should be asking if you find yourself resisting this but continuing to get frustrated is, "What is going to make me feel more confident and competent in the long run, and how can I get there?" instead of the question that may be more common, "How can avoid looking stupid?"

Life Style Changes: Body and Soul

Body

Healthy changes in your life style may help you get along without medication by boosting both your mood and your optimal brain functioning. You have a sensitive instrument to learn to take care of when you have AD/HD! Life style changes include sleep, nutrition, exercise, and finding ways to calm your mind. They also include taking time to enjoy yourself and others and taking time to nurture and care for yourself. Putting balance in your life is an ongoing challenge for women and even more so for women with AD/HD.

From Shake, Rattle, and Roll to Sleep, Rest, and Renewal

Falling asleep, getting up in the morning, and staying awake all day are problems that often confound women with AD/HD. Often these difficulties may stem from or be exacerbated by hormonal changes. AD/HD itself may be playing a role in this. You may want to speak to your doctor about medication to address these issues or to see if your medication might even be adding to the problem.

Aside from these physical issues, getting into regular sleep habits is essential. Obviously, a good night's sleep helps you get up more easily and helps you stay awake during the day. In order for you to begin to ease into sleep, you may need to begin shutting down gradually, transitioning to sleep time in a regular way that relaxes and calms you. Just like if you suddenly turn off your computer, you get messages that the computer was not turned off properly and that there are systems that need to be turned off in sequence. It is the same with your brain and body; they need to be more gradually slowed down. So experimenting with routines or rituals that are soothing and inviting can be quite helpful. The idea is to feel enticed to slow down rather than fighting it.

I always encourage women to have a "room of their own" or at least a place of their own or a time of their own in a room. This is a time or place for yourself where you can turn off the noise and demands of the day. This may include a warm bath, a special chair to curl up in, a special book, soothing music, something soothing to sip, a fire, candles, aromas, or relaxation exercises, meditation of some type, or time with pets. Think soft, soothing, nourishing. If you have an organizer come to your house, try taking some time away from setting up files to setting up a sanctuary like this.

It will be different for each of you, and you don't have to have a big space or loads of time. Just some routine you look forward to that will help you break away from the computer or the long list of stuff to do. You can even put this on the list of things to do if that helps. You may want to prearrange with partner or friend to call you or to come get you at a certain time. If you have an organizer come to your house, try taking some time away from setting up files to setting up a sanctuary like this.

Eating and Moving

In their book, *Delivered from Distraction*, Drs. Hallowell and Ratey continue to emphasize life style changes such as sleep, proper nutrition, and exercise as essential elements of treatment. They encourage adults with AD/HD to eat a balanced diet with protein as part of breakfast since protein is the best, long-lasting source of brain fuel. While this is good for anyone, individuals with AD/HD need all the extra brain fuel they can get consistently throughout the day! I always a carry protein bar with me, and I find that nothing works better to help alleviate those feelings of starvation. For loads of good information on supplements and nutritional advice, look at *Delivered from Distraction*, Chapter 25.

Hallowell and Ratey (2005, pg.16) also say that "Regular exercise is one of the best tonics you can give your brain. Exercise stimulates the production of epinephrine, dopamine, and serotonin, which is exactly what the medications we treat ADD with do. So exercising is like taking medication for ADD in a holistic, natural way."

One strategy is to set something up with someone else such as a class or a routine with a friend, a trainer, or a family member. This helps you when moving is the last thing you want to do!

Also for you inattentive low activation types, be realistic about the time of day you schedule this for long-term success. For women with families and jobs, it is often very difficult to find time. It is rewarding to arrange for your husband or partner or a babysitter to watch your kids so you can get out to a classes or exercise together with a special friend. Make it fun! Go out for coffee after or do something you enjoy. You won't do anything for long if it isn't rewarding in some way.

Soul

Modifying your inner world requires changing your view of yourself and your AD/HD. It means allowing you to do things differently by giving yourself permission to make some of the lifestyle changes discussed above. This strategy is about changing what you say to yourself that allows you to set up your world in a way that makes you feel good and allows you to use your brain effectively.

Strategizing effectively means taking into account your real difficulties and *letting* yourself set things up so that you have a better chance of succeeding. Below are some examples of modifying your thinking to make changes that make your life work better. They may sound simple but are often not easy to put into effect. They are all about knowing yourself and what works for *you* not what others may tell you about what you should feel or think. Even between women with AD/HD there is a huge variety in how each woman will need to set up her life to work right for *her*.

*Even if people think you're weird, if possible, don't plan too many different activities on the same day if you are the kind of person who doesn't do well with this. *Too many* is whatever makes you feel overstressed and overwhelmed on a regular basis. For some, multitasking is energizing and just the right kind of stimulation.

*You can *allow* yourself to set up a quiet area that is just your own. This might strike you as odd about modifying your outer environment but this personal strategy means changing your thinking first, allowing yourself the possibility of doing this. This is what women struggle with most often.

*You may need to prepare in detail the night before what you will need the next morning if you are the kind of person who finds it difficult to think in the morning when you are under pressure and tired. Others may be way too pooped at night to do anything and are better off getting up very early to do their best planning and preparation.

Remember, there is no best way, just a best way for you! Permission to do things differently is what we are after here.

*You might let yourself to go out for dinner on holidays or actually go on vacation if holiday seasons are a time of overwhelming stress for you. If multi-tasking is a big problem for you, allow yourself to get a mother's helper to come in chop up vegetables and get dinner going while you spend time with your children. Or allow yourself to hire a babysitter to take care of the kids while you cook if you would rather do it that way.

Fun: The "F" Word

Another important way to give yourself permission to care for yourself or approach life in a new way is one of great conflict often for women with AD/HD. I refer to fun as the "f" word because it is almost a dirty or forbidden word among women with AD/HD in my groups. Even though women with AD/HD have a great time when they get together at conferences, fun often gets put on the bottom of the to-do pile. Pleasures get equated with guilt because women feel that they have too much to do. Learn to tolerate a little guilt while taking a some time for pleasure, even if is to just read a novel, listen to music, tell jokes with your kids, play cards, or go out with friends. Make a call to someone you love. Have a soothing special time with a partner even for a few minutes a night, as well as a time on the weekend not devoted to problems or schedules—a problem free zone. Nurturing yourself is often the most difficult thing for a woman with AD/HD to do.

Helpers for the Messy Internal World

Interpersonal strategies mean letting other people help you such as AD/HD coaches, therapists, personal assistants, and organizers. (See next chapter discussion of professionals, organizers and coaches). Sometimes, though, you will have someone in your life who's accepting, non-judgmental, calm, and organized and can help you think through what you want to accomplish and gently (or not so gently if that is what you want) keep you focused. A good, trusted friend or family member or acquaintances with whom you can barter services can help. You may also work in a buddy system in which you both decide you're going to do a task and call each other to check in at the beginning and the end of the agreed upon period. You can help each other think through what you need to do and check back at the end of the day to review and regroup.

Extra Strategies

Below are more explanations and suggestions for a variety of challenges to expand what you may have seen in the section above. Use these suggestions as take off points in your own planning when you use the grid at the end of the chapter.

No Tech: In addition to paper planning devices such as calendars, lists, Post-its, buzzers, beepers, and timers some women have thought of unique ways to approach their challenges.

One woman decided to create a huge wall of corkboard so she could keep notes or instructions right by the phone. This way she could remember the questions she wanted to ask or the procedures to go through. Another woman decided to line her wall with hooks for her clothes instead of using hangers and drawers. There are special products for highly sensitive people such as shirts with no labels or socks with no toe seams.

A Touch of Tech: For distractibility, I use white noise machines everywhere to block out ordinary noise that makes it impossible for me to concentrate. Experiment with higher tech aids like computers, spell-checks, organizing software, PDAs, electronic reminders, or computerized memo pads. Terry Matlen's book, Survival Tips for Women with AD/HD has lots of interesting ways to use these.

I use my cell phone to leave myself messages on my home phone (which is programmed in for safety) with all the ideas I have and reminders of things to do that occur to me while driving. This is safer than risking what I call a, "WWD," a WRITING WHILE DRIVING violation!

Use your voice mail instead of being disturbed by the phone. You do not need to pick up every call. Since I first wrote this book, more people use caller ID so this makes it more feasible and comfortable for women to screen calls. Here's a chart you can use to fill in to help you approach your challenges.

Strategies Grid

Areas Needing Support	No Tech	A Touch of Tech	Personal	Interpersonal
Time				
Money				
Stuff				
Hyper-sensitivities				
Impulsivity				
Activation				
Hyper or hypo activity levels				
Writing				
Organizing				
Distractability				
Memory				
Sequencing				
Planning				
Decision-making				
Others of your own				

Conclusion

Remember, if something isn't working, do it differently. Whether you live or work alone or with other people, don't keep on doing it the same old way, only trying harder. If you're always trying to go to New York but keep winding up in California, then get on a different bus!

Later we will go into more depth on the necessity to rethink and reorganize your life beyond the use of these strategies. These will include eliminating and reconsidering things that you have been doing automatically for years.

For now, think about what strategies you need to put in place to stop the drain on your cognitive energy and resources. There are thousands of strategies once you put your AD/HD brain to the task. The harder part is how to put them in place, get support in doing them, and maintain them. For complete information on other great tips and strategies see the Resources section in the back of the book.

In the next chapter "The Rest of the Middle of the *MESST*," we look at support, both emotional and physical. Years of negative experiences cause negative expectations and difficulty setting limits and boundaries. That can make setting up a life that works for you as a woman with AD/HD even more challenging. Personal and professional support can often make a world of difference.

CHAPTER SEVENTEEN

The Rest of the Middle of the "MESST"

Support

In this chapter we will look at *support*, another essential piece of the treatment puzzle. This ranges from emotional support in the form of support groups to paid help for specific functions you have trouble performing to professional services such as coaching, organizing, and personal assistance.

Support Groups

Support groups most commonly take place on a regular or drop-in basis; however, there are now some online groups. Either can be led by peers or by a professional facilitator. Whichever form or structure they take, when members share their stories, struggles, and triumphs, this can often play a pivotal role in early treatment.

During the first stage of diagnosis and treatment for AD/HD, it's often difficult to find the kind of support you need from your family and friends. They haven't been educated about it or been working at it as you have, and they have their own emotional responses that they need to work through; it is often hard for them to understand it or accept it. This can be an isolating, upsetting, frustrating experience.

Ideally, you want to get support from your personal circle, but until then, it's important to find outside support from those who can provide a positive environment. The better you feel about yourself in relation to your AD/HD, the better you will be able to talk to the people close to you about it. The more you accept yourself and the AD/HD, the more they will in time. You may also be more willing to take risks and move toward new goals when supported by others who understand your experience. Hearing other people's stories who are at different places in their diagnosis and treatment can bring hope and help you understand the process to get a better idea of where you're headed. Hearing others' stories may also help you stop the blaming and shaming you experienced when you were dealing with your issues alone, in secret. Eventually, it may also help you to rethink your own view of your differences and difficulties.

Adults with AD/HD tend to gloss over the things they do well and focus only on what they consider to be their failings. Being with people who see your strengths can make you pause to take in your strengths and successes. Typically, support groups give you more opportunity to tell your personal story and interact at a more personal level than educational meetings; although often the distinction is blurred, the benefits are similar.

Where to Find Support Groups

There are support groups through CHADD and other national and local networks listed in the *Resource Section* at the end of the book.

Support Services

Just like in a workplace in which many people couldn't function without support staff, a woman with AD/HD at home or at work will benefit from support services to begin or continue to function well. For some people this might mean help cleaning house, doing laundry, paying the bills, running errands, doing paper work, making dinner, organizing closets, shopping for clothes, or de-cluttering on a regular basis. You must figure out which areas are seriously draining your vital cognitive and emotional resources—your time and energy—and find the kind and level of help you need to meet your challenges.

Do Not Try This at Home Alone

Women newly diagnosed with AD/HD often say with great determination, "Now that I know about this, I'm going to go home, and

I'm going to try harder." They try to apply this new approach to tasks they have found overwhelming and daunting their whole lives such as keeping their purses organized, cooking dinner every night, or organizing their paper work. While this motivation and determination may be admirable, in the long run it can often be self-defeating. Doing the same thing they have always done but "trying harder" just sets them up for frustration. For example, women will experiment with multiple new organizational systems, but that is not the whole picture. It doesn't account for the real level of difficulty their AD/HD causes them, and it shorts circuits the process by the hope that "somehow, with will power, I will just do it." They often put all their energy into this, which takes away from the energy that could be used to work through their emotions and develop a new life. I worked with a very talented female client who had spent *seven* hours a day for 30 years trying to master all that is involved with cooking a meal. The sequencing involved in planning menus, shopping, cooking, and cleaning up was excruciatingly difficult for her. When she overcame her internal barriers and got support, she was able to turn some of that energy and attention to her writing, which was her gift.

I don't want to imply that you must have special talents in order to justify getting help. You all have gifts, talents, interests, and strengths. But you need to put more attention on them or if you don't know what they are, take time to discover them to balance out your difficulties with positive experiences.

The Right Kind of Help

Because you often feel vulnerable regarding your AD/HD, it is essential to find someone who can work with your special challenges. The kind of help you may need might not fall into an easily described category or be what others think you need. For instance, you may need someone to help you organize your household rather than clean it. Just make sure whoever you hire to help you is not critical, judgmental, scolding, or shaming.

Personal Assistant

You can hire a very part-time, economical assistant to help you in a variety of ways, again depending on your individual needs. It might be another mom, a college student, or an older, retired person looking for part-time work. Some of you may need someone energetic to run around and do errands. Some of you may need someone to do filing on a regular basis or pay bills. You may need to try a few people before you work out the process since you may not know what works for you at first. I have found that it is necessary for me to have a personal assistant sit with me once a week for 90 minutes and assist me in the painstaking process of deciding what to do with each paper from the huge amount of papers that accumulate. I decide, and she puts it away. You may need someone to come once a month and help pay the bills even if he or she just sits there while you write the checks. When you set something up to occur, you have selected the time and created the space.

Think through what you need to do and try and write out a specific job description. Ask people you know or put a flyer up in a local coffee shop or day care center you feel familiar with or in a local neighborhood paper. Some of you may want more distance from a person that will come into your home. In that case, look for someone at a college or advertise in a different area.

Professional Organizers

The field of professional organizers has grown rapidly in the last several years. Some in their national organization, called National Association of Professional Organizers (NAPO), even specialize in chronic and severe disorganization and AD/HD. The key is to find someone by word of mouth, online, in the paper, or through professional organizations with whom you feel comfortable enough to communicate your special needs and who will be responsive to them in a non-judgmental way.

Whatever system is devised, it has to be personalized to fit your needs. If a professional wants to put everything away in pretty, colored, labeled files, and you need to see papers in order to remember they exist, you need to communicate this and work together to find a creative solution. If you hire a professional organizer to create great systems for you, make sure you also create a structure for someone to help you maintain the system. It's in the maintenance and routine that adults with AD/HD often have the greatest problems.

Emotional Issues Related to Getting Support Services

It's critical that you constantly work at remembering the concept that it isn't a luxury to get help for your AD/HD and if you do, it doesn't mean you are immature or spoiled. AD/HD causes serious disorganization for many people; it is not even in the same ballpark as getting help with ordinary domestic chores. Even though getting support for your deficit so that you can focus on your strengths is essential, it is important to understand some of the emotional blocks that might interfere with getting this kind of support.

Many women feel a range of painful emotions attached to the idea of getting help. They may feel embarrassed or ashamed about letting someone see the disorder in their home or work life. Having someone come in and see a backlog of clutter can be intimidating. Women can also feel guilt about letting others do things for them that they think define what it means to be an adult or real woman. They have deeply held beliefs about how getting help in certain domestic areas makes them a failure as a mother or wife.

Women don't like to have help in these areas because they don't want to feel dependent. In the end, it may cause them to remain even more so because they aren't giving themselves the chance to grow and shine in ways they may be able to if they had more support. Until women embrace this concept of interdependence versus dependence, until they become willing to confront their barriers, they may find themselves becoming more depleted, depressed, and down on themselves even after diagnosis and treatment with medication.

Often a woman with AD/HD will become emotional in an organizing session. *Going through unpaid bills can bring up feelings of guilt and shame and going through half finished projects can bring the sorrow of unfinished dreams, lost opportunities, and mistakes with each new pile uncovered.* This can work well when a counselor is in the picture because then an individual can take the feelings that arise in organizing back to a counseling session to work through.

Keeping Pace with Success

Letting yourself explore your strengths and be successful in new ways brings with it new challenges and may require a new level or kind of support. It's necessary to continually keep pace with success.

I discuss this in depth in my book *Journeys Through ADDulthood* and call it the "crisis of success." For example, let's say you let yourself have organizational help at home a few hours a week and that frees you up to start a small, part-time business or to go to the gym and get in shape so that you have more energy to think about taking a class. You start a new positive cycle in which some of the seeds you plant begin to grow. Then your part-time business takes off and before you know it, you are inundated with new orders. Or maybe you volunteer for a committee at work or at your child's school. You feel better because you are using your computer or people skills but then you find yourself overwhelmed again. At that point you have to reassess your new needs for support. More success also brings more executive functioning challenges, and you may need more or different kind of support such as an office assistant a couple hours a week. There are also other things you will have to do at that point such as saying no, making difficult choices, or letting go of other things.

Spring Cleaning the Internal World

Women with AD/HD often need help with planning and ordering their inner worlds if only for a few minutes a day. Some women say they are able to look organized on the outside but that they need straightening and ordering on the inside. The picture "Spring Cleaning the Internal World" illustrates what some women have found to be

SPRING CLEANING THE INTERNAL WORLD

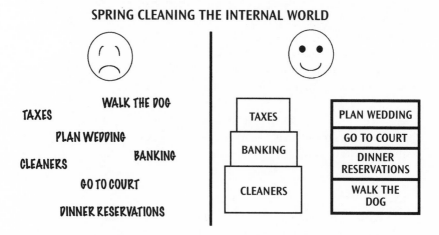

helpful in bringing order to an internal world that often seems chaotic. On the left side of the diagram, everything seems to be of equal importance, which can be confusing, disorganized, and messy; on the right side, the whole picture feels less overwhelming because it is more orderly and structured. Other useful images might be that of pulling down the shades to block out extraneous thoughts or wrapping up less important concerns in boxes and putting them back on the shelves to take down and open as needed.

Coaching and counseling for AD/HD can help you mentally box up and prioritize what's important. Then you can make a plan of action broken down into small steps. If you are seeing a counselor experienced in working with adults with AD/HD, he or she will perform some of these coaching functions as well but less frequently with more emphasis on the emotional components of the tasks. Your counselor may be able to recommend a coach to work with outside of your sessions if she or he feels that it would be helpful, thus creating a team approach. There will be more on counseling in the next chapter but since more and more people are turning to personal AD/HD coaches, I have devoted a special section to it as follows.

Coaching for AD/HD

It has become increasingly common for adults with AD/HD to work with a professionally trained AD/HD coach. In the last ten years there has been a proliferation of training programs, for AD/HD coaches, each with a particular philosophy and approach. AD/HD coaching as a profession was spearheaded early on by Nancy Ratey, M.Ed. and Sue Sussman, M.Ed. who in 1994 formed what was named at the time the National Coaching Network. Also in 1994, *Driven to Distraction* presented a model for ADD coaching called the HOPE model. Since then, many models have evolved, most of who have their own websites or advertise in magazines. See the resource section at the end of the book for more on coaching resources. You can also ask around for personal referrals. There are a range of personalities, training, and education so you need to research them as well as to ask about fees, ways of working with you, and frequency of contact. Many coaches work on the phone or online so it is not necessary to find someone in you local area; this opens up the possibility of working with highly trained coaches from anywhere in the world.

Different Focuses

Coaches often have certain areas of focus or specialization. Some are more focused on performance issues like task, time, or household management or completing assignments and projects. The coaching may be focused on performance, strategies, or skill building. Some focus on business or on writing whereas others place more emphasis on helping you lead a balanced life or finding a life path.

Coaches sometimes also work as professional organizers but more frequently these are separate services. Coaches do not typically come into your home. Coaching groups are sometimes available on the phone or online; this works wonders for those living in isolated areas. The groups help participants make commitments or goals and have them check in regularly for support.

How Coaching Can Help

Sue Sussman and Nancy Ratey (2002) described coaching to me this way.

"The coach is an emotionally neutral person in the life of an individual with AD/HD . . . Thus the coach can offer suggestions, and reminders, provide structure and boundaries and be perceived by the client as helpful and supportive . . ."

Having the structure and external stimulation of an encouraging coach with whom you develop goals creates an external structure that can help you move ahead and stay on track. A coach can also help a woman bring a few tasks to the forefront since women with AD/HD often have a great deal of trouble choosing from all the myriad ideas in their heads. All these variables can seem to be of equal weight. Many people with AD/HD have to hear themselves think out loud to process their thoughts or internalize a concept. Coaching can involve daily or weekly check-ins on your plans and how to accomplish them, making sure your steps are small and manageable, and can help you get back on track when you get off. Women with AD/HD also can have a sudden loss of perspective when it comes to their strengths and weaknesses, and a coach can help them regain a balanced perspective.

Self-check to Determine if Coaching Is for You

If you answer yes to the questions below, you may want to consider finding someone (other than your partner) be coach you.

_____ Would it help to have someone to call every day to help plan the day with you?

_____ Would it help to have someone check in with you to help you set limits on activities or tasks before you create too many plans and set too many goals?

_____ Would it help to talk through decisions you need to make with a non-judgmental person?

_____ Would it help to have someone assist you to focus on a few of the many projects that you want to do?

Possible Roadblocks

If an individual begins certain types of coaching too early in the process, I find there are often too many emotional conflicts that may interfere with their ability to stick to the commitments made in this process. Coaching is often performance oriented, and an individual has to have worked out some of the shame and negative expectations that may arise. If you find this is happening, you may need to work in counseling for a while first or with a coach in conjunction with your counselor. Coaches will, when necessary and appropriate, refer back to the client's counselor or doctor when problems arise that are out of their scope of practice and training.

Summary

It takes most women a long time to overcome internal barriers to putting support in their lives. The goal for women with AD/HD is to focus on their strengths a majority of the time since that will ultimately lead to satisfaction and success rather than spending all of their time coping alone with their deficits or feeling like they must only use the support until they are "strong enough" to do without it. Women with AD/HD may benefit and need some form of support mechanisms all of their lives

At this point, you can get started by letting someone in close enough to give you a little more support in some of the areas we mentioned or in areas that are holding you back and keeping you chronically depleted or depressed. This is a big internal barrier so be patient with yourself if you feel resistant to this idea. And be somewhat patient with your partner or family if they feel resistant to it. As we discussed earlier, both these barriers will be easier to push through when you get emotional support from others. If doing the above is not enough to let you overcome these barriers, you may consider counseling for a while to confront these more in depth. It often takes counseling to bring about a shift in your self-image and your view of your unique challenges before you will accept household assistance, coaching, or professional assistance with daily tasks or organizing.

For other great tips and strategies and for other educational and support resources, look at end of the book in the Resource section. In the next chapter, we will look at the *end* of the MESST, which focuses on individual, couple, and group counseling for AD/HD.

CHAPTER EIGHTEEN

The End of the "MESST"

Therapy

The last letter of the *MESST* model stands for therapy, which is often the next step in figuring out what you need and then being able to move toward it. Years of negative experiences can result in negative expectations and difficulty with setting limits and boundaries. That can make setting up a life that works for you as a woman with AD/HD even more challenging. Professional guidance can often make a world of difference.

In this book, when I use the term counseling or therapy for an adult with AD/HD, I mean a process (in groups, with a partner, your family, or individually) that addresses the emotional barriers to making the changes you need to make your life work better. Even though there are many different kinds of mental health professionals with different kinds of training and approaches, when we talk about an effective process, it is strength-based, interactive, and collaborative. That's true whether the mental health professional is a psychotherapist, mental health professional, social workers, or psychologists. The "T" in the MESST model stands for *therapy*, but for consistency, I will use the term counseling here as I have in much of the book.

Ideally, counseling for issues stemming from AD/HD strikes a balance between focus on real-life matters and the feelings that prevent you from taking the steps you want to take to meet your goals. These issues can be effectively addressed in couples, group, individual or family counseling or in some combination of these.

In this chapter, I will talk to you as I have throughout the book, but this material is intended to be helpful to your partner and any

mental health professional who is interested in effectively interven-
ing, supporting, or guiding women with these challenges.

In part one of this chapter, we will look at individual counseling
for women with AD/HD. We will explore the internal barriers that
may prevent them from moving forward and common themes and
goals that are often the focus of counseling for women.

This section will also discuss what happens in the family system
when you make changes in individual counseling. I will also point
out what to look for in effective AD/HD counseling and potential pitfalls. In the second part of the chapter, we will look at two other
counseling settings you might benefit from at certain times such as
couples counseling and group counseling.

PART ONE: INDIVIDUAL COUNSELING
FOR WOMEN WITH AD/HD

Internal Barriers that May Prevent You from
Moving Forward

Some people with AD/HD have an easier time moving forward
after diagnosis whereas the road for others may be a little more complex due to secondary effects from years of living undiagnosed with
AD/HD. The *strategies* and the *support* we discussed in the last two
chapters may seem easy to employ to the outside observer but are
often quite challenging for women with AD/HD to utilize. These
seemingly concrete tasks bring them up against such strong internal
barriers that they often stop cold. Feelings about themselves and
their difficulties have sometimes become so interwoven with their
self-image by the time of diagnosis that education is not enough, and
counseling is needed to facilitate change.

A woman who has been struggling undiagnosed may carry with
her an emotional legacy that makes it difficult to make the changes
that she desires. When she "hits a wall" as she tries to restructure her
life, both she and her partner are often baffled as to why she doesn't
take the needed and desired steps. This can be about seemingly simple
things like asking for more time on a test or getting help in the house.
The point at which her "neurology meets her psychology" is the
point at which counseling for a woman with AD/HD can be helpful.
For example, let's say a woman with AD/HD agrees she needs to hire
an organizer to help her with her piles of paperwork (caused by her

neurology). In this case, even though she may want to avail herself of this help, she may feel too much shame or guilt, feel undeserving, or be afraid to bring it up with her husband (her psychology).

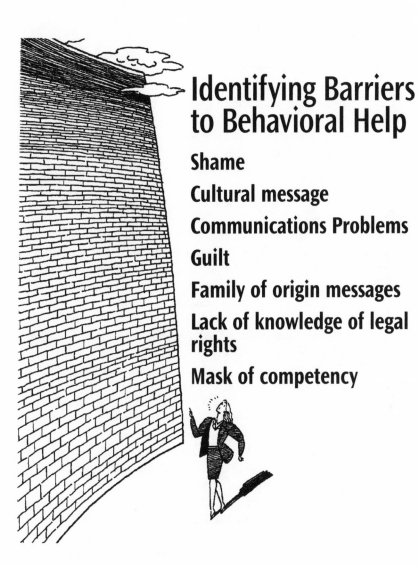

Identifying Barriers to Behavioral Help

Shame

Cultural message

Communications Problems

Guilt

Family of origin messages

Lack of knowledge of legal rights

Mask of competency

Common Themes Addressed in Counseling for Women with AD/HD

Even though each woman is different, there are some common themes among women seeking counseling for AD/HD. The effects of living for a long time with undiagnosed AD/HD include a distorted self-image, the pain of underachievement despite strengths and talents, and difficulty with mood or relationships. The challenges of AD/HD also often compromise friendships because of the difficulty of maintaining them. Overwhelmed by daily life, these women often become isolated, depressed, and ashamed of their perceived failings.

As we saw earlier in the book, the woman with AD/HD comes to expect "maligning messages" with her behavior. In an effort to avoid such reprimands, she often avoids requesting the very assistance that could help her. She is driven to keep up a "mask of competency" at all costs in order to avoid the re-emergence of early painful feelings of "not getting it right."

Women with AD/HD also tend to have difficulty with communication and assertiveness. Since they have come to expect the worst, they tend to misinterpret interactions in relationships or even create self-fulfilling prophecies by employing defense mechanisms that move them away from other people, instead of healthy, assertive self-protection requiring setting limits and boundaries.

Louise was a good but disorganized teacher. She had functioned for many years with the support of a trusted classroom aide. When this aide retired and another aide took her place who was judgmental of Louise's unique ways of doing things, instead of telling her what she required, Louise let this aide dominate her and all her insecurities surfaced. She became overwhelmed, her self- esteem and health plummeted, and she eventually left the job she loved, instead of setting limits and asserting the power she actually had in this situation.

After diagnosis, a woman may also find she has a tremendous backlog of anger or regret that may interfere with her ability to move through the grief cycle or that may interfere with her employing the techniques or tools necessary to manage her AD/HD symptoms.

At some point, she may feel as if she is stuck between two worlds. She hasn't yet integrated a new identity, but she has outgrown the old one. She may feel alone or stuck if the people around her resist the process of redefining her image. Counseling can support and guide a woman while she works through the many feelings associated with this process and until this strange new identity of being a woman with AD/HD is more firmly rooted.

Counseling Goals

A mental health professional must validate a woman's difficulties yet never lose sight of the whole picture that she is more than just a "problem" but someone with strengths and possibilities. Eventually, the woman with AD/HD will internalize a new view of herself and a new view of her difficulties. Having a supportive relationship that holds up a mirror for you to help you repair your self-image and see yourself whole and accurately again without the distortion that living for many years without explanation can bring is critical. The mental health professional must see you in this way.

As a result, when you are confronted and confounded by an AD/HD moment, day, or week, your self-talk will be much different. You may still be very frustrated, but you won't see this as a reflection of your character. When a woman slips into thoughts like, "I'm really just lazy or immature or irresponsible . . ." even long after she has been diagnosed, a good mental health professional can steadily maintain and reflect the more positive image for her that she has both great strengths and great difficulties until she is able to do this self-talk on her own. Your goal then is to work with your mental health professional to learn to make choices that lead you to live a more satisfying life.

What Happens When You Make Changes in the Family System

In addition to individual changes and struggles, a woman with AD/HD may also have to deal with the stresses that come about when any one member of a family makes a significant change. Even if her changes are positive, people close to her may resist or react in unexpected ways. Women with AD/HD can benefit greatly by having the support of a mental health professional to deal with such stresses within a system.

The challenge to a family system when someone begins recovery of some kind is quite common. For example, when someone stops drinking, there is a lot of what we call "change-back" messages. Families live by an invisible regulatory system. Everyone knows the unspoken rules of behavior and the roles each is expected to play. They play them out automatically without any thought. Even if someone is unhappy or things could be better, at least it is familiar to everyone. When someone makes a change for the better, it disrupts this way of operating. The family becomes anxious and uncomfortable because everyone is forced to give up their familiar ways of behaving. They then try to "hook" the one making the changes into returning to the status quo. Women are often especially vulnerable to this because other people's feelings are involved, and they are very sensitive to those. Unfortunately, these "change-back" messages and behaviors can sabotage a person's recovery.

Let's look at one common scenario by way of illustration. When a woman is treated for AD/HD, she may for the first time be able to hold her own in an argument instead of folding like she may have done previously because she was too overwhelmed or confused to put her thoughts together in a cohesive way. Before she was on medication and/or getting outside support, she may have settled for peace at any price, but now she may be able to tolerate more conflict. She may be unwilling to continue to take all the blame for what is going on in a relationship or family and begin to make her own decisions more easily or with more clarity. Her family members may say things to her like, "You're not yourself any more. You're always making trouble now. I thought the medication was supposed to take care of that," as if the medication was a tranquilizer. People may tell her to "take a pill," when she might be displaying real emotion for the first time now that she can focus and express herself more clearly. If she doesn't have outside support from someone such as a knowledgeable mental health professional, she may take the bait and revert back to her old, unproductive, unfulfilling ways.

Power Shifts

Such changes for the woman with AD/HD might create a real power shift with her partner, which is good, but hard on the relationship for a while. Medication can give her both the wherewithal to take action and also give her the power to stick with her feelings and express them, even though they might not all be positive. When a man takes medication, quite often his changes in behavior come as a relief to those around him because he might become more responsive and attentive; for a woman, however, people often experience her becoming more assertive. This is often uncomfortable for others if a woman who has been under-active suddenly becomes a force to contend with.

At first, a woman might be afraid to understand the way she feels about her partner or to confront other issues in their relationship. She may have been suppressing her feelings before, not having the energy to deal with them or becoming too overloaded to face her feelings. At this point, a woman might be confronted with all her internal prohibitions about the power and the danger she feels when making someone angry. She may be tempted to go back to the way she was before and give up some of her clarity or assertiveness. If, however, she is in individual counseling during this transitional period, she can work through these feelings and get support to maintain positive changes, or she might seek out couples counseling to help them do the same as a couple.

Effective Approaches and Pitfalls in Counseling

What to Watch out for in Individual Counseling

Here are three ways that counseling can be less than effective for women working in individual counseling for AD/HD. It is good just to be aware of these so you can identify when problems arise and explore with your mental health professional what might be happening to keep you feeling stuck.

1. Stuck in the Organizational Piece of the Treatment Pie

Sometimes mental health professionals unwittingly set up a client to feel like a failure. Without understanding the complexity and depth of the problems and barriers, both the mental health professional and the client often get stuck in the organizational strategy part of the treatment. This interaction might then re-create a situation in which, once again, the woman feels she is disappointing a significant person in her life.

2. Stuck in the Child Treatment Approach

Another pitfall occurs when methods often used with children with AD/HD are applied to adult clients. Because AD/HD counseling calls for a much more directive approach than traditional psychotherapy, a mental health professional may fall into a pattern of over-suggesting and over-advising, focusing too much on behavior modification. When this happens, women with AD/HD can feel they are being treated like naughty children instead of intelligent adults. For example, one very experienced mental health professional who worked with AD/HD children began treating adults and tried to apply the same methods using charts and stars and structure. In an effort to motivate a mature, creative, vibrant woman, she said, "If you keep your desk clean eighty percent of the time this week, I'll have a chocolate-chip cookie waiting for you." The client felt demeaned to say the least. Obviously, the complexity of her life went beyond this simple, condescending sort of attitude that she perceived as lacking in empathy.

3. Stuck on the Surface of the Treatment Pool

Another common pitfall is when the mental health professional truly doesn't understand the depth of difficulties that a woman's AD/HD presents in her life. This lack of understanding is often perceived by the client as a lack of empathy. For example, when a woman desperately tries to communicate that she is drowning in backlogs of unattended business, she may feel invalidated when she is simply told to try harder to get organized, to make lists, or to get a new Franklin planner. The layers of emotions around these issues are often completely missed.

What to Look for in Individual Counseling

Appropriate and effective counseling for AD/HD adults is as follows:

- Proactive
- Interactive
- Educational
- Supportive
- Strength-oriented

One of the most important characteristics of appropriate counseling for AD/HD is it's focus on helping the women confront the emotional barriers that are preventing her from taking the steps she wants to in order to move forward with her life.

The focus needs to be on what the woman wants to do and what small steps she can take to move toward that goal. If there seems to be a barrier that prevents her from taking that step, it needs to be examined. Often at the root of these are shame, guilt, difficulty with communicating, or setting limits. Until and unless these are addressed, all the strategies in the world won't work because she won't be able to take the next step.

What's important in counseling for AD/HD is to strike a balance between coaching, helping someone stay on track, and exploring emotions when they get in the way of these goals. Extremes of over-controlling, over-suggesting, or over-directing should be avoided. Exclusively exploring the early psychological roots of AD/HD as well as only focusing on the organizational and strategy parts of the issues are both unhelpful. What is helpful is for a mental health profes-sional to convey an understanding of the complexity of the process so that the client trusts that her mental health professional is able to guide her through this journey. The mental health professional can normalize and support her through the rough spots as well as point out the beautiful *attractions* along the way. (Solden, 2002)

The mental health professional is helpful when she can pull out the most effective options from what seems to the client like hun-dreds of possibilities. Then she can help to organize and prioritize these with the client. This reduces feelings of anxiety in the client from having too many free-floating ideas and helps her form a simple plan of action with a few clear steps. It is critical that after a client decides on steps she wants to take and assumes that it will be easy, that the mental health professional approach the emotional side of this by asking the client to explore what might in fact be difficult emotionally about taking these steps such as fear or embarrassment. (Solden, 2002, pg.154)

PART TWO: OTHER SETTINGS

Couples Counseling

In addition to an individual's patterns, especially if she has been in her current relationship before diagnosis and treatment, a couple's interactions may have become organized around the undiagnosed difficulties. In this section, we will focus on some helpful approaches to couples counseling when one or both of the partners has been diagnosed with AD/HD. This will be helpful for you and your partner as well as for the mental health professionals you may be working with.

Goals for Couples Counseling

The ultimate goal of couples counseling is for both partners to accept and understand the AD/HD and to see themselves, each other, and the partnership as larger than those symptoms. Sometimes getting an official and thorough diagnosis can serve the purpose of breaking through the denial of a partner. For partners to be able to look at scores and the evaluation in black and white and to see gaps and disparities can make the AD/HD more concrete and real, which can begin a move toward acceptance.

Both partners will go through a grief cycle in a different way. You can read more about the grief cycle for the partner without AD/HD as it pertains to the partnership in Chapter 23. The partner without AD/HD must deal with disappointment and a loss of expectations. He must rearrange his view of marriage and partnership. He might also have a backlog of resentment and anger, which will have to be addressed before the couple can move forward. He will need to come to a new view that although life will be different, it can be rich.

I once heard the story of a man who came to see the beauty and miracles that happened every day living with his wife with AD/HD. He described coming home after one of his wife's grocery shopping days where she often spilled the contents of the bags. One day, after his view of her had shifted, instead of feeling frustration with the "mess," he opened his eyes and saw the miracle of chocolate cake "growing" on the trees of his front lawn where it had landed after she became distracted and tripped, tossing the cake she was holding onto the branches of the nearby tree.

She spills the contents of bags making what could be looked at as a mess, but he sees it as beauty. His view has shifted. He has reached acceptance. Acceptance doesn't mean he will always be so good natured as this or that he won't still be frustrated often or irritated, but it does mean he can now accept the reality of her challenges and not personalize them, just as hopefully she can accept the reality of whatever his challenges are.

Effective Approaches

As mentioned earlier in this chapter, when a woman is diagnosed and begins medication, shock waves of change can reverberate throughout the "system." During this transition time sometimes only the mental health professional can hold onto a larger view and support the couple until they establish a new way of relating to each other in a positive and healthy way.

Balance

An effective couples mental health professional should always strive to maintain a balanced approach so that neither partner feels that he or she is "the problem." Instead, the focus is on the way the partners understand, interact and communicate with each other. The mental health professional must remain vigilant that the woman with AD/HD does not become the "identified patient" or the partner to be fixed. Remaining neutral is complicated by the fact that the partner without AD/HD will often want to see his partner as "the problem," and the woman will sometimes collude with this view! She may feel so ashamed or guilty about her "failings" that she may be willing to let the sessions focus on her and accept all blame for the problems of the relationship.

Calming Things Down

The couple will be more likely to relax and listen and be less likely to blame or be defensive in the beginning of treatment *if they understand the following*:

- Certain kinds of problems are to be expected during and after diagnosis and beginning of treatment and are a normal part of the process

- Executive functioning problems explain why it is so hard to follow through with agreed upon plans

- It is a long journey rather than, "Okay, you've been diagnosed, now change."

- Shared understanding will be less than perfect and accepting that will make things easier

- A portion of their support should come from outside the partnership. This will decrease the frustration of trying to get perfect understanding from one person and take some of the pressure off the system

- They will have a tendency to underestimate both the difficulties and strengths of the partner with AD/HD

Communication and Empathy

Focusing on communication and empathy is more effective in the long run than only focusing on irritating behaviors and getting organized. The woman with AD/HD needs to ask for acceptance but also needs to understand, empathize, and validate the struggles of the non-AD/HD spouse who continues to be affected and frustrated by the AD/HD even if he understands and accepts it. She needs to do this without blaming herself.

An effective mental health professional assists the woman with AD/HD to explain to her partner what it's like in her brain and what she needs. It can also help her partner to listen so she feels heard and understood. For example, she might say, "Sometimes I feel like I am drowning. It feels very frightening when I can't think of what to do. When you turn away from me at those times, I feel abandoned. I need some kind of anchor at those times. When I am having an AD/HD meltdown I wish you would . . ." or "What would be helpful is . . ." Sometimes she doesn't even know what would help and yet she expects her partner to provide it. Her partner then feels like he's being asked to do something impossible or is being blamed for something he doesn't understand, thereby increasing the chances that he will walk away or withdraw just at the point she needs him. Counseling can be a helpful place for both partners to understand what goes wrong, to work out new ways to recognize those situations when they arise, and to strategize about what to do the next time to break a negative cycle.

Partners sometimes worry about how they can be supportive without being codependent. Counseling can help them understand true support, how to set limits in a healthy way in order to protect themselves and the relationship, and how to keep them from feeling overloaded or resentful.

It is important to understand the non-AD/HD partner's areas of weakness as well in order to find out what the partner with AD/HD can contribute. Each partner has strengths and weaknesses of some kind. It is important to form a respectful partnership that is balanced in giving and receiving even though each may be giving and receiving completely different kinds of things in the exchange they will each be of value.

Attributions and Wounding

It is extremely important for the mental health professional to recognize that couples tend to attribute personal meanings to the AD/HD symptoms and behaviors. Each person will react to particular AD/HD symptoms in his or her own way, depending on his or her particular background. Both partners can feel rage or hurt that comes from re-experiencing an earlier wounding. Even if the original wounding was completely unrelated to his present partner, the feelings may be the same.

This is true for all couples, but with AD/HD there are certain symptoms that can be wounding and misinterpreted in ways particular to AD/HD. For example, behaviors like forgetting, not listening, hyper-focusing, being disorganized, or being distractible may all be interpreted as a lack of caring, abandonment, selfishness, immaturity, irresponsibility, being spoiled, not interested, thoughtless, controlling—shall I go on?!

These are some of the examples I have seen:

- *If a non-AD/HD partner had a mom who was an alcoholic and needed caretaking, he might feel (fill in the feeling), e.g., angry, resentful, worried, scared) if his partner with AD/HD seems like she needs caretaking from him*

- *If his parent was narcissistic and the partner with AD/HD is very self-focused or hyper-focused just trying to survive, he may feel used*

- *If his parent was bipolar and the AD/HD partner has or is acting on a flood of ideas all at once, he might feel afraid that she is manic*

- *If he was emotionally abandoned by a parent, he may re-experience abandonment when his partner has trouble listening*

The partner with AD/HD can also easily be wounded again when her AD/HD symptoms elicit responses from her partner that are similar to those she received as a child. For the woman with AD/HD, raised by parents who scolded, ignored, misunderstood, discounted, or criticized her for being clumsy, messy, disorganized, etc., she may be extra sensitive to criticism from her partner and vulnerable to re-wounding, for example:

- *A woman always criticized for being messy feels scolded and ashamed when her husband comes home at end of the day complaining about the condition of the house*

- *A woman who ideas were never taken seriously because she couldn't express herself clearly feels invisible when her partner talks over her to others as if she is stupid or inconsequential*

- *A woman who had always been told she was causing too much trouble withdraws when her husband calls her "high maintenance." She stops telling him her needs and doesn't ask for help and becomes depressed or anxious instead*

Through couples counseling, partners can learn how to set limits on the frustration and hurt that spills over into critical, destructive behavior in order to build a safe and nurturing relationship. Each partner needs to expect and request empathy and mutual respect because this forms the basis for any solid couple relationship, no matter what the struggles are of the individuals.

Positive Relationships

In addition to setting limits on criticism and emphasizing empathy and communication, couples need to spend time together away from the areas most impacted by the AD/HD and to create a cushion of enjoyment to buffer the inevitable and continuing impact of AD/HD. Couples need to create AD/HD free zones where they just have fun together.

Help for "Mixed" Marriages

I like to think of counseling adults in which one partner has AD/HD (or even both have AD/HD but have different types) as counseling a "mixed" marriage. I believe that adults with AD/HD have a sub-culture with understood ways of talking, behaving, thinking and interacting. Thinking in these terms help everyone involved remember how critical it is to respect and understand differences.

Group Counseling

Group counseling can be another highly effective tool to help a woman redefine and accept herself in spite of her difficulties. Such counseling can help her become desensitized early on to the issues surrounding AD/HD and to put them in perspective by coming to respect other women with the same difficulties and strengths as hers. This is similar in many ways to the benefits of support groups that we discussed earlier, however, support groups are usually different in form and function. Support groups can be large meetings, attended on a drop-in basis, and are sometimes peer led. Support groups encourage socializing afterward and tend not to be as controlled or focused.

I define group counseling for as small groups (maybe 5–8) of people that meet at regular times with the same people with a commitment to a specific number of sessions. To build and maintain emotional safety, members are often asked not to meet outside of the group. Typically these groups are formed by a mental health professional who carefully screens and educates participants regarding the group's purpose so as to make sure they are suited to that particular group. Some people may not be well suited for a particular group due to other difficulties or issues they may have. Sometimes groups are set up to achieve homogeneity, for instance, a group may be made up of all women, moms, teens or by interest. On the other hand, they may be deliberately composed for diversity. Of course, for a group devoted to dealing with AD/HD, all the members would have AD/HD. Often people in the group are current or past clients of the mental health professional, or have been referred to the group by another mental health professional participating in group counseling as an adjunct to individual work.

The mental health professional structures, directs, and monitors healthy communication and flow. By attending to the interpersonal dynamics of the group, she or he also helps people work through any problems that arise within the group. AD/HD is by no means the only subject discussed, especially after the group has been together for a while and has developed feelings of safety and cohesion. Everything from relationships to children and work may be discussed as well as life stages and transitions such as birth, aging and death.

The consistency and continuity of this kind of group allows members to know each other and note changes and growth in each other. For example, women with AD/HD often gloss over their accomplishments, small and large. A group can freeze-frame them for a member so that she can pause to really take notice of her success. This typically becomes a more natural part of their process over time. Another example might be that a woman may get encouraging feedback week after week about her interesting ideas, the enthusiasm with which she presented them and the connections that she made, even though she may never have thought of herself as creative. She may have thought of these as useless meanderings, but with this kind of enthusiastic feedback, she may integrate this into her belief system about herself and start to make choices based on this new self-identity.

Summary

Working with a mental health professional can provide an anchoring relationship to help a woman address the feelings that arise when she begins to get help with her AD/HD. This is often the missing piece to help a woman rebuild her sense of self, see herself in a new way and allow her to move on to make healthy, meaningful choices and form more positive relationships.

AD/HD is a chronic stressor, as I have said before; each new level of success can sometimes break down a coping strategy that doesn't apply to that new level of success. Depending on your situation, you might need weekly, bi-weekly, monthly or occasional "tune-ups" when things go wrong, to get supportive help.

A woman who brings this more complicated life experience with her might need counseling to explore or work through these feelings so she continues to learn to live successfully as a woman with AD/HD.

In the next section, we will look at look at the 3 R's , the process of restructuring, renegotiating relationships and redefining your self-image at work and home.

For mental health professionals looking for more information on working with Adults with AD/HD see the special section of the Resources at the back of the book.

PART IV

EMBRACING

Diamonds in the Rough

I view women with AD/HD as diamonds in the rough. Their disorganization on the surface can hide the beauty underneath, even from themselves, and keep them locked away from others and from their own potential. The point of diagnosis and treatment is to unearth those special qualities hidden deeply below the surface, like uncut diamonds. It is to recognize the brilliance waiting to shine beneath the rough exterior and to make the beautiful facets visible so that they can be seen and treasured.

The encyclopedia says "with skilled cutters and polishers, these rough diamonds can be transformed into brilliant jewels." This signifies how those working with AD/HD women can play a role in their revelation. It also mirrors the important fact that women with AD/HD must accept help from other people in order to restructure their lives to reach their full potential. This need for help does not diminish their worth. As with the diamonds, the help (mining, cutting, and polishing) allows them to achieve their full worth and value.

Despite their great strength, diamonds also have great vulnerability. With the wrong kind of blow, they can split and fragment in many directions. They can even be destroyed with intense heat. So, too, it is with these women who must understand what they need to do in order to live in a healthy way that protects them. As the encyclopedia says, "Even in the richest ground, many tons of earth must be taken from deep in the earth and sorted out to obtain one small diamond." The potential is locked away but definitely worth the search.

It has become clear to me from my talks with women with AD/HD all across the country that what is valuable to disorganized women (and is often overlooked) is this kind of validation and hope. What happens for a woman in a successful course of treatment is an internal shift in her sense of self; this ultimately affects her patterns of relationships, mood and success from that point on. I have seen many AD/HD women fruitlessly and obsessively search for what I believe to be a false, dead-end goal. Or they set themselves up for failure, waiting to be "normal" as a measure of whether or not they are succeeding. While it is critical to focus on organizing one's life, I have come to understand that the real goal is not about becoming "cured" but about using this reorganizing as a vehicle to develop uniqueness and strengths not as an end in itself. The point is not to become a different kind of woman but to become more of who you really are and to make visible more of your own beautiful facets.

Ultimately, women with AD/HD must begin to see themselves from a different perspective. As one young AD/HD woman said after eight weeks in a group in which she got to know other women like herself for the first time, "I used to think of ADD women [especially herself] as bumbling and embarrassing. Now I see them as warm, exciting, interesting, and compassionate."

CHAPTER NINETEEN

From Chaos to Creation

Learning to Embrace Disorganization

Embrace Disorganization?

You might think that I'm crazy to tell you to *embrace disorganization*! Well, I could tell you to fight it. I could tell you to overcome it. I could tell you to ignore it, hate it, or hide it. But none of those things would work because you would still be keeping a big part of you split off from the rest of yourself. Hiding takes a tremendous toll in terms of time and energy. *It's both unhealthy and counterproductive to hide and hate a big part of yourself.*

Embracing all of what you are is one of the important keys to healing self-esteem, improving your mood by improving your self-talk, and giving yourself a strong sense of an inner core that doesn't reel from shame when AD/HD symptoms inevitably occur. The truth is that you are *all* of your strengths and *all* of your difficulties—and it is all acceptable. Embracing helps you move through the grief cycle to a deeper sense of acceptance and *beyond* to actual *enjoyment* of your AD/HD and your creativity. Embracing actually means "to hold, to surround, to contain." When creative energy is harnessed and directed, it can grow much stronger. You can wrap yourself up into one cohesive self-image, not just scatter parts of yourself that you or others find unacceptable.

I'm not talking about a "Pollyanna" sort of acceptance because without real acceptance and understanding of your true level of difficulties, you won't begin to approach getting enough structure or help to support your considerable strengths. It's only when you are able to reach out and embrace both your strengths and your difficulties that you will be able to move ahead with your life and begin what I call a "Cycle of Success."

Disorganizationally Gifted

I want to emphasize that people with AD/HD have great abilities to *disorganize*. In fact, I think they are *"disorganizationally gifted."* While I do say that tongue in cheek, any artist knows that an essential step in creativity is the ability to disorganize. It is this same ability, this giftedness at disorganizing, that you can use to your advantage to break down your systems and dismantle your life the "way it's always been."

In this book, I have emphasized the need to restructure your life in order to live successfully with AD/HD. When I say that the goal is to restructure your life, I mean that you won't just cope and get by like you always have. I mean that you will completely rethink the way you live and work. It doesn't happen overnight, and it doesn't happen without difficulty.

To help you achieve this, you'll use your ability to "disorganize" in order to generate fresh ways of working out new solutions. You can create many options. You might not follow them all, but in that hyperactive mind of yours, you have a great ability to think of ways to make things work. You will often run into barriers and have to break through them in order to make things happen in a new way. But if you start to think of embracing this disorganization, if you think of yourself as having great abilities for disorganizing the status quo, then you don't have to walk around saying, "What a disorganized mess I am!" all the time. You can say "How can I use my creativity in thinking of new ways to help solve these problems?"

The reason that common AD/HD strategies alone don't always work is because they usually focus on merely controlling the negative and difficult part of the AD/HD. You want to focus on supporting the new growth, not just taking care of the difficulties. As you grow and become more and more successful, you'll constantly think of new ways to form cushions of support and structure underneath you. *The emphasis should be on nourishing your successes, not just managing your deficits.*

What I'm talking about is breaking up the old order. It means challenging and changing traditions, roles, and rituals and shaking up the balance of control and power held sacred in your house for years. It means figuring out where the limits are in the system, *really* talking to your partner, and challenging the way you've worked things out in the past. You will have the wherewithal now that you're on medication. You will be able to stay in the argument and confront the issues, not ignore the way you feel or the way you want things to be. It isn't going to be easy, and it will cause anxiety. It would be easier *not* to act. Therefore, you may have to enlist professional facilitation at some point because embracing disorganization means letting go of some of those cherished ideal images and that is difficult.

What I am suggesting is similar to the way stimulant medication helps AD/HD. It is paradoxical. Instead of fighting disorganization, embracing it calms you down. When you relax into it, a certain order comes about. Embracing disorganization does not just mean controlling it. The irony is that until you feel better about your AD/HD, you're not going to be able to get the help you need.

At a certain point, when you have truly integrated these disparate ideas about yourself, you will begin to create successful experiences, and the success will take on a life of its own. You will start to hold on to your successes and build on them as they compound rapidly. At some point you will cross a line after you've embraced all parts of yourself and embraced the AD/HD. You will understand that it is a necessity and not a luxury to get the help you need, thus freeing up your time and emotional resources, allowing you to focus on your strengths. You will understand the need to break down barriers and find healthy ways to protect yourself. You will understand that you truly can start pursuing goals that really suit you. When you embrace yourself, your AD/HD, your strengths, and your difficulties, it won't hurt as much when other people don't accept it or understand you. You won't have to apologize or over-explain. You'll be able to talk to others about what you need and set limits without putting yourself down. This validates other people as well as shows respect for yourself, even when your AD/HD symptoms appear.

Ultimately what I'm talking about is *living with controlled disorder*, not trying to get rid of it or waiting to get over it. It is not done in a day, and it is not done with medication alone (although it is usually not done without it). You need to ask yourself, "How can I make my life work? How can I make my relationships work? How can I make my career meaningful?"

If it means doing things a bit differently than other people, then be different; it takes courage to break through the barriers of shame and guilt to ask for support. If it means breaking the mold, then break it; it takes courage to accept that you can't do what other people can do. If it means challenging the "way it's always been," then challenge it; it takes courage to celebrate that you can often do what other people can't.

You will have to ask yourself, "How can I make life work for me even if it upsets other people in my family? How can I change the rules and roles that haven't been working? How can I tolerate the anxiety of making others uncomfortable in a way that doesn't disregard their needs but doesn't trample mine?" Many times this will take professional facilitation.

When I say *embrace disorganization*, I am not saying to *not* be organized or to not focus your attention on the creation of organizational systems. I *am* saying *don't keep trying the same things that haven't worked before and don't keep coping alone*. Expand your idea of organizational help to include other people, other people to coach you. You need to get over the obsession with being an organized person or trying to "keep it together" in the same way that non-ADD people do. Don't just try harder. Don't just get another fancier organizing method. You can't compare your life to what other people can handle because you have a disorder. A disorder means that something is not of average difficulty. It's not productive to compare yourself to others and how they live their lives. What is productive is to talk to people who have the same kind of difficulties and abilities that you do and to understand that you might need a much higher level of organizational support than other people.

Embracing disorganization means taking things apart and putting them back together in a new way. It means taking your AD/HD seriously. Don't wait until you're over your AD/HD to start your life because you never will be over your AD/HD. Don't measure your success in terms of how un-AD/HD-like you have become because you never will be completely un-AD/HD-like. Know that your AD/HD symptoms will appear from time to time. What you do about it, what you say about it, and how you feel about it is going to influence whether or not things get better or worse. I've come to understand that the ultimate goal is not about becoming cured or becoming more organized as an end in itself. Organizational strategies should only be used as a vehicle for your talents, your uniqueness, and your strengths. Your goal is to begin to see yourself from a different perspective. I encourage you, then, to stop chasing an impossible, culturally approved dream. Step off the perpetual treadmill, embrace all the parts of yourself, and begin to take back your life.

The 3 R's

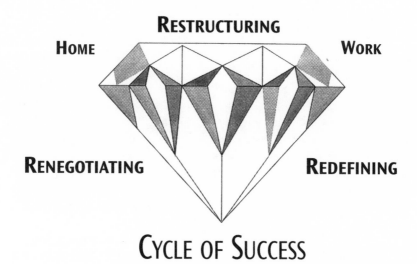

CYCLE OF SUCCESS

The Three R's to Successfully Living with AD/HD

This section is about the need to go beyond strategies and support. It is about the need to go beyond medication, education, and even therapy. The goal of all that we have talked about is to *restructure* your life to such an extent that it *really works for you*. As you see in the 3 R's chart, you often need additional tools to accomplish this. These include *renegotiating* your relationships at home and in your personal life, as well as *redefining* the image of yourself, of your work, and of your partner. You'll do this in order to more closely align with your real strengths and to deal more effectively with your real difficulties.

The strategies we talked about earlier often employ paper aids and technological tools that address the primary symptoms of AD/HD. They are helpful and necessary. But these strategies and support systems often fall short of helping you live successfully with AD/HD because *they don't go deep enough, they don't go on long enough, they don't continuously keep pace with your growth*. And they usually don't involve the other people in your life in a meaningful way or to the extent necessary to make long-term changes.

Restructuring

Restructuring includes balancing three primary areas of your life: your strengths, your needs, and your time for fun and recreation. For women, the way these three areas usually get divided up leaves them off balance and on a treadmill. Restructuring helps you regain your balance.

Renegotiating

Renegotiating your roles and your relationships is challenging but essential because changes in one member of a system, at home or at work, will cause changes in the entire system. Other members often will resist *even when the changes are positive*. Renegotiating at home and at work involves setting limits and protecting yourself while at the same time moving toward relationships instead of backing away from them. It also involves learning how to get help without sacrificing your self-respect.

Redefining

Even after you have learned how to renegotiate your relationships with improved communication skills, you may still keep getting stuck. To clear that barrier, you will need to take a serious look at *redefining your self-image*. You need to look at the negative messages you unconsciously deliver to yourself when you don't meet the cultural ideal you may have internalized. This idealized image may miss your essential strong qualities as well as the adjustments and accommodations you need to make for your difficulties.

At home, your partner or family may still be holding on to certain kinds of cultural images and stuck in their own grief cycle(s). Redefining is also about working through *their* issues. At work, you may have to revisit your entire concept about what kind of work is appropriate for you, replacing some old dreams with new ones. Both at work and at home, working through the 3 Rs will ultimately help to define what it means to be a mature, competent, woman of value, even though you have AD/HD.

CHAPTER TWENTY

Are You Staying or Going?

Restructuring Your Work Life

As we introduced in the last chapter, the critical part of treatment now is to focus on the 3 Rs: *Restructuring* your environment, *Renegotiating* relationships, and *Redefining* your self-image. In this chapter, we will look at how restructuring applies to work. In the next chapter, we will look at restructuring at home and in your personal life. All restructuring, whether at home or work, involves renegotiating and redefining, which will be explored in Chapters 22 and 23.

To begin, let's revisit Lucy, who we met a while back, and look at how the elements of restructuring come into play in someone's work life. When Lucy was thirty, she went to community college where she studied fashion design and art. It was there that an alert teacher noticed her difficulties and suggested that she get tested for learning disabilities. In the process, she was diagnosed instead with AD/HD and began taking Ritalin. She got accommodations such as extra time for tests, and eventually she earned an associate's degree. Lucy got a job in a nice department store as a window dresser, designing the windows and dressing the mannequins. She loved this job because she could be active, and she got to use her creative abilities. Even though she loved the designs, Lucy had trouble with other parts of the job. She was a little clumsy; she tended to knock over the mannequins and drop the pins. There were a lot of required reports and paperwork. Lucy also had trouble with the other women in the department because she spread her stuff all over the workroom. She began to think they were getting a little annoyed with her. She thought they were looking at her disapprovingly and the tone in their voices seemed harsh when they asked her to move her things to her own area.

Though she was on medication and could concentrate better, she started to feel like she was bothering people and getting in the way. She began to think they didn't like her and even started to not enjoy work. Lucy felt the other designers were laughing at her when she dropped things, and she felt bad about the little jokes they made regarding how much space she was taking up. She began to forget about all the great, creative, beautiful things that she was doing and started focusing on her anxieties instead. She thought that perhaps this job was too big for her or that she just wasn't smart enough. She thought that perhaps she should transfer out of this department and get a job that didn't have so many responsibilities.

The danger was that Lucy would decide she wasn't talented enough, when in reality she probably would do better at a higher level of design rather than at the lower level that pulled on her weaknesses. In order to show her true strengths and continue to rise to her proper level, she'd have needed to ask for accommodations that would give her more space, a different work area, or an assistant for an hour a day to help with some of the detail work. These would have made a huge difference. For this to happen, though, Lucy would have had to be willing to risk some acknowledgement of her needs. Unfortunately, this was the very thing that she tried to hide because she felt it was too embarrassing to stand out from the other women in that way.

Getting through these lower levels of achievement, the entry- and mid-level jobs are usually the downfall for women with AD/HD, even with medication. A woman needs to work toward asking for accommodations or at least be able to state her needs. She needs to understand herself, know what her strengths are, and value herself sufficiently to present the idea that she and her boss both have the same goal: for her to do her best work. Presenting this in a way that preserves her self-respect and focuses on her strengths is quite a challenge for women who are especially sensitive to these issues. Restructuring applies to any woman's work life whether she is currently working on her own, thinking about what kind of work to pursue, or actively employed.

Balancing Your Work Life

The Priorities Pie Chart illustrates an example of the time and focus women with AD/HD spend in three different areas that are frequently out of balance.

1. Time focused on strengths as opposed to just coping with deficits

2. Time focused on own needs as opposed to those of others

3. Time focused on fun or personal life as opposed to work of one kind or another

Strengths and Deficits

Let's look at the balance between strengths and deficits as it applies to the area of achievement and work for woman with AD/HD. It's essential for women not to confuse their strengths and abilities with their difficulties. *It's very common for women with AD/HD to hold jobs that are considered simple because the tasks involved are simple for most people, fail, and then assume it means they need to do even simpler work.* Another common scenario occurs when women have demanding jobs that suit their abilities, but they can't handle all the organizational tasks needed to support the job. They naturally assume that they are no

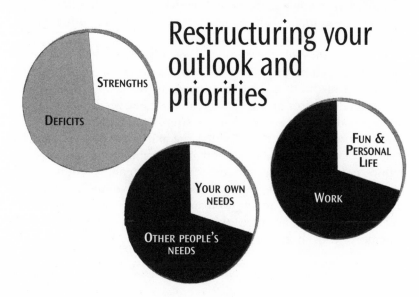

Restructuring your outlook and priorities

STRENGTHS

DEFICITS

YOUR OWN NEEDS

OTHER PEOPLE'S NEEDS

FUN & PERSONAL LIFE

WORK

good at that kind of work. Eventually, they work their way down the scale until they find jobs that allow them to meet the organizational demands. In other words, they are constantly trying to match and meet the requirements of their level of difficulty rather than their strengths.

It's not hard to see that a sense of underachievement would result. If they don't have the organizational abilities to back up their conceptual ideas and don't realize that they need assistance and support for those ideas, they might be severely underachieving, constantly working in the areas of their greatest disability. The resulting frustration can affect their self-esteem and mood to a great extent.

There are a number of factors that hold women back from asking for accommodations. Sometimes they experience internal barriers such as shame or guilt when they consider asking for such help. Sometimes they lack the communication skills necessary to state their needs in an assertive but non-defensive, non-blaming way. At other times, they don't know what is reasonable to ask for, what their rights are or even whether or not they are deserving of them. Often it is the overriding feeling that they are not being fair to other people. Instead, woman with AD/HD need to be aware that they are requesting an even playing field, a way to make the best contribution they can to the organization.

Until women are presented with new ways of thinking, they have no real belief that each of our unique brains make us good at some things and others good at different things. We grow up in this culture thinking that intelligence is identified with quickness of presentation. Because people often confuse processing speed and/or organizational skills with intelligence, it's essential for women with AD/HD to separate their intelligence and abilities from their organizational difficulties. Then a woman can say to herself, "This is my organizational difficulty. This is my AD/HD. This is not my intelligence." Only when women do this can they understand and continue to pursue their areas of strength. They will need to work continually to build a cushion of support under themselves from other people.

As women become more successful, their demands are going to increase. The coping and compensating strategies that they used before are not going to work for them any more as they rise to their full capabilities. For example, in college, a woman might have had a great deal of trouble organizing ideas and putting them on paper. She might have "pulled it off" by staying up all night, spending fifty hours on a project that might have taken others only five hours. Even though she is just as smart, the structure that comes more or less automatically to others is not there. It takes enormous amounts of processing for her to pull it all together. This may have exhausted her in college, but she was able to survive.

As she moves from college to grad school or into a career, or when she tries to combine schooling or work with a relationship, social life or family, she will find that her compensations do not work any more. It becomes mathematically impossible to accommodate all the new demands with her old system. Something has to give. Either she has to slow down or stop her career advancement or give up on the idea of a family or social life.

A woman who's having difficulty needs to figure out that she and a particular job are often simply a bad match. She may need to walk away, but if she quits, she may take with her the self-image that she couldn't "cut it." Perhaps there is a way for her to keep the good parts and create a better match for the difficult parts. Then she doesn't have to throw away the whole job. With such big gaps between her abilities and her difficulties, it is unlikely that she will easily find a perfect match.

If she does decide to leave the school or job, it is critical that she leave with the understanding that her problem is not a matter of intelligence or ability. The job might just have too many organizational details attached to it with little support available. When she thinks about rebalancing her strengths and deficits, she must remember that she has gaps in her abilities. I think of ability as a very tall ladder. Her ladder might be taller than most people's. It might even reach to the top of the Empire State Building, but it has gaps between the rungs or even missing rungs. If she doesn't find a way to fill in those gaps, to get to the next rung, she's not going to go anywhere, no matter how great her ability. To be successful at work, she must find the balance between strengths and deficits. She must honor both of these so that she can make both of them work for her. The point is for her to thrive and be successful, not to become overloaded, depleted, or to stay up all night.

Your Needs vs. Other's Needs

Another area that typically needs balancing, is the gap between the needs of women with AD/HD, and other people's needs. At work, this often means learning to say no and setting limits to direct supervisors, as well as coworkers. This applies both to actual work assignments as well as to those other unwritten expectations that exist for women at work. It's difficult to learn to say no and to protect and project a sense of competence at the same time. A woman who has coped with AD/HD all her life often feels that if she says no to a request, this will wipe out other people's good opinion of her. Sometimes, however, by saying yes to everything, she creates the very situation that she has been trying to prevent. If she keeps saying yes and not setting limits, she will eventually make mistakes and not be able to keep up.

If a woman does a good job and continues to be successful, people will ask her to take on more. Customers won't say, "Linda, you did such a wonderful job on this deal for me that I'm not going to recommend you to my friends." In some sense, it feels heady and great (after medication and treatment) to finally be successful and recognized. But there comes a point of diminishing returns as she tries to keep up the pace. She must figure out how to structure her life to make it work.

Restructuring may mean getting more assistance or actually having to say no or set limits in a way that doesn't reject others or put herself down. She can do this by validating the importance of wanting to do a good job, something she and her boss can agree on as a common goal. A woman must figure out what will work best for everyone involved and then find a way to tell others.

She may have to shut her door or put a "do not disturb" sign up for a certain amount of time per day. It's all right for her not to answer her phone every time it rings. She doesn't have to respond to everyone else's needs, even for charitable or good causes. She can learn to say to people, "I wish I could participate in your project, but I'm working on something I'm very involved in right now. I'm excited about it, but it's taking all my time. Perhaps we could schedule an hour next week to sit down and talk." In that way, she validates the importance of the person making the request and her own needs. Once she has defined her needs and set her limits, she is free to suggest alternatives that may be beneficial to both. Setting circumscribed times to deal with the requests of others is especially important for people with AD/HD so that their flow is uninterrupted. They might not have the time to talk to other people on an as-needed basis, so it might work to create a non-distracting, non-interrupting environment. Whether the strategy is to move away from distractions, to set up a later time to handle requests, or ask for more time or assistance, remember that the question always is: How can I make my job work for me?

Balancing Personal Life and Work Life

Setting limits in order to get work done is fine, but that doesn't mean that you now have a reason to block out people and fun, even at work. Setting limits means that you can get your work done without feeling guilty or pushing people away. What you also need to figure into the equation, though, is when to stop working and let things go a little. Recognize that with AD/HD, you will never really feel that everything is organized and done. Just as important, you must set limits with yourself about how much time you are going to spend on a project. Once you have fulfilled your own expectations for work, it is then important to interact with others in ways that are truly enjoyable, replenishing, interesting, or just plain diverting. In other words, lighten up!

Once you are meeting your own personal needs for pleasure and relaxation, you can look at how to help out others. You may feel overloaded at first, but if you do this on your own terms, carefully choose the things that interest you, and spend the proper amount of time with the people you really care about, then giving to others will nourish you and replenish you. Giving that comes from the heart and from your genuine interest is stress reducing and healthy. It is very different from giving out of exhaustion and guilt, saying yes to everything at your own expense. You must constantly balance these areas of your life. Check in on these areas with yourself or a coach frequently.

Examining Your Current Work Life

If You Aren't Currently Working Outside the Home: Time and Space

If you want to be working outside of your home and are having trouble figuring out how to make this transition, this is a section for you. Especially if you aren't working outside of your home right now, you need to take time to examine your choices and options. Make sure that part of your day or week is earmarked to think about your work life, whatever that might currently mean for you. It might mean going back to school, making a plan to look for work such as starting a resume and assessing your talents, or just taking time to imagine a satisfying future.

Sometimes it's even harder to focus on yourself and figure these things out if you're not working outside the home. A woman I know had a coach come to her house once a week to help her stay organized. She wound up using that coaching time to focus on her children's schoolwork and household details rather than move toward her goal of going back to graduate school. She had to learn to carve out a part of each coaching session to focus on herself and her goals.

You might get messages from others that may be difficult to cope with. For instance, in order focus on your self and your work life, you might need a housekeeper once week, someone to watch your children after school, or day care for your younger children. This may elicit negative comments from your husband, family or friends, as if these things were luxuries for someone not working outside the home. The woman with AD/HD has to become desensitized to these comments and to realize that these are not luxuries for her. She has a disorder for which she is being treated, and if she ever wants to enter a venue in which she can use her abilities, she must find a way to plan and strategize. Because of her difficulties, she, more than anyone, needs to have a distraction-free space for some time each day. For example, she may need to make phone calls to gather information. It is essential for her to do something on a regular basis, even if it is only for ten minutes a day.

Start to carve out time and space for yourself. This might mean blocking off time in your calendar for appointments with yourself! Blacken them out so you won't be tempted to discard them at the first outside demand. It might mean having a friend come over and sit with you while you do information processing, having someone call you at the beginning and end of your personal time to provide some external structure, or signing up for a class and paying in advance so that you will attend. Sometimes it's useful to get involved in an activity with another person; you may be less inclined to put it aside. Go to the bookstore alone and look for what interests you. Take any small step in relation to your interests, strengths, and abilities, anything to increase the time that you spend focusing on your strengths or discovering them. Remember, you're trying to break a cycle, a system, to get off a treadmill. You have to do something different! You don't have to do big, dramatic things that take a lot of time. Even a small step makes everything around you shift. And when the system shifts, people shift, and then you can become the person that people work around rather than you working around everybody else's needs.

A physical place for you at home is a must. Even if it's just a corner of a room where you can keep your stuff, it will be a place that represents you, your strengths, your hopes, and your future. You've got to have some breathing room. Imagine yourself in a collapsed building; you'd need to find an air pocket to start breathing again so that your creative force, strengths, and abilities aren't snuffed out. No one else is going to do this for you. No one else is going to say, "Okay, I won't ask you for anything anymore." You're going to have to find a way to say no, or say, "Not right now. I'm sorry, I'd like to help you, but this is my private time." Turn off the phones, do whatever you have to do. Don't respond to other people's needs for as long as you can manage. Fifteen minutes a day at first is fine. If you have to get out of the house to do it, do it! This can be nerve-racking at first. You may be anxious, but as you get used to it, your anxiety will be reduced when people see that you mean it and that you take yourself seriously. If you can't afford childcare and your children aren't in school, trade time with a friend. Find every way to seize time for yourself.

Thinking About Jobs

It's essential to consider not just what kind of job you are qualified for, not just what you are good at or what your interests are, but also what the actual work environment might be like and what an actual workday requires. When you think of a job or career, try answering these kinds of questions and exploring the following issues.

First fill in the blank as in the example below and then think about the reality of that kind of work in this detailed way. It's important to think through the small details that make up a typical day at a particular job.

1. *What does it really mean from an AD/HD perspective to be a _____ on a day-to-day basis? (e.g., lawyer, writer, secretary, nurse, teacher, CEO)*

    • *How much boring paperwork or filing is involved?*

- *Would you work outside or inside?*

- *Would you move around a lot?*

- *Would you move from office to office, location to location, or desk to desk?*

- *Would you have to move all your materials with you and move quickly?*

- *Would you have to go to lots of meetings?*

- *Would you have to write lots of reports?*

2. *What if you decide you do have enough interest in a field to pursue it despite some unappealing aspects?*

   - *How could you use assistance or accommodations to design a way to work in that environment?*

   - *If it doesn't seem as if it would be easy to restructure a traditional work setting, how might you do the same kind of work in a way that's more independent, perhaps as a consultant or on your own?*

   - *How could you take the same skills, abilities, and interests that attracted you to that field and apply them to another field that could better accommodate your organizational difficulties?*

Always remember that you want to continue to move toward your strengths not merely to accommodate your difficulties. When people only consider their difficulties, they eliminate a whole range of occupational options that might allow their creative abilities to emerge. For example, many people with AD/HD have a great ability to conceptualize—look at how you can capitalize on your strengths even if it means moving up the ranks through some middle-level positions.

3. *How can you begin to explore what kind of work, school, or interests you're going to pursue?*

   - Who could you interview, or talk to, who works in a field you're interested in?

   - What kinds of organizational demands are associated with each organization you explore?

Roadblocks to Career Information Gathering

Because information processing is often a problem for women with AD/HD, a great deal of anxiety and fear can arise at this point. They're afraid they might not know what to say on the phone or that they might go blank. They may be afraid they won't remember the information or that they'll lose it, and, if they lose it, they're afraid to ask for it again. These situations trigger all the old feelings of being thought weird or stupid, of asking the wrong questions, of losing things, and of being irresponsible.

Strategies for Successful Information Gathering

- *Write down instructions to yourself before you make a call*

- *Write down information as soon as you get it, possibly keeping a bulletin board by the phone as a place to put this information*

- *Call during "off" hours and leave a request for information on an answering machine until you build up your confidence. You can also email or fax people to get through that initial period of anxiety*

Women also resist the information-gathering stage because of fears that ultimately they won't be able to succeed at a new job or school. They fear they won't be able to meet the demands of these situations. Using their highly creative AD/HD minds, they sometimes think through their entire future and every possible obstacle that they might encounter. This kind of thinking can be counterproductive. They need to take the first, small step and stay grounded in the present because things unfold in unexpected ways.

If You Are Currently Working

If you are working currently at a job or for yourself and trying to improve your conditions, or you are trying to decide whether or not to stay at your current job or move to a new one, you will need to assess your situation. Ultimately, you need to answer yes to one of the following questions:

1. *Can I stay at this job and make it work? or*

2. *Do I need to find another job that does work for me?*

It should not be a long-term solution or option to stay at a job that doesn't or can't work for you. You may need to explore whether internal barriers are preventing you from making these changes.

Some of the factors involved in this exploration process include thinking through reasonable changes to improve the physical nature of your work environment and the barriers that may arise, both external and internal, to improving your workspace. This discussion is followed by a new *Work Decision* to assist you in thinking this through. In Chapter 22 on renegotiating, we will also look at communication strategies to help improve your work environment.

Reasonable Changes in Your Physical Environment

Here are a few suggestions to make to your workspace better meet your needs, starting with reducing distractions. This includes simple things such as shutting the door of your office, using a sound blocking device if you work in a cubicle, or arranging to work at quieter times of the day, if possible. Of course, as Kathleen Nadeau says in her chapter on AD/HD in the workplace in A Comprehensive Guide to Attention Deficit Disorder, it's essential to make this strategy work for your personality type, as well as for your AD/HD. She emphasizes that introverts and extroverts with AD/HD are going to have to find approaches that don't ignore this important variable. Here are a few questions to consider:

- *Do you work better with high stimulation?*

- *Do you need a job where you move from location to location to keep yourself focused or does that overwhelm you?*

- *Do you need to work in an environment that's very quiet, i.e., do you need sound blocks to block out any extraneous noises?*

Whichever way works for you, you've got to honor that you have AD/HD. You can't spend 98 percent of your day trying to block out distractions and feeling anxious from the effort. Don't be chained to a desk if you need to be moving around. Learn to know your particular balance between being overstimulated/understimulated and overwhelmed/underwhelmed.

Structure and Stimulation

Whether you are considering working at home or on your own, or you already are, it's essential to consider the amount of structure and stimulation that you need. There's a narrow band that works well for women with AD/HD. The challenge is to stay within that narrow band. Once you move outside it, things can often go wrong. The paradox seems to be that women with AD/HD who need structure are able to have that in a large corporate organization, but sometimes the much needed structure can feel constraining to their creativity and independent spirit when it includes more limits, rules, deadlines, demands, bureaucracies, paperwork, or boredom and frustration.

Whereas you might feel suffocated in a bureaucracy or a company, when you are working alone with nothing external to come up against, you might fall into an abyss of nothingness. You may fade away, get off track, or get overwhelmed with details and paper. The key is to set up structure and external stimulation in advance. You can hire assistants to provide organizational support for your business or your independent work. You can get a partner who has the opposite kinds of skills from yours. In *ADD: A Different Perspective*, Thom Hartmann calls these other types of people "farmers." They can help with the daily maintenance, record-keeping and detail work that's so difficult for people with AD/HD, and they provide a great complement to your "hunter" skills. The other human strategy that you might integrate into your independent work life would be to get a coach to check in with you every day, keep you on track and provide you with needed stimulation. Working for yourself provides a great way to capitalize on your strengths, but it's important to understand in advance that it will pull directly on your deficits as well. Focus on your strengths but prepare for your challenges.

Activity/Energy Levels

No matter how you work, at home, on your own, or for someone else, recognize and honor your particular activity levels. Learn to know the kinds of jobs you can't work at for a straight eight hours a day. Come to terms with variability in your energy levels. Perhaps you can't sit still all day, or you can't stay alert the whole day without a break. Even though medication will help tremendously in these areas, these variables might still continue to be factors in your life to consider. This might mean going through another grief cycle because women say, "I don't want to have to consider all of these things! Why do I have to be so different?"

External Barriers to an Effective Working Environment

At this point, you may want to try to write down a few changes that might make your work life better. Then think how you will go about trying to make these things happen. What actions would you have to take?

If you find this is difficult or are having trouble putting these changes in place or asking for what you need (whether it is the above mentioned or any of infinite possibilities of ways you may think of to make your job more AD/HD friendly), you need to determine if your barriers to making these changes are external or internal. You are trying to figure out if your job's environment is too toxic to fix regardless of what you do. *Is this a place where people are so non-accepting of you or your AD/HD or so inflexible that even if you were legally able to get accommodations, it wouldn't be worth it?* The co-founders of the AD/HD coaching movement, Nancy Ratey, M. Ed. and Susan Sussman, M.Ed., emphasized in their presentation at the 1995 *ADDA Conference on AD/HD in the Workplace*, that accommodations are worth asking for if the work situation is good in general and if your relationship with your employer or supervisor is productive. Otherwise, if you and the job are a bad match in the first place, accommodations probably won't be effective in the long run.

So again, your choices are either to stay *if you can make it work, or if you can't, leave and make it work.* Either way, *the goal is to make it work!*

Knowing When it's Time to Leave and Preparing for This Change

Determine criteria for leaving and set a deadline for yourself. For some the criteria will be financial, for others it will be interpersonal, for some it may be the negative effect it has on your emotions such as anxiety or depression, and for others it may be family related.

Determine an interim course of action. You might need to prepare by going back to school or taking a training course while you are still at your job or immediately after you leave. You may need to make changes in your personal life to accommodate a possible financial change, or you may need to think about self-employment or temporary employment. Your family will have to be consulted and considered, as well.

Internal Barriers to Change

Are you aware of any internal barriers such as embarrassment or the need to protect your sense of competence that might contribute to your difficulty in making these changes? Women often confront a wall of shame or guilt that makes it difficult to ask for help, accommodations, or assistance at work because they feel that others might think they are not very smart or that they are asking for some special advantage instead of understanding that they are asking for a level playing field. This can lead to avoidance and lack of communication with their employers or coworkers. This often happens when people haven't sufficiently integrated and understood what AD/HD means in their lives. See renegotiating and redefining in Chapters 22 and 23 if you are struggling with this.

A Work Decision Tree

Here is a decision tree to help you think through if you should stay at your job and if so how to make your job work for you.

SOLDEN'S AD/HD WORK DECISION TREE

© copyright Sari Solden, 2005, not to be reprinted without permission.

Is Your Work Life Working For You?

Yes or No

If you answered yes—great! Skip the rest of the chapter.

If Your Work Life Is *Not* Working For You, What Reasonable Changes Could Help?

____ Non-distracting environment

____ More structure

____ Accommodations to activity/energy levels_____

____ Informal or formal coaching

____ Communication strategies

____ Support

____ Others such as _____

Can You Ask For Or Make These Changes?

Yes or No

If no, are the reasons due to the following:

EXTERNAL OR INTERNAL BARRIERS?

External Barriers:

____ Too toxic an environment.

____ Not a good enough fit

____ Too resistant to accommodate what you need

____ Other such as _____

If you said yes to external barriers, you may need to do the following:

____ Determine criteria:

    ____ Financial

    ____ Interpersonal

    ____ Depression/Anxiety as a result of the external factors.

    ____ Family related

Determine a deadline.

____ Make interim plans:

    ____ Training

    ____ Classes

    ____ Career counseling

    ____ Temporary employment

    ____ Self-employment

    ____ Financial

    ____ Family

____ Other _____

Internal Barriers

If you find yourself unable to take these steps to make these changes, either to make your job work better or to leave work if you need to, ask yourself if something inside you is preventing this.

____ Shame

____ Embarrassment

____ Guilt

____ Fear

____ Family tapes

____ Cultural messages

____ Feelings of incompetence

____ Fear of conflict

____ Fear of being overwhelmed

____ Other _____

If you said yes to internal barriers, you may need to do the following:

____ Get professional coaching or counseling to help work through this barrier and then try again.

____ Talk it through with a trusted friend or partner

Summary

We've looked at some of the critical elements involved in restructuring your work life. You need to find a new balance between the time you spend on your strengths versus your deficits, the time you focus on your own needs versus those of others, and the time you focus on fun or your personal life versus work of one kind or another.

Next, if you are not currently working outside of the home and you want to move toward that goal, you need to put time and space into your schedule to make that a reality. You need to spend a great deal of time thinking about what would be a good fit for you. This goes beyond your abilities and interests to thinking about what would work for your AD/HD, as well. Finally, if you are presently employed, you need to decide if you can make your situation work for you or if you need to make a change. If you decide you need to make a change, you can work toward setting some criteria for how and when you will accomplish that. Whatever it takes, you can restructure your work life to make it "work for you." (Fellman, 2000)

In the next chapter we will look at restructuring at home. Then in Chapters 22 and 23, we will look at renegotiating relationships and redefining your self-image both at work and at home.

CHAPTER TWENTY-ONE

Shake, Rattle, and Roles

Restructuring Your Personal Life

Let's go back and visit Jodi and see what has happened for her since she was diagnosed and began taking Ritalin.

Jodi finds that the medication gives her much more energy for her daily tasks, and she feels calmer when the typical daily frustrations arise. She has even begun to read again, starting with several of the latest books on AD/HD. She has a good "feel" for what AD/HD is about and what she needs to do to make her life work better. Her husband thinks that this is great and is happy that she's feeling better. He's especially glad that Jodi doesn't seem to cry so easily any more.

Once a month, he baby-sits while she attends CHADD meetings where she hears speakers on AD/HD in adults. Sometimes Jodi now notices, however, how little help her husband actually gives her around the house and with their daughter. They're beginning to fight about this issue whereas before they never did.

Jodi now has a housekeeper who comes in once a week to do the major cleaning. She feels hopeful because she has a new organizational system installed in her computer to help her with bill paying and time management. In addition, her mother now comes over once a week to help her organize her papers piled up in the house and also to arrange some of the backlog of clutter accumulated over the years.

Three months after being diagnosed and starting medication, Jodi goes back to her therapist, whom she hasn't seen since just after she began medication. Jodi is upset and confused because she's still not organized, and on top of that, she's feeling angry and lonely. She wants to know why the medication isn't working better.

Throughout the rest of the book, we will look at what a woman like Jodi may need to do and think about in terms of restructuring her environment, renegotiating her relationships, and redefining her self-image. We'll start with restructuring.

This first "R" involves making deeper changes in the way you live your life, beyond the strategies we discussed earlier in the book. The first step is to balance the focus on the AD/HD in the family, as well as balance your focus on your own needs and strengths with focus on other people's needs and time spent in your areas of deficits. This is much like we talked about at work, but now the focus is at home. Next you will examine the division of labor in your household and find new ways to make that work for you. Step three is to *take a fresh look at* the rules and roles by which you and your family have been operating. This often means going to a deeper level and actually altering or eliminating the way you have always done things.

A Balancing Act

The balance in families and partnerships affected by AD/HD often needs attention. The diagram called *AD/HD in the Family System* shows the different ways that AD/HD is handled in the system. When a person has AD/HD, one of two things usually happens either before or after diagnosis. The system can become totally

AD/HD IN THE FAMILY SYSTEM

System totally organized around AD/HD

No acknowledgment of AD/HD

organized around the AD/HD; in other words, everybody is some-what of a slave to it because everything stops whenever family members become overwhelmed by the disorganization, impulsivity, or activity of the AD/HD person. Family members spend their energies trying to solve the AD/HD individual's problems by taking over all the tasks. Eventually, they begin to feel like their needs are going unmet, and they become resentful.

At the other extreme, there is little or no acknowledgment of the AD/HD. There is superficial recognition after the diagnosis, as well as superficial support, but no real willingness to change the way the system operates. This often happens to women, especially to those without hyperactivity, who haven't had the energy or power to assert themselves. Through the years, because of her failure to meet "the woman's job expectations" we talked about earlier, a woman may have lost self-esteem and been identified as the problem in the immediate as well as the extended family.

This detail from a portrait of a man and a woman by Degas expresses the loneliness that a woman can feel in a marriage or a partnership when she is diagnosed with AD/HD and then continues to cope on her own at home. She is trying to "fit" her AD/HD in around everything and everyone else. Even though she feels better as a result of the medication and may employ some new strategies (as Jodi did), she may still have a sense of loneliness and even resentment.

Balance of Strengths and Deficits at Home

Just like we looked at in the pie chart in the previous chapter when discussing work, you need to look at the same three areas at home: strengths vs. deficits, other vs. self, and fun vs. chores. It is no secret that focusing on your strengths is a key element on the path to success. This has been validated in educational psychology, career development, or any kind of personal growth training. The focus in AD/HD treatment, however, often becomes "managing the AD/HD," which often translates to over-focusing on deficits and not strengths. Obviously it is critical to get help for these deficits. But it is frustrating and counterproductive to spend all your time and efforts trying to manage your weak areas. This keeps you on a treadmill where you can get weaker, with lower and lower self-esteem. As an alternative, find a way to put a little more energy each day into your areas of strength, or into your dreams. Managing your deficits can then be for

the purpose of moving toward goals that reflect who you really are and your true abilities.

Carve out a little space each day and each week for the purpose of discovering what those strengths or dreams are, if you don't already know. These don't have to be work related just what brings you joy, reconnects you to more of what feels like your real self, the self you may have lost contact with all these years coping with the demands of undiagnosed AD/HD.(Solden, 2002)

New ideas about yourself will emerge when you shift your focus to your strengths. It will then become much easier to figure out how to manage your difficulties because you will have created an internal structure for yourself, and a new internal picture to move toward.

Your Needs vs. Other's Needs at Home

Setting limits on the kind of time you expend on other people's needs doesn't exclude the kind of giving that nourishes you and others. The setting of healthy limits on your time and energy, instead, will allow you to have more time and energy to connect and engage in real relationships. This "true" giving of yourself is different from giving because of the difficulty of "saying no." Healthy self-protection and the healthy setting of limits will allow you to feel safe enough to venture into a close relationship. Learn to set limits, not as a defensive way of pushing people away, but as a way of enriching yourself, and keeping yourself focused on moving toward your own goals.

Remember, you can set limits even when others keep asking you for help. You can set limits even when people are nice to you or ask you to help a good cause.

Don't wait until you have a month, a year, the perfect environment, or other people's cooperation before you focus on yourself. If you just start to make one small change where you focus on yourself, eventually other parts of the system begin to shift around you.

Balance in Home Life

Work at home means chores, tasks, routines, or other stressful personal activities. By play, I mean time spent in replenishing activities such as creative, fun, recreational, relaxing, social, or spiritual arenas.

To accomplish this, you might have to make a commitment to other people or pay in advance so you actually follow through on the activity. Put a date in your appointment book, an anchor to involve another person so you can't get out of it. Women have to learn to push the envelope of work versus play, beginning to tolerate the guilt of having fun when their work is undone. You need these recharging times, but set them up in a way that won't overwhelm or drain you.

I know women with AD/HD can't believe this, but it's true. Even though you take time out from work, which you are already overwhelmed with, you'll find that to engage in recharging activities will give you more emotional and physical energy.

Consciously make choices to allow you to take care of your mood, knowing that you have a sensitive system and that you react easily. Even with your best efforts, if you do occasionally start to feel overloaded, keep a few ideas in mind to allow you to get back into balance. These can be simple things, such as taking a walk in the middle of a party, or finding a quiet place to be alone for a while, as you regain your balance. The point is that you don't need to reject opportunities for fun and socializing because you feel you might become overloaded.

I hear many women say, *"I'm waiting for the demands to stop,"* but the demands never stop. I've even heard them say, *"I realize that I need to sleep, I need to eat."* These are basic things. Women with AD/HD are desperate to find time in their schedules "to get their lives done." Rebalance your "time budget" and stop taking it out on your own emotional and physical health.

Examining The Division of Labor

As the diagram *Restructuring your Environment* indicates, the second area of restructuring involves dividing up labor in the household according to each person's strengths and difficulties. This sounds simple but is really quite complex, as the emotions that this restructuring brings up are more difficult to deal with than the actual tasks themselves. The division of labor is necessary for each woman regardless of the family structure. Even if a woman lives alone, she still needs to find someone to help her figure out how to compensate for her deficits and get the right kind of support and structure.

The process begins with a series of initial restructuring meetings followed by shorter follow-up meetings to make adjustments and to take stock. Ideally, these follow-up meetings will take place on a

RESTRUCTURING YOUR ENVIRONMENT

TASK DIVISION
AD/HD Partner • Non-AD/HD Partner Together
Outside person

Changing, Eliminating & Simplifying
Roles, Rituals and Traditions

regular basis if not weekly. Keep them short, especially in the initial set-up phase to prevent burn out. If someone is burning out, take a break, but *always reschedule* even if it's fifteen minutes later or the next day. During these dialogues, it is important that the spirit be one of cooperation and team work rather than adversarial. This is more of a business-meeting model and not designed to focus on feelings.

Meeting of the Minds: Eight Talking Points

1. Figure Out Your Strengths and Challenges

At the beginning of this process, you, your partner, your family members, or even your roommates as the case may be, will determine each of your strengths and areas of challenge so that you can make better decisions about the division of labor. For the purpose of these meetings, it's crucial to not just to focus on your difficulties but to know everyone's strengths and difficulties in order to assign the right person to the right job. This is both in terms of the tasks themselves and the qualities they bring to the family unit. As in any well-functioning business, assigning appropriate tasks to the right person is the smart thing to do.

Use the common strengths and difficulties listed below as a starting point for your own discussion. The purpose is to increase communication, not just to mechanically divide up tasks like dealing out cards. It may take several conversations to come up with some workable ideas.

Discuss these in the following order:

Strengths

- Your strengths: e.g., creativity, spontaneity, enthusiasm, conceptual abilities, or brainstorming abilities
- Strengths of those in the family without AD/HD: e.g., organizational abilities, dependability, planning skills, or follow through

Challenges

- Your challenges: e.g., time, money, clutter management, paperwork, prioritizing, getting started, or distractibility
- Challenges of the family members without AD/HD: e.g., being overly responsible, too controlling, lacking spontaneity, or getting lost in details. These qualities won't be the same for every non-AD/HD family member. In fact, the non-AD/HD family member may have some of the same problem areas as you do even if they are less severe. This is when a family may have to turn to outside help, as we will see later

Try to be as specific as possible when discussing strengths and difficulties because people can have great organizational skills in some ways and poor ones in other ways. A woman with AD/HD may have great planning and conceptual abilities and can mentally plan a complete trip from start to finish, deciding each step that needs to be taken, but she might not be able to manage the details of putting that plan into action. So when you are specifying your area of difficulty for this exercise, don't just say "poor organizational skills," but specify difficulty in carrying out many small details.

2. Pick Tasks with the Greatest Impact

Next pick the top three tasks that most impact either you or the family. Below are a few discussion starters. The important thing is to find out what the critical areas are for you.

- *Grocery shopping*
- *Financial management*
- *School and child-related schedules and activities*
- *Clothes shopping*

- *Social obligations*

- *Household maintenance*

- *Food preparation and clean-up*

Determine *the level of difficulty*, whether it is mild, moderate, or severe, break up the tasks into distinct phases, and then identify the different skill sets that each aspect of the task requires. In the next phase of task division, you will use this information about level, severity, and specificity to decide the different ways a task can be accomplished.

3. Get the Right Kind of Help

For each task you address, use the list below as a scale to determine where your level of difficulty may fall in order to generate options about how the task can be altered to fit and accommodate your particular family.

1. Should you do the task at all?

2. Should you do the task alone but with supports such as Post-its, calendars, planners, beepers or written supports set up by a non-AD/HD family member such as instructions on how to balance the checkbook or diagrams of where the dishes go in the cupboards?

3. Should you do the task alone but have a non-AD/HD family member in the room, not to do the prescribed task but to help you focus?

4. Should you have the non-AD/HD family member as co-participant in the activity as long as the non-AD/HD person can assist in a non-toxic, non-controlling way?

5. Should you be an assistant to the non-AD/HD person in completing the task?

6. Should you remain in the room in a non-participatory role doing other tasks while the non-AD/HD person does the primary task? (This gentle presence can give a feeling of support, which can then help reduce resentment that may have built up).

7. Should you let the non-AD/HD person do the task but offer to reciprocate in some other way?

8. Should an outside assistant be brought in if none of the family members are willing to do a task?

Simple interventions work for the least severe deficit. If there is a minor organizational challenge, Post-its, planners, or new calendars may do the trick. A moderate level of difficulty may require someone to be in the room. The next step may be part- or even full-time help, especially if areas of difficulty overlap. Just because a family member is not AD/HD doesn't mean he or she may not have his or her own difficulties in certain areas. Just pushing tasks onto him or her isn't going to work either. As you proceed, you will be able to figure out exactly what interventions will be necessary to accommodate each challenge and who will do it. There are many ways to structure this that doesn't involve all-or-nothing thinking like, "You do the cooking, and I'll do the bills."

4. Determine What to Do When Nobody Wants to Do a Task

If nobody wants to do certain tasks or has the necessary abilities, what are the options? Together think of friends, family, or professionals who might fill in the gap, either on a "paid or trade" basis. Trading tasks with a friend or neighbor can be a workable solution with the right person. If you're going to pay for help, what kind of adjustments in the budget or family time will this mean? Obviously, this can only be done by family members who are willing to talk and renegotiate. If they can't, they're going to have to have some help talking through these things, as we'll see in the next section on renegotiating. But really think through the benefits and costs of paying someone to help out. *Isn't it possible that hiring a bookkeeper once a month may be more cost effective than couples counseling every week to argue about the bills not getting paid?*

5. Brainstorm Together!

Try brainstorming together as a means to problem solving like you would in a business. Think each process through in detail to figure out what is really causing the difficulty. For instance, is cleaning the kitchen really impossible, or is prioritizing the different tasks (as other people do automatically) the real barrier? Maybe having a supportive family member present in the kitchen while you cook or clean may be the thing that works for you. Is it cognitive processing, sequencing, prioritizing, inattention to detail, or a need for stimulation and/or outside structure? Is it impulsivity and shifting, visual spatial issues, or motor difficulties? It's necessary to identify the problem before you can find the right solution.

6. Break through Traditional Gender Roles

Examine the areas below that have typically been assigned to one gender or another and discuss them thoroughly as to who is best suited for the task and/or how you might strategize to support each other.

- Household/yard maintenance
- Coordinating individual schedules
- Buying clothes for the family
- Talking to teachers
- Maintaining the cars
- Handling the finances
- Making social engagements or recreational plans
- Managing papers
- Intimacy

Time eats away at these when you are living with AD/HD. And remember, there may be areas that you don't view as a problem but your family members do.

7. Reward Yourselves

Always reward yourselves after having one of these restructuring sessions. Decide on some kind of fun, mutually agreed upon activity. These meetings can also be a good way to get to know each other better on a deeper level. If your relationships have lost some of the communication you once had, these meetings' can be a vehicle to start talking again. Don't turn these sessions into drudgery. You might want to hold them away from home in a place that you both consider fun. If something happens, and one of you can't make it, take the time to reschedule.

If you do this effectively with the purpose of making it work for both of you, not just for the purpose of getting chores done, you'll be surprised by the effect that it has. Your restructured life starts to feel better. You are more in control, thus you have less resentment. And if you have a partner, your sex life or romantic feelings may even improve, as well. It is quite likely that you will be in a better mood and have more emotional and physical energy.

8. Accept the Support of Others

Support from other family members does not have to mean co-dependency, which is taking responsibility for and being emotionally in charge of everything. Family members don't have to do everything for you, but often helping to strategize about how to get help or thinking through plans can be tremendously helpful. Along with reassurance, this provides the feeling that "We're in this together." With this understanding of the meaning of support, none of you will feel bombarded all the time with demands that may then lead to feeling a need to retreat.

Another way to avoid co-dependency for the non-AD/HD family members, particularly spouses, is for them to go out and have a good time on their own or to engage in some kind of social activities they enjoy that might be too overwhelming for the AD/HD partner. The point is to make life work without draining anyone and without allowing resentment to build up.

Sometimes you might have special needs and mini-panics during the week but knowing that this will be addressed during the weekly meeting can help you feel more supported and calm. There also needs to be a mechanism for managing daily panics and daily centering. Maybe the spouse can give five minutes at the beginning of the day to assist with centering and prioritizing. Often mini-panics are just a sudden loss of perspective, and a reassuring word helps enough to get a woman back on track.

If this happens frequently, it would be a good idea to get a third person involved. A coach can facilitate this process. The more you can get needs like this met outside the basic partnership, the more energy and interest remain with the spouse or partner, allowing for deeper work and help within the relationship.

9. Reciprocate

You might want to think about reciprocating in some way when it comes to tasks, exchanging some chore you could do, or providing some special favor to your partner in return for assistance with your weak spots. Always remind the members of your "support team" that you really appreciate them. Actually, doing something special for them will keep the system healthy and prevent resentment from developing.

Taking a Fresh Look at Rules and Roles Within the Family

The deepest level of restructuring is to actually alter and often let go of the way you've always done things. *This means simplifying, eliminating and/or redesigning the roles, rules, and traditions often held sacred in families for years even when they no longer work.*

Too Many Tasks

Sometimes there are just too many tasks to go around for working people, especially those who have children. If there are too many tasks, or those that you have are too complicated, rethink them. Is the way you do them too time-consuming? Do they use up too much emotional and physical energy? You probably don't have to do all that you're currently doing. You might be doing all that you expect of yourself but you're not having any fun or recreation. You might not be socializing enough or having enough nourishing or romantic time with your partner.

If there's just no way that you can meet all your obligations, consider omitting tasks or changing the requirements. Below are some questions to assist you in reexamining your tasks.

Reexamining What You Do and How You Do it

1. In terms of simplifying or eliminating tasks, consider these kinds of questions and alter them to fit your own situation.

2. Do you always have to drive to the grocery store, or can you order or make arrangements by phone and have the items delivered?

3. Can you hire an assistant, a college girl, perhaps, to help pick up the cleaning or take your children after school for an hour or two?

4. Could you shop through catalogs and shopping networks instead of always going to the store?

5. Can you buy purchase clothing in quantity so that when you lose a sock you'll have plenty of others to match?

6. Can you stop subscribing to so many magazines or newsletters in order to reduce the clutter?

7. Can you have baskets with big labels for mail or keys?

8. Must you have in-laws over for brunch at a certain time every month? Can you take them out instead?

9. Can Grandma buy some of the necessary school supplies?

10. Can your husband be the one to call the school when you need information?

11. Can the family members who want special things at the grocery store make their own trips if they're old enough?

12. Do you have to cook that big dinner on Friday night even though you've worked all day and you're overwhelmed and exhausted?

13. Do you have to give the most elaborate theme birthday party in town?

Rituals, Traditions, and Holidays

I'd suggest sitting down again with your family with a list titled *Rules, Roles, and Obligations for Rituals, Traditions, and Holidays.* Together try to come up with what those mean in your family. Do you have to do Mother's Day exactly the same way every year? For example, can you take your mother to a play instead of entertaining her at your home? Think of that yearly family vacation that might be a nightmare! You may have to challenge areas in your family, religious, or cultural life that you previously thought were untouchable or unchangeable. Are there any obligations that you can eliminate, change, or simplify? Too many rules, roles, and obligations can stop you from fully engaging in life. Changing the "sacred" things in life doesn't come without a price, however. To achieve these changes, you will have to communicate with your family in deeper ways than you ever have before because these alterations can affect many other people. Giving up traditions entails going through a grief cycle. It's upsetting to think that you can't do whatever you want because of your disorder. But you'll learn that there's another side to life, different from what you've always done. You're not necessarily denying your traditions or giving them up (unless you want to) but rather supporting your strengths in freeing your energy for what you most want to do. You don't want to dissipate the newfound energy you have now that you are on medication. Changing traditions doesn't mean giving up nourishing activities. Remember the Priority Pies. You want to restructure to meet your needs to get the desired pieces of the pies, not to just get rid of tasks.

Start out at your weekly family meetings discussing these rituals in depth. It can be fun to talk about multi-generational issues or how such traditions got started. Talking about the past takes some of the focus and blame out of the present, helping you understand everyone brings to the family. Talk about what these traditions mean to each family member. Once you have developed a new plan, write it down, and then discuss how you're going to maintain it. What's the first step you need to take as a family? Discuss any internal barriers such as family-of-origin messages that might be interfering with your abilities to restructure. Some families take a step forward and then the extended family comes over and makes disparaging comments about the new roles and rules. This can send the family right back to the way things always were, even though the new way was working for them.

You can use the Task Division Chart to structure the discussions I've outlined in this chapter. The best way to use this is to make a copy for everyone so that each of you can fill it out alone and later use it as a basis for discussion and comparison. In the first column, write down a few areas that you think are the most important to work on. Then put either your initials or a check mark under the columns that apply to your willingness or ability to do these tasks, either alone or together. After all your discussions, you may decide that an outside person may be most appropriate. In the last column, indicate if you feel that the task should be eliminated, simplified, or drastically changed.

TASK DIVISION CHART

Tasks or Areas of Conflict	Able/Willing Alone	Able/Willing To Do Together	Not Able, But Will Be There	Outside Person	Change Task

Summary: And Now,
For the Rest of Jodi's Story . . .

At the beginning of the chapter we saw changes that Jodi made after diagnosis. Though these were good and necessary, they didn't go deep enough or far enough to help her integrate all her experience. They also didn't allow her family to come to a new level of reorganization to accommodate her AD/HD. Once her family could break out of their old patterns of relating and thinking about Jodi, then they could thrive.

Jodi's mom has been coming over every week to help her. It's hard for Jodi to deal with the anger she feels when her mom says things like: "I don't know how you can live like this! What kind of example is this setting for your daughter? Actually, I don't completely believe in this AD/HD stuff. I think you're still not trying hard enough." And then her husband says things like this to her: "Why are you still like this? I thought that with the medication you wouldn't be like this any more. Now you are going to therapy, both your mom and I are both helping, you have a housecleaner, and it's still not enough!"

We've covered a lot of ground in this restructuring discussion, but an important point to remember is to go slowly, individually, as a couple, or as a family. Don't set yourselves up for failure by taking on too much at one time. Counseling can serve as a support if you run up against barriers. (See Chapter 18)

If you get stuck at this point in the division of labor, you may need to work with your family and friends to set limits in a non-defensive way and to set up an environment that works for you without pushing others away. You need to find ways to communicate with your family that allows you to maintain your self-respect and equality while considering their needs, as well. In the next chapter, we'll look further at how to make your communication more effective and assertive in the process of restructuring by learning to renegotiate your relationships.

CHAPTER TWENTY-TWO

Yours, Mine, and Ours

Renegotiating Relationships

In order to go further in restructuring your life, you often need to renegotiate relationships in your personal life with your family, partner, extended family, and friends or parents, at work with employers and co-workers, and in college with instructors. Wherever and whenever your AD/HD *happens*, you will need more than strategies about how to set up your environment. You will need communication strategies that help you renegotiate with other people. In this chapter, we first look at renegotiating in your personal life. This will include how to set limits and communicate in healthy, non-defensive ways as you go about setting up your environment to work for you and others. We will also explore what interferes with setting limits. You will find a *Four-Step Model for Renegotiating*, as well as information on how to find common ground. We will look at the cycle of misinterpretation presented earlier and see how that cycle can be broken with good communication. After that we will look at renegotiating relationships and the necessity of communicating clearly and assertively for success at work and at college.

Renegotiating In Your Personal Life

Toxic Help

How do you get assistance from your spouse, partner, mother, friend, or even a professional helper without getting *toxic help*? The *Toxic Help* symbol represents help that is harmful. In the attempt

to move toward structuring a helpful relationship, it's difficult to reject negative words while still communicating appreciation. You might think, "How could I be so ungrateful as to criticize somebody who's helping me?" But you must not allow yourself to be put down in order to get help. That's too high a price to pay. It's important to separate out that which is authentically helpful from that which is not.

The initial period after diagnosis is an especially vulnerable time because you are trying to build your self-esteem and focus on your strengths despite the fact that a part of you still believes in the negative attributions. When helpers comment on your difficulty with tasks, you may still be easily triggered into those old feelings of shame and incompetence such as those delivered by Jodi's mother: "You are living like a child," or "What a bad parent you are," or "I thought you were over this" do not contribute anything of value. Others may try to motivate you with behavior modification such as rewards or stars, as if you were a child, or even worse, a pet. They might set up their own goals for you to accomplish or attribute psychological reasons for your difficulties in meeting those goals. None of these things work for adults with AD/HD. Instead, they make them feel diminished and misunderstood, as if they have disappointed somebody important.

Even though friends and family members may not understand your AD/HD, you don't want to walk away from relationships that are valuable. You may eventually decide that you have to, but if there is potential there, try to nurture that which is good in the relationships through renegotiation.

It is important at this time to change the way you measure success. You may have difficulty with tasks, but the new basis for measuring your success is not how well you do things but how well you manage to get things done. Professional facilitation is often quite helpful at this point.

Setting Limits

It is important to communicate effectively when someone's behavior is not helpful. You need to tell them that even though you appreciate their efforts and intentions, it would be more effective if they could avoid "spicing it up" with derisive comments. Be specific about the kind of the communication you'd like and give examples.

The "I" messages, basic building blocks of communication, are essential here. You can say, for example, *"I appreciate that you're helping me. It's a great relief to have you sweating through these things with me, but at the same time, I find myself becoming somewhat depressed and anxious and even angry sometimes when I hear myself being put down."*

Or you might say, *"Since I know you want to be helpful, it would be great for you to encourage me and focus on how well I'm doing in general or on some of my positive attributes. Because I'm not always sure how to get what I need, it would be helpful if I were more control of the way we're going about this, or at the least, to work as a team."*

If you're close to the person, you might go on to tell him or her that negative messages bring back a lot of bad feelings. However, a functional working relationship is not always possible with a close friend or family member who may bring a lot of resentment from the past. In that case, it's better not to have that person with you, especially at the beginning. You want to avoid a situation that recreates old feelings of frustration, of disappointing people, or that you're doing something wrong. Perhaps later, when he or she better understands the AD/HD and what's helpful, he or she will be able to work collaboratively with you more effectively. After you feel more comfortable in your new skin, you will be better able to communicate in a non-defensive, clear manner.

You need to surround yourself with people who are helpful and encouraging and who notice your successes until you are able to hold onto them yourself. Eventually, when you have had enough positive reflections and enough successes, you'll be able to remember them and build on them yourself. It will then be much easier to attract *non-toxic* help for yourself.

Globally Dismissed

When someone discovers that you have AD/HD, you may then subtly be thought of as *globally* less competent rather than having specific areas of weakness. I call this being globally dismissed. Many clients report others being overly solicitous, treating them like a child or being overprotective once their AD/HD is known. For example, an employer might not assign certain tasks. For example, a woman with AD/HD had trouble prioritizing. Each morning, her husband sat down and helped her prioritize her tasks for that day into a schedule. Other than this difficulty and other kinds of organizational difficulties, she was a competent, intelligent planner. This couple was preparing to make a cross-country move that required much planning and coordinating. The woman had her responsibilities and the man had his, but without even realizing it, he began making decisions in her assigned task area without consulting her. He even *undid* her decisions. Later in counseling, he realized that he had been unconsciously *globally dismissing* her, feeling she was incompetent across the board because she a specific area of difficulty.

In order to avoid allowing others to *globally dismiss* you when dividing up tasks, it is important to keep a sense of self-respect and not to insist on dividing things up 50/50 in terms of sheer numbers. There might be a lot of qualitative help that an AD/HD person can

"I only know how to do two things. Garden and paint."
Claude Monet

give back in terms of emotional support, creative or conceptual help, even if she doesn't take on the lion's share of the work.

Monet said, "I can only do two things well—garden and paint." As you see in Monet's picture of a woman surrounded by her beautiful garden, he was able to accept that his strengths were more about quality than quantity. This point so strongly expresses the focused band of abilities that people with AD/HD have; they may not have as wide a range of competencies as others without AD/HD, but they usually have a number of specific areas in which they excel.

Dominance, Dependency and Other Fears

As we have discussed, *renegotiation* regarding the division of tasks often brings up a lot of issues around power and control that are present to some extent in every relationship. With AD/HD, this can sneak in and play an important role without you recognizing it. When a spouse or partner who is able to do daily tasks in a more organized fashion starts to dominate the relationship, exerting more and more control, power can slowly slip away from the AD/HD partner, thus diminishing self-esteem. She may begin to think thoughts such as the following:

- *I'd better keep my mouth shut and not express my feelings. I don't want to rock the boat*
- *How can I tell him I'm angry when he's helped me so much?*
- *If I don't watch it, I can turn him away*
- *Eventually, he'll get sick of me and leave*
- *How far can I push this whole thing?*
- *I'm not a good partner, anyway*

Many women with AD/HD have fears of loneliness or abandonment that turn into dependency. They may then push away feelings of anger or avoid setting healthy limits needed to get appropriate help and support. I've seen women with AD/HD stay in emotionally abusive relationships because they feel they can't be completely independent and take care of things on a daily level. For example, they might not be able to work a nine-to-five job in a traditional way because they easily get overwhelmed and exhausted. Of course, many women feel this kind of strain, but women with AD/HD experience this to a greater extent, which in turn impacts their decisions to stay in painful relationships.

Again, what is needed is assertive communication that expresses their gratitude but also their feelings and needs. They need to learn how to say, *"I'm really appreciative of everything that you're doing, and you're really helping me, but I still find I am angry about this other issue."* To do this often takes professional facilitation.

Four Steps to Renegotiating Relationships

The four main things to remember when renegotiating your relationships as outlined on the *Four-Step Validation Chart* are as follows:

1. Validation

2. Negotiation

3. Appreciation

4. Reciprocation

Validation

When someone is helping you, first validate the importance to you of his or her feelings and needs, the relationship, and the importance of the issue for him or her.

Negotiation

Negotiation is all about finding common ground. The focus should be on problem solving, not on you as the "problem" to be solved. In every relationship, both partners have different needs, but with AD/HD, it's often more extreme. Find a healthy way to protect, validate, and honor your needs but to do the same for your partner so that neither one's needs are sacrificed in the process. This involves a real understanding and acceptance by both of you of AD/HD and your combined strengths and weaknesses. Your solutions may not be like other people's solutions but that doesn't matter as long as you work on them as a team. This means being solution-oriented and generating lots of options versus black-and-white thinking. Again, this can require professional facilitation, especially at first, to be able to maintain a non-blaming stance as you're trying to problem solve and to really listen to each other.

Appreciation

Obviously, when someone helps you with an actual task or listens and compromises it is appropriate to appreciate him or her verbally.

Reciprocation

After that, reciprocation can keep the balance so that you are not just on the receiving end of help or identified as the person who is causing the problems in the family. These might not be in the same areas as the original task that was done, but she can reciprocate in other areas. Reciprocation can take into account all of a woman's strengths.

Putting the Four Steps Together

Here is a sample conversation incorporating each of the four steps. In this scenario, the woman with AD/HD feels much too overloaded to keep up the kind of socializing and entertaining her husband would like them to do. He is starting to feel resentful as he really misses this kind of activity. First we will hear the perspective of the woman with AD/HD, and then we will hear the partner's point of view. It is important for both partners to develop these partnership skills.

~~~~~~~~~

Woman with AD/HD

Validation

I understand your need to have people over to the house. I know it's important for you to socialize more and that you wish we would socialize together. It's important to me that we work together to figure out a way to get both of our needs met.

Negotiation

Since the way and amount you want to socialize is difficult for me, we need to find a way for you to be able to socialize without me sometimes. If you want people over more, maybe you could make more of the arrangements. In addition, maybe we can socialize more outside of home. These are a few ideas I have about it. Maybe a combination of these would work. What do you think?

Appreciation

It felt so good for you to understand this dilemma and to work with me on this. I really appreciate how you compromised on this.

Reciprocation

I would really like to do something for you in return. I know how much you want a little time for yourself to work out, relax, or go to the game with your friends. Why don't you take some time after work to go to they gym a few days a week? I know you need that down time just like I need to do things a certain way for my well being.

~~~~~~~~~

Partner without AD/HD

It is also just as important for the partner without AD/HD to do this. It is not a one-way street. Here is the same situation with the partner following these steps.

Validation

I know how my wanting to socialize and entertain is overwhelming for you because of your AD/HD, and I don't want you to feel more over-loaded.

Negotiation

Since I really like to socialize and entertain more, how about a combination of these? We could meet friends out more often even if it is for shorter times such as for a movie or for coffee. It doesn't always have to be long dinners. When we have friends over here, it doesn't have to be for dinner. Or if we do dinner, we could order in and watch a movie. Also, I'd like to meet up with some people alone sometimes if you don't want to come. I have friends I could see on my own if you don't mind.

Appreciation

I really appreciate the way you have tried to compromise on this. It feels good, and I can see that you care about me.

Reciprocation

I know you are really trying this on, and I would like to help you out. How about every time we go out or have someone over, I'll clean your desk or wash your car? I could help you with something that is overloading you a little that would be easy for me and helpful to you.

~~~~~~~~~

Looking for Common Ground

We'll now go into a little more in depth on the subject of negotiation. Mediators look for common ground between two parties in terms of goals. They aren't looking for their differences or for someone to blame. This is not easy, and it takes a lot of practice.

These are the steps involved in negotiating:

1. Really hear what the other person wants

2. Say that back to him or her

3. Take in what you like and what doesn't work for you

4. Suggest your own solution

5. Repeat the process as needed until you have reached a workable solution that, at least on a trial basis, is acceptable. Realize that it might not work out as planned but that you will come back to the negotiating table without blaming each other.

If you feel stuck or if you need more information before coming to a decision, decide what the next step should be. Who is going to be responsible for it? Mark it down on your calendars and determine how to do follow-through. After every session, follow with verbal appreciation and offers of reciprocation. Set this up so that you have fun with it. Do it over a glass of wine or ice cream. Do it in the bathtub when the kids aren't around and then take a walk afterwards.

The following is a fictional negotiation session. I suggest you read through the script together for fun and then substitute your own area that you need to work out. You can do this time and time again with different issues that arise. Eventually, you won't need the script, but it's an easy model to follow when you are trying to problem solve a specific area. Start with something fairly concrete at first and then move into more difficult areas later. This couple is discussing how to handle their finances.

The Negotiation Script

Joe:

> Since this is my area of strength and not yours, why don't I just take over the checkbook? How does this work for you?

Linda:

> I like the part about not having to deal with this since it's so difficult for me, but what doesn't work is the feeling that you will have all the control. I may feel like a little kid and get resentful. How about if we do it together?

Joe:

> That may work, but it sounds a little vague for me. I feel more comfortable when things are clearer. How about since I have an ability to do things regularly, I will set up a schedule, for instance, to look at finances every Sunday night? You will be able to depend on that and since structure is important for you, this may be helpful for you, as well. You could come into my office at that time and sit with me as I do this so you will feel more in control and won't be in the dark.

Linda:

> That sounds good. How about if you remind me, though, since I'll probably be so caught up in something else? Even though I definitely want to do it, I have a feeling it's going to be hard for me to get there since it bores me.

Joe:

> I don't mind reminding you, but I don't want this to turn into nagging and resentment.

Linda:

> Ok, how about if you remind me just once or twice, even with a Post-it or a message on the phone a day or two before? Then if I don't come, the consequence is that I won't know what's going on but at least it will get done.

Joe:

> And then I won't have to feel as though I have to make you come to this meeting. It's all agreed to in advance.

Linda:

> Sounds good. Thanks for working this out. Why don't we see if there's something I can do that's difficult for you?

Joe:

> Okay, well, I would appreciate if you would help me think through this problem I'm having with my boss at work. You are good at understanding the big picture. Maybe you could give me some insight.

Linda:

> I'd be happy to. Let's get out our appointment books and write in times for both things, the money meeting and a time to talk over this situation at your work.

Joe:

> I'll even pencil it in two days before to remind you. I'm really glad we sat down and discussed this. It's really been bothering me. Let's see if this works.

Renegotiating Social Obligations with Friends, Family and Other Groups

In addition to renegotiating at work and with your partner, you may also need to renegotiate your boundaries with other groups, as well. Friends and extended family will also need assertive communication when you eliminate or change rituals. It will be important to learn how to communicate these things in a way that validates the importance of your relationships and also tells others what you need to have a good relationship without moving away from them.

Staying Over with Friends or Relatives

Sometimes women with AD/HD find it difficult to stay in the homes of friends, relatives, or people they don't know well because they find it much more difficult to arrange and maintain their belongings. They are self-conscious about their disorganization, feel bombarded, don't get enough down time, and can easily get over-whelmed.

If possible, an AD/HD woman needs to be able to make other arrangements that will work for her such as leaving early or staying at a hotel if she can afford it. She needs to set it up in advance and not constantly put herself into situations that work against her AD/HD. Sometimes this requires saying no, setting limits, or assertively describing your needs.

But I'm No Good in the Kitchen

For many women with AD/HD, social events involving a lot of domestic, routine tasks such as food preparation, setting the table, washing dishes or participating in other domestic activities may be especially stressful. In addition to having difficulty with the distraction and bombardment inherent in these group activities, women also have difficulty staying focused and figuring out what to do in these unstructured situations. Such situations can bring up a great deal of anxiety and shame because they feel like their fail-ures at these basic jobs traditionally assigned to women are made public for all to see. This often leads to avoidance of such gather-ings, unfortunately causing the loss of important relationships and opportunities.

Instead, these women may have to learn to ask for directions or to find informal coaches. They need to state clearly what they can contribute, for example, "If you tell me exactly how you'd like me to help you and give me the instructions, I'd be happy to help. I know everybody has their own way of doing this." Ask for specifics and say what's difficult for you. Always try to focus on positives and what you can do well, instead of putting yourself down and highlighting your insecurities. Validate the other person's importance to you. Always keep your own sense of what your corresponding strengths are. "I'm not good at chopping vegetables, but I'm great at organizing games for the kids."

Social Gatherings

Women with AD/HD also sometimes have difficulty with their relationships when invited to parties or family gatherings. Quite often they feel bombarded by too much stimulation, especially women without hyperactivity, and therefore withdraw, sometimes offending people without intending to as we discussed in earlier Chapter 9.

They feel overloaded and exhausted, and they can't keep up. They might have difficulty carrying on a good conversation, trying to think of what to say in the middle of so much activity. Many women with AD/HD mysteriously retreat to another room, become quiet, upset or withdrawn, or just don't show up for these kinds of events. All these responses may give the message to others that you don't care about them. They don't know that you're having a hard time or why.

You don't have to go around screaming AD/HD all the time, but you can explain to them that you get overwhelmed, that you need some down time, and that you'll be back in a little while. If you do want to talk to somebody, you might say, *"I really do want to talk to you, but I find that I can't block out the noise here. Why don't we find a quiet space?"* In response to a party invitation, you might say, *"I get overwhelmed by parties, but I really would like to talk to you more in depth. Why don't we make a date for Friday?"* If you go to an event, give yourself permission to leave early when you're worn down, knowing that you want to go and connect to people, but that you want to leave before you stop enjoying the situation. Set it up and think it through in advance so you don't feel anxious. Plan for your AD/HD.

Committees, Boards, and Other Volunteer Groups

When asked by others for a contribution of time or energy, many women with AD/HD say yes and feel overloaded or say no and feel guilty. They don't know how to communicate their caring, stay connected, and maintain their limits. They feel they must give an answer immediately before they have had time to think through a decision or response.

There are a number of ways to handle these situations. Instead you might say, "Let me think about it. I'll call you back tomorrow." Don't feel you have to make a decision right then because that's when you're going to feel more pressured. Give yourself time to figure out the best way to handle it, knowing that even if you want to contribute, you may not be most effective at that time because of your other commitments. Write things down so that you will be able to remember them in your next conversation. You might try to come up with solutions that aren't all-or-nothing such as offering to donate money or other items in place of time and energy or simply asking them to call you next year. You might say, *"I can't donate time to go on a campaign around the neighborhood, but if you give me flyers, I'll hand them out at work,"* or *"I'm really not good at doing these mailings, but I wouldn't mind making ten calls."*

Earlier in the book in Chapter 9, we looked at a diagram that showed the misinterpretation cycle that can happen in these kinds of situations. We see a better outcome in the bottom half of that chart. Once you have more self-acceptance and understanding of yourself and your AD/HD, you are less likely to compound your problems by how you react to your AD/HD. Instead of avoiding people because you fear they will be critical or think you're weird or stupid, you may be able to talk about your struggles and needs in a direct and self-supportive way, thereby preserving valuable relationships.

SECONDARY EFFECTS

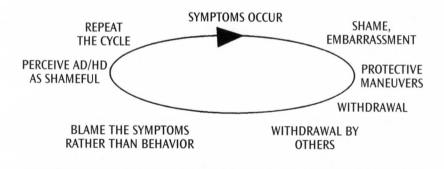

SYMPTOMS OCCUR

REPEAT
THE CYCLE

SHAME,
EMBARRASSMENT

PERCEIVE AD/HD
AS SHAMEFUL

PROTECTIVE
MANEUVERS

WITHDRAWAL

BLAME THE SYMPTOMS
RATHER THAN BEHAVIOR

WITHDRAWAL BY
OTHERS

WHEN THE FEELING OF SHAME DIMINISHES, THE CYCLE IS BROKEN

LAUGH   EXPLAIN

STOP BEING LONELY   MOVE TOWARD PEOPLE

Even though you may have worked through many of these communication patterns and divided up the household tasks, you may still feel stuck. This might necessitate a serious look at what images you and your partner may be holding on to. Are either of you insisting on a culturally approved ideal of what a mature, successful, competent woman should look like? Are you waiting for that time to arrive before you begin to enjoy yourself or your partnership? If so you will want to look at these questions in more depth in the next chapter on redefining your image.

Renegotiating At Work and College

Whether you are trying to make your present job work, thinking about new ways to work, or are working in college, the other strategies needed to make your work life have to do with communication. You need to know how to set limits, how to communicate in a positive way about yourself, and know how to maintain your self-respect while getting what you need at work.

It's going to help if you've worked through the shame you may have attached to AD/HD. Then you'll be more effective in getting what you need by communicating in an assertive way without over-defending and explaining, trying to convince others or moving into a position of self-deprecation to get what you want.

A young woman, Bridget, had spent more time than expected on a project that she didn't have ready for the meeting the next day. She started acting defensive and separating herself, creating an aura of doing something wrong, when actually what she needed was a positive way to state the truth: she had created something very special, but to get it done on time, she would need an assistant to help her with the details, make copies, and collate it. All that she could focus on at the time was that her AD/HD difficulty in completing projects on time was going to bring her negative responses. In actuality it was her behavior that brought the negative feelings from people, rather than the AD/HD problem itself. She needed to learn to say: "I've done something really special and I'm excited about it. I think you're going to love it. I need some extra time," or "I need some assistance." The situation already existed and she needed to be able to reframe it to convey that she was sorry for any inconvenience, without putting herself down.

Positive Communication

When the symptoms arise in any kind of AD/HD problem, instead of sending the message, "I'm really messed up, I really don't deserve to be here, and I'm not doing a good job," do your best to employ strategies that are going to help you take control. When the inevitable happens, and you're late or you forgot or mislaid something, don't make it worse by avoiding the situation or putting yourself down. You want to be able to communicate that you are sorry for any bad effect that you have created, that this person or the project is important to you, and that you want to be able to do the best job you can under present circumstances. *"Yes, I was late, and I'm sorry it has had a bad effect. I think having assistance would help avoid that in the future. Right now, what we can do to make this work is . . ."* emphasizing the positive nature of what you have accomplished.

Positive communication to other people also involves setting limits. Women are afraid to set limits, to say no, because they think it's going to mean criticism, rejection, a bad message to the other person. What needs to be communicated is that what the other person is asking is important to you, that you wish you could accommodate them, but right now it's not going to work. You may suggest another way to make it work — for example, if it's a big lunch that you can't attend, you might ask the person to meet alone with you. Let them know it's important for you to talk, but you find it difficult in a distracting environment.

You don't have to go around telling everybody you have AD/HD. It's very off-putting. You only need to go to that length if you need some legal accommodation or if there is somebody in particular whom you want to know for some reason. Describe what you need, validate that you and the other person both have the goal of doing a good job. You can say something like, *"When you explain this to me, it's very important for me to get it. What really works better for me is if I could have it written down so I can refer to it. I sometimes have difficulty with remembering these kinds of verbal lists. I don't want to have to interrupt you all the time, so perhaps you could leave the instructions typed up next to the computer."* If you need to be alone and you're afraid of appearing rude to people, of shutting them out or saying no, it's always better to try to state it first, tell them how you're feeling and that you don't intend to be rude. With AD/HD often your attempts at self-protection can look as if you're shutting people out.

It's important to find a way to make it work for you, but you don't want to do it in a way that they can misinterpret or react negatively. You might say things like the following.

- *I don't mean to be rude but I'm really going to be buried in work for a couple of hours so I'm going to shut my door. I'll open it when I'm done with this report*

- *When I get interrupted, everything leaves my mind. I'm going to turn my phone off for a couple of hours every day*

- *I'd really like to answer those questions. How about if we schedule a time, maybe on Friday at one o'clock, so that I can prepare and give you a lot of attention?*

- *In the middle of my day, I'm sometimes distracted and I can't give you the kind of attention that I'd like to*

- *It's really important for me to do a good job, so I need you to write down the instructions*

- *I know I'm hard to follow sometimes. I get so carried away with enthusiasm for this subject. Let me know if I lose you. Please interrupt*

- *I have trouble keeping track of time because I get so involved in my work*

- *This discussion with you is so important to me, but I have difficulty blocking out the noise in here. Let's find a quieter spot so I can really concentrate and give enough attention to what you're saying*

If someone is trying to explain something to you and you're not getting it, you might say, *"Thank you for being so patient"*, instead of, *"Sorry I'm so dumb."* If you bump into something, say, *"I'm sorry I messed up your books"* instead of, *"I'm sorry I'm so clumsy."* Instead of saying, *"I can't,"* or *"I won't"* do such and such a task, you might say, *"This kind of task is very difficult for me to do."* Then make a suggestion as to how to proceed, either with other kinds of instructions, more time, or with assistance.

Always *validate the other person, validate yourself,* and then *suggest another situation* instead of feeling that you have to be available on demand. If it's a boss that's asking you for more and more work, *you can say that you feel good that they're asking you to do this work, and you really enjoy it, but you feel that to do the best job you either need an assistant or a different time frame. Even though you hate to give this project to someone else, it might be the best for the company to do at that time.*

What you don't want to do is hide, pretend that everything's okay, and then overwork, taking things home and not doing a good job. Things will slip by, and you will get more and more anxious about it. This buildup of anxiety underneath anything good that you have done feeds either the feeling of being an impostor or the feeling that things are going to fall apart. That's going to affect your behavior and your relationships.

Ways to Get Coaching at Work

Even if you don't ask for legal accommodations, there are other ways of creating structures to get some of the help you need. Informally, this might include setting up ways for people with whom you work to remind you of important things. For instance, this might include asking a co-worker in a positive way to stop by your office on the way to a meeting to serve as a reminder for you to attend.

More Formal Assistance

You can request regular check-ins from a supervisor to go over the projects that you are currently working on in order to help yourself stay on track. You might request regular, short meetings that would help you be realistic about the amount of work that you agree to take on. This can be framed in a positive way with your stated intention of meeting your mutual goals, which include you doing the best work you can. In these check-ins, especially at times when you feel the work load is increasing to a point where you will be unable to manage it, you can try to reach an understanding together of what the priorities really are.

The focus of these sessions should be to generate alternatives that satisfy the goal of getting the work done well. Instead of an all-or-nothing attitude, for example, you might suggest the following: First, you could accept a lesser assignment and do high-quality work on it. Second, you could complete all the work in an expanded time frame. Or, third, you could do all of this work with assistance. This clearly defines your limits and also leaves the decision-making with the supervisor instead of you trying to meet impossible demands and being unable to produce the quality of work that you want. Again, this is not a pass-fail, all-or-nothing, either-or situation. You want to focus on doing a job well rather than on what you don't do well. Sometimes you just need the communication skills to know how to set limits and communicate in a positive way about yourself.

College: Open Lines of Communication

Despite all the extra work they may have done, all the hours they have put in, if they are late with papers and not communicating, they get incompletes, fail, drop out, or are asked to leave eventually. This happens with traditional college students, well as with adults who are retuning to school. The most important ingredient for success in college for students with challenges is to employ effective communication strategies.

If you are in college, communicate with your teachers about your difficulties instead of hiding them, because otherwise they have no idea how hard you are working. They just know that you don't turn papers in on time, and don't know you have spent hundreds of hours on a paper because of your difficulty in pulling your ideas together. If you don't communicate with your instructors, they might have an entirely different image of you. When it comes to a point at which you might have to ask for an extension, an incomplete or extra help, you will have a much better chance of being successful if your professors know the kind of difficulties that you have as well as the kinds of effort that you make. You don't want shame or guilt interfere to the point where you make things worse after you miss a test or deadline, by avoiding the whole subject. This just increases your anxiety as well as sabotages your chances of success. If you do work through your feelings of embarrassment and get legal accommodations at school, establish good working relationships with your professors; you will increase your chances of success greatly.

Before You Go to College

Investigate the attitude and accommodations offered by a particular college that you are considering so that you know which schools are more special needs friendly. Students who have been diagnosed can arrange with the student disability office for accommodations (extended time on tests or non-distracting test-taking environments). You can be given help to figure out a balanced or reduced class load.

You can get tutors and coaches to help you stay on track or help you in your writing assignments. But you have to ask for them.

If you are a young woman going away to school, it's ideal if you can enlist the support of your parents; involve them in your AD/HD diagnosis and treatment. This will help them understand why you might need to or might have already changed programs, schools, or directions. You'll need your family's and your school's support if you are to get accommodations, a reduced load, and a balanced program. But it's going to take talking about this to make it happen.

In the next chapter on *Redefining* there is a section about work. If you still have trouble with communication at college or at work asking for what you need, you will need to go further in redefining your self-image. Once you have worked through some of the embarrassment, you will find it easier to ask for you what you need and to have mutually positive relationships. That means relationships in which both your needs and the person you are in relationship with are met. At that point the focus can come off of your deficits and onto your enjoyment of your work and relationships.

CHAPTER TWENTY-THREE

One of a Kind

Redefining Your Self-Image

At some point in the process of restructuring and renegotiating, you will have to redefine your image of yourself, your work, and your partnership. Even if you've worked through a lot of these issues, if you're still waiting for the day when you're going to look and function like a person with a different kind of brain, you will constantly be set up for failure. This can stall your progress and prevent you from taking that last step toward a creative, interesting, satisfying life. In this final chapter, we will first look at changes in your core self-concept that happen as a result of the entire process we've traced in this book and the change in self-talk that brings. After that we look at the need to redefine your work self-image so that you can allow yourself to change course when needed in order to find more satisfaction in this area of your life. Then we will talk about the importance of your partner redefining the true value of a woman in a partnership. Finally, we describe the brand new "cycle of success" that is initiated eventually after you truly reach acceptance of your differences and an appreciation of your strengths. This chapter also recaps both the grief cycle and the success cycle for you and your partner.

REDEFINING YOUR CORE SELF-CONCEPT

As you see in the following Self-Concept illustration, after a long period of support from other people and through professional facilitation, you can ultimately embrace or incorporate all your strengths and difficulties, even though none of them completely define you.

REPAIR OF SELF-CONCEPT IN TREATMENT OF AD/HD

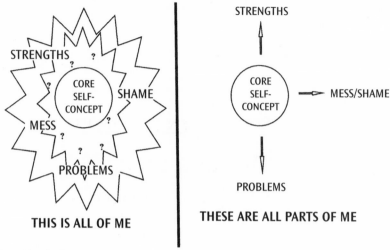

THIS IS ALL OF ME   THESE ARE ALL PARTS OF ME

© copyright Sari Solden, 1994

The picture shows the feelings associated with difficulties and strengths clumped together with the sense that "This is all I am." The picture on the right, however, shows the core feelings separate from the feelings about the AD/HD. After a long, positive process, the sense of self becomes more cohesive and stable.

At this point, you can say, whether at home or at work, *"Boy, I have a lot of big gaps here. It's a long stretch, but I can now hold onto the idea that I have great abilities as well as difficulties that are way out of line with my strengths, and they are all part of me. I must remember both sides and not deny or minimize either. The shame that I used to feel when something AD/HD-like happens doesn't completely disappear, but it doesn't define me any longer. I'm sensitive to it, but I know why I'm being triggered. I've planned for it. I know how to work with it. It's external to me now."*

As mentioned earlier, this is a long process that can be greatly facilitated by a skilled counselor who can hold onto this idea of you as a whole person until it is incorporated into how you see yourself. When this happens, it will color all your choices and decisions, including the jobs you apply for and the relationships you pursue. Before this, your self-image did not allow you to clearly see opportunities or choices.

Self-Talk

Two essential things can happen when you redefine who you are in a positive way. When you understand your AD/HD, you are able to sort out your primary symptoms, your neurology from your psychology, and your core self-image.

Previously, in Chapter 8, we discussed negative self-talk. The illustration, *Self-Talk*, shows the effects of both negative, and positive, self-talk. AD/HD symptoms will continue to emerge; you have to expect them. Your occasional AD/HD symptoms are not what is going to cause the biggest problems, though. The negative self-talk that accompanies the AD/HD is what makes it worse because it degrades your mood, as well as affecting your relationships. In the left half of the diagram, when experiencing symptoms of AD/HD in which you might blunder, be disorganized, or shut down, you would go into negative self-talk such as "I'm stupid. Forget all this garbage.

SELF-TALK

AD/HD Happens	When AD/HD is MORE ACCEPTED
BLUNDER	
DISORGANIZE	AD/HD Happens
SHUT DOWN	
Negative Self-Talk	**Positive Self-Talk**
"I'm so stupid!"	"It's that AD/HD again"
"Forget all this garbage"	"I'm mad at the AD/HD"
"It's just an excuse"	"It's just an AD/HD attack, ride it out!"
"What's the matter with me?"	"I give myself permission to relax?"
"What a jerk!"	"It's a signal that too much is going on!"
"I'm a mess"	"Take time to think it through"
"It's hopeless"	"Box it up, Put it on hold, Get help!"
DEPRESSION	You are able to separate from the AD/HD

What they're saying about AD/HD is just an excuse. What's the matter with me? I'm such a jerk." But when you're able to separate out your self from the AD/HD, you might say something more along the lines of what we see on the right hand side of the chart such as, "Oh, it's that AD/HD again! It's just an AD/HD attack; ride it out." You will use your strong feelings that emerge at these times as cues to what you need to stop a negative cycle by saying things such as, "I give myself permission to relax. This is a signal that too much is going on and that I'm not having enough help." You will know that it's a signal that you need to take action and that it's not a disaster. When you're able to calm yourself down with this kind of self-talk, the episode will pass.

Redefining at Work

Changing Your Image

Sometimes even if you renegotiate, and you're able to say what you want and your communication is good, even if you have accepted your AD/HD as above, things still don't always work when thinking about the way you want to work. Perhaps you've been taught to believe from a very young age that a certain way of working, a certain kind of career, is appropriate for someone of your education, intelligence, or abilities. You might really want to change jobs or change niches, but you might be holding onto a corporate, academic, artistic, or other type of early internalized and idealized work image that just might not fit for you. It might take a while to find new mental or real work role models. This might mean coming to terms with redefining for yourself other ways of working that can also mean you are a mature, successful, competent woman. You may need to ask yourself questions like:

- *Does your deeply held work image or ideal mean you can't stay home part-time if you want to?*

- *Must you work full-time, even if you don't need the money?*

- *Would you see it as a failure if you found yourself exhausted by working a forty-hour week?*

You might need to work on accepting that you can work in different ways with different spurts or kinds of energy levels, even after medication.

Through counseling or support groups, you might find incredible talents, strengths and creative abilities that you might not have ever explored. Maybe working in corporate America and having a three-piece suit and a briefcase has been your image of success and maybe it is something you would like. But on the other hand, maybe that kind of work life wouldn't work for you, and something more entrepreneurial would suit you better, especially if you had a partner or assistant.

Self Image for Young Women

Self-image concerns at a young age make it especially complicated to accept the idea of having AD/HD. The whole idea of thinking that "something is different about your brain" is also more threatening to someone who is struggling with self-esteem and the natural insecurities of this stage of life.

If you are a young person, you may see getting help for something like this to be making a statement about sanity, weakness, or intelligence. In young adulthood, you're just forming your issues of independence; this might make you feel more dependent, cause anxiety about your ability to be in the world, to take care of yourself, and to get the right kind of job. Since it adds a whole layer of pressures, it's very important for you to seek support and meet other women with AD/HD who have become successful. They've worked through these problems of self-image, gone on medication, and made their lives work for them. The good news is that if you do it early enough you'll be less likely to develop confusion later on. You'll pick a career and an atmosphere in which to work that can support your strengths.

Redefining In Your Personal Life

Partnerships

We've talked about your grief cycle in Chapter 13, but I've also written one for non-AD/HD partners because they often get lost or ignored in this process and because they may need to redefine the image of what a valuable partner truly is before you both can move forward together. For those of you who are not currently in primary relationships, this will help you talk about it with new partners and help you both understand the critical factors in any view of you and your AD/HD that a potential partner may have or needs to come to terms with.

Grief Cycle for Non-AD/HD Partners

It's important for your partner to know the stages of the grief cycle in order to understand that it's natural to feel these feelings and to know what to expect. Even more, it's essential for partners to go through them in order to work through their feelings so that your relationship can begin to work for both of you. Ideally, you can read this together, and perhaps it may trigger a discussion about your partner's view of AD/HD, as well as the effect of AD/HD on the partnership.

Denial

Even if partners accept the AD/HD diagnosis, they still have difficulty accepting the neurobiological explanation for behaviors. They may deny the degree of impact this will continue to have in your life. They may deny the kind of change the whole family will need to make, both physically and emotionally, to live successfully with AD/HD.

Anger

Partners often personalize the AD/HD behavior as if it's "being done to them." Even if they get past this, they feel anger that it is happening and anger at the impact it is having on all parts of their lives. They often feel resentment and may begin to blame and devalue you. They can have feelings of betrayal; this was not the life they had envisioned. They may feel embarrassed around other people, become focused on changing your behavior, or feel as if everything revolves around you.

Bargaining

They hope that if you take your medication and go to support groups that things will be more normal. They may read some books and attend some meetings in order to figure out how to help you "change," or they may just try to take over your life to get some sense of control.

Depression

That this situation doesn't appear to be as easily controlled as they had hoped can bring up a wide range of feelings. They may feel overwhelmed, depleted, or used. As the demands and pressures increase, they may feel increasingly hopeless. They may even start to consider the viability of staying in the relationship. They may have forgotten all of your strengths or feel great loss over what they had expected in the partnership. They may feel no partnership or no way to work things out together. They may become overly focused on your problems or responsible for everything. They may feel embarrassed and isolated as a couple from friends and family who don't have these kinds of problems. They may feel increasingly isolated from you.

Acceptance

As partners work through these emotions, there comes a shift in outlook. Expectations become more realistic; areas of deficit become more circumscribed so they don't affect the good areas of the relationship. Together you learn to control problem areas. The AD/HD becomes externalized and does not define who you are as individuals or as a couple. They may still get frustrated and angry at times but they no longer feel as if the symptoms are directed at them. Positions become less polarized as you both become more solution-oriented. As a couple, you begin to relate again as peers with areas of strengths and difficulties. Expectations of each other become more realistic. When a partner has worked through grief and loss and accepted that you are different from non-AD/HD families, you are able to form a different concept of a mature, loving, valuable partner. You combine areas of strength to form a partnership, find solutions, minimize effect and access strengths. To do this, both partners must agree to that common goal.

When Your Partner Feels Stuck

Sometimes partners get stuck when moving through the grief cycle for a variety of reasons. Typically, the partner does not move through the grief cycle as rapidly, get help from support groups, or be as involved because the AD/HD is not something he is trying to integrate or come to terms with inside of himself in the same way you are. The grief cycle means moving through a range of difficult emotions, but it's also ultimately about accepting and even *celebrating* you just as you are. Partners often object to this phrase, "celebrating your partner" because they think means they shouldn't experience feelings of irritation or frustration. But it is really an opportunity for them to celebrate you as a person, not to celebrate the difficulties—in the end, this is the only way to make a relationship work.

Going through a cycle of grief allows a partner to appreciate and embrace you as a whole human being, as a full woman, and to cherish your unusual mix. Once partners work through the painful feelings, they realize that the AD/HD is not being *done* to them; they understand this isn't a passive-aggressive act or a failing as a mature person. Additionally, they realize that they don't have total responsibility for the other person and that it's not necessary for them to sacrifice their own needs. They're able to let go of a lot of frustration and anger.

Validating each individual's variations, strengths, and weakness and becoming comfortable with them would be helpful for any couple, AD/HD or not. Understanding that each of us has a personal biochemical makeup that influences our behaviors can provide an additional "lens" through which to view our relationships. Because people involved in AD/HD partnerships have to squarely face these issues, they have an opportunity to reach a higher level of marital communication, acceptance, and understanding

A Whole New Cycle Begins

The *Cycle of Success*

At some point, it all crystallizes. You see yourself as a person with great creativity and ability who has organizational problems. That's all. You lose the shame, or if you don't lose it, you are able to act anyway. The Cycle of Success begins a new dream. At some point, you cross a mysterious invisible line and become proactive, having integrated the idea of AD/HD deeply into your identity. Because you feel more secure, you are able to reveal more vulnerability. This in turn helps you to ask for necessary accommodations or personal help without as much shame. The shame doesn't disappear completely, but you are able to take necessary actions in spite of these feelings. You really get and can communicate that you are not asking for a luxury, a special favor, or something you are trying to "get away with," but something you need to make your life work.

The goal of all AD/HD treatment is to move through the grief cycle and then beyond it to a new cycle with a life and momentum of its own. Things don't always go well, of course. People don't always give you the help you ask for, but there's a whole new set of possibilities. For the first time, there's an idea of, "Yes, I have these difficulties, but I'm also all these other things too. They're all part of me. Even though I do all I can to minimize the negative effects to other people, I'm through apologizing for who I am."

Shame separates from core

Unusual rather than defective

Creativity harnessed out of chaos

Communication becomes assertive

Energy returns

Self-talk changes, mood improves

Support easier to get

Shame is Separate from Your Core

The shame you feel about your AD/HD symptoms become separate from your feelings about yourself. You may still sometimes feel some shame when your AD/HD symptoms arise, but it doesn't color your feelings about yourself.

Unusual vs. Defective

You start to see yourself as an interesting, unique person rather than defective. You have the same symptoms, but you almost (believe it or not!) start to enjoy them to a certain extent.

Creativity Harnessed out of Chaos

Instead of creativity gone wild, you can imagine possibilities as you direct and harness your creativity to make it productive by putting boundaries around all that energy. When this creative force is harnessed and directed, it feels exciting and satisfying instead of chaotic.

Communication Becomes Assertive

You've learned to state your needs in a non-defensive, non-aggressive way. As your self-image changes and you lose the shame, you are able to set limits. You're able to protect yourself in healthy ways by stating your needs and becoming solution-focused through increased communication options.

Energy Returns

As a result of getting needed help, medication, and some control over depletion and overload, you don't feel as if life is an overwhelming burden anymore. As a result, the rest of your life becomes more regulated. You don't spending so much time hiding. You're sleeping, eating, and exercising more. You're more able to make time for entertainment or recreation and nourishing relationships. You're taking in energy from the work that you're doing, or the activities you're involved in bring out more of your creativity and your strengths.

Self-Talk Changes, Mood Improves

You don't go into a downward spiral when you make a mistake, making the situation worse. You recover your balance much faster. You can separate out your neurological difficulties from your character, and you can figure out what you can control and what you can't. Depression and anxiety are no longer pulling you down.

Support Is Easier to Get

You now have an image of yourself as a creative person who needs help to fill in some of the gaps. You know that you need coaching, structure, and support. You know you need people to speak to you in a helpful way and that you need to demand respect.

I'd like to end by comparing the Picasso portrait of a woman with the Mona Lisa. You can see that they are both wonderful works of art, both beautiful images, but they represent very different kinds of women. The Picasso presents a completely different vision of what beauty is, one that the woman with AD/HD can hold onto as she redefines for herself what it means to be a woman. This new dynamic image can be a symbol to replace the Mona Lisa's traditional image of womanhood and beauty. The calm, serene look of Mona Lisa is a beautiful, organized, stable kind of figure. But it's certainly different from this exciting, vibrant picture of Picasso's multifaceted image of a woman, who represents the woman with AD/HD, a *diamond in the rough*. You can easily see what a set up for failure it would be if the Picasso woman spent her whole life trying to be like the Mona Lisa.

My message to you then, in closing, is . . . If you are a Picasso kind of woman, wear your bright colors and your bold shapes proudly. Don't hide yourself away behind a little smile.

A woman of depth, of vision,

moving and changing,

surprising.

A woman of many facets,

exciting, engrossing,

engaging.

Impossible to predict.

One of a kind, doesn't quite fit the mold,

but definitely priceless,

and a treasure . . .

if she could only see it.

AFTER WORDS

Women's Voices

These are some of the questions and answers that appeared over the years in my online column.

Question – September 2002

A woman asks if I still struggle with AD/HD symptoms and discusses her own good relationship with her husband.

Sari's response:

Yes, I still struggle with the same primary symptoms as anyone else but I don't have the worthless part that you asked about. That is the place where you have to work in order to meet the goals you mentioned. You need to get the support you need in order to be able to focus on what your good at so that you can continue to build your self worth. In terms of having a great relationship with your husband for so long, that is a great plus as Ed Hallowell, states, "The best treatment for one with ADD is to marry the right person."

Question – August 2002

A man writes in about what to do in a family where everyone has AD/HD.

Sari's response:

Since you have online capabilities you may want to contact a resourceful and reputable site **www.addconsults.com** for books on couples with ADD. My advice is to hold on tight. You need support, both emotional and physical and may find it with friends, relatives, professionals, coaches, tutors, or household help. Figure out exactly what is the great need. You probably will need some coaching or counseling to figure out a plan. Please don't try and do it alone. Laugh a lot and value your differences. Make sure everyone is doing something they are good at some of the time. Protect your time together as a couple away from the areas of chaos and conflict. Work on accepting that you will be different than non-ADD families. Find other like-minded people.

Question – June 2002

A woman writes to say she still loses her temper even after medication. She would like to laugh instead of getting upset and learn other ways to handle frustrations such as being logged off her computer just as she was about to win a game.

Sari's response:

Here are some suggestions:

1. Share these kinds of stories with other people with ADD and have a joint laugh, in order to gain perspective, which is easy to lose with ADD. Listen to other people's stories. This could be in online groups, or my discussion forum - www.sarisolden.com. You might write an article, read what others have written, go to support groups or conferences such as **CHADD (www.chadd.org)** or **ADDA (www.add.org)**.

2. Protect yourself as much as possible from what you know causes these sudden losses of perspective. Minimize the potential frustrations by using,, for example, sound blocks or notes on your door telling people not to enter during a certain time period. Operate your brain like a fragile rare instrument that needs proper care and delicate handling.

3. Make sure your medications are working optimally and you are on the right ones.

4. Watch your self -talk, such as "that's the ADD again" instead of for example "what a loser I am". This way you won't add to the frustration barrage of self-blame.

5. Program yourself to laugh every time you find your dog looking as you say he does after one of your outbursts.

6. Make sure you have enough to do in your life that is meaningful and important to you to counteract these difficulties.

Question – July 2002

Question was whether any women feel better before learning they have AD/HD. This woman is going on 40 and has been diagnosed for four years and feels worse about it now.

Sari's response:

If you have not been diagnosed until adulthood and then get a diagnosis without the kind of treatment that can help you sort out and come to terms with this kind of experience then it makes sense that you would feel worse. That is why I have written my new book, *"Journeys Through ADDulthood"*. This unfortunately is a common experience although most people don't talk about it. Even though many feel relief and hope at first, months and years later many are not feeling better. Medication is critical and I don't know if you've found anything helpful. Beyond that you need to find a therapist or coach that can help you sort through your self image feelings about your differences, your choices, relationships, etc. These are complex issues that you need to confront in order to make this transition. Investigate help in your area, such as support groups and conferences.

Question – May 2002

I am a 30-year old mother with ADD. My 11 ½ year old daughter is starting to realize my inefficiencies and unorganized traits that so many of us with ADD have. I can't remember dates, names, appointments, etc, unless I write them down on the BIG calendar in the kitchen. I keep a daybook, but often forget to look at it. She is at that age where she is asking a lot of questions about anything! She also talks a lot and she notices when she loses me (my mind wanders). I often say "I don't know" and "huh?" and she gets frustrated and angry at me and thinks I am uninterested in what she has to say, and I think she thinks I am stupid! She knows our house is not as organized as her friends' with their Supermoms'. And she wonders why I never make it on time to appointments and why the laundry rarely gets completely finished. Since I was only recently diagnosed, I haven't told many people, and those who do know act like they don't believe me. Even my sisters, mom, dad, everyone doubts it. They think I am just playing some sort of game. A lot of therapists even look at me strange when I mention it. I am on medication and it helps but it is not the "cure all." I seem to be getting a lot more done but am still very forgetful. Anyway . . . because of all the negativity surrounding my diagnoses, I am not very apt to tell people. Should I tell my daughter about it? I think she should know, but I don't know how to explain it to her. And I am afraid she may be ashamed of me. And also, since she shows some of the signs of ADD, I don't want her to think there is something wrong with her as well. Although I am watching her closely, I don't want to put anything into her head. What can I do? It's embarrassing when she has to remind me about things all the time (doctor appt's, school activities, signing off on homework, conferences, etc.). Any suggestions would help.

Sari's response:

I too am the mother of a preteen daughter. I think it is so difficult for any mother of a girl this age because they frequently meet with disapproval from their daughters at a stage in their life when they are often faced with the loss of their own ideal images. On the other hand, how valuable it can be to be a role model for your daughter at a time when she is struggling with the pain of feeling different or that she doesn't fit in or does not match some perfect image she is trying to live up to. You can model that having differences or difficulties, even though painful, is something to be coped with but not crippled by and that the goal for each of you is to strive to be a whole person. You can join with her in this way or at least convey your own personal efforts and challenges. Model the struggle of someone living with differences without letting them color your self-concept in a negative way. In order to do this you must first work internally to really feel strong and whole despite your difficulties. When you are able to feel whole in any way you won't feel so vulnerable. You will be able to get support such as a coach or organizer. People take cues from you and remember all moms feel stupid and vulnerable around preteens who recognize our imperfections, ADD or not.

I received this email but I found it so helpful that in addition to answering it, I asked for permission to print the writer's comments as well.

Dear Sari – April 2002

I feel acutely uncomfortable when I am having company at my home and my female guests try to help me in the kitchen.

Some women are considerate enough to ask if they may help, and if I discourage it, will say, "Let me know if there's anything I can do," and go back to the living room to chat with the others. I do have a few friends who are determined to help, and that is where my problem is.

I have a hard time doing certain tasks with others present. Some kitchen tasks are like that for me. Also there is a sense of real "stimulus overload" with another woman in the kitchen who is asking "where do you keep your (name of kitchen implement or food) which impedes me no end in doing my own tasks. I don't know if other ADD women do this, but some of my kitchen items don't have a "place" - it is wherever I have room to stash them when I unload the dishwasher. It's those infrequently used items that I bring out at parties, such as the chip and dip dish, that tend to get put away any old place I have room. I feel like I am constantly being pulled off-task by these questions. The kitchen help would be easier to manage if I didn't have the distraction of the questions.

Some women can prepare food for guests and chat at the same time. I have trouble with this, unless it is a simple snack. I find that having to hold a conversation and do complex jobs in the kitchen with several dishes demanding my attention at once to be really difficult to handle.

I would really like to be like other women and function well with others in the kitchen. Do you think it would be help to plan in advance what people could do to help me, put the required materials where they can find them easily, and give them these jobs to do? Another thing I could do, would be to have help in the kitchen with tasks that gradually increase in difficulty for me, and work up to the dinner party kitchen help.

Or should I just be frank and tell people that having someone try to help me in the kitchen for more than a short period of time just distracts me and gets in my way and I would prefer them not to?

I don't have this problem with cleaning up - it is very helpful for people to stack plates and silverware in the dishwasher and throw out trash. The only problem there is when people try to put away the food and ask me various questions regarding that.

My ADD affects me mostly in the areas of distractibility and stimulus overload. I feel like I am about to "short-circuit" when I would like to enjoy my company. I am reasonably well-organized. I am not particularly impulsive (except sometimes under stress). I tend to tire easily and have little energy. I also can tune out when something doesn't interest me, or shut down with too much sensory overload.

I would normally try to have a simple snack rather than a whole meal, but I have several friends who live more than an hour away, and I feel like I should at least offer a meal.

I would appreciate any advice you could give about how I should handle this problem.

Sari's response:

You have beautifully explained the problem that so many women face as well as offered great alternatives for handling this situation including alternatives such as direct communication to advance preparation for a situation that you know will need special handling. You know your brain well and are handling your ADD challenges as best as can be expected. The goal is not to get over your challenges but to handle them in this kind of experimental way. Obviously, you are moving more and more toward accepting yourself and this is what is allowing you to brainstorm so well.

Dear Sari – March 2002

What is your advice on whether to inform your employers that you have ADD? I am a customer care consultant and sometimes I just want to tell them but on the other hand I don't want to jeopardize my position. I have been doing the same job for eight years and believe me my ADD could explain to them a lot of my shortcomings.

Answer to this question was provided by ADD Coach Nancy Ratey. (www.nancyratey.com)

Thank you, Nancy, for your input!

Generally speaking I always advise people not to disclose unless it is done with a very specific purpose in mind, meaning if you need an accommodation. If not, then it is not advisable. It sounds to me your employer values your work despite your own feeling about your performance since they have kept you on for eight years! Maybe setting some time aside to brainstorm some ideas with your boss about how you could improve your performance would help? That way it will show initiative on your part and involve him/her in the process.

Question – March 2002

A woman writes to ask what a non-ADD husband might expect to notice in his ADD wife. She was the inattentive type in the back of the class. She has also struggled with depression. Things are coming together now that she is in her 20's and married but she thinks her husband has trouble understanding her.

Sari's response

It is difficult for people to really understand a woman who was inattentive instead of acting out as having ADD since the difficulties are often so internal especially when combined with depression. I don't know what your particular kind of ADD looks like but in general these things are common among adult married women with the inattentive type ADD:

Difficulty getting up and getting started in the mornings.

Overwhelmed easily by too many demands or variables even though it might not seem like a lot or very difficult to the outsider given a woman's level of abilities in other areas or education or intelligence. Because of this she may overreact easily to one more even simple request because it might put her over the top emotionally. Having to do simple tasks which may seem to be stress reducing actually may increase her difficulty because it may reduce needed stimulation and structure. For instance a woman might be better off at a demanding job in an area of skill than at home with no structure or stimulation because she might not know how to prioritize or organize even a very simple day. It is the executive function or management function of the brain that makes it hard.

Socializing may be difficult, making small talk, going to parties with a lot of background noise or where her attention is pulled in many directions. Shopping or cooking are often difficult although not always. So basically, simple, everyday living may be demanding. This may include organizing the house, difficulty with laundry, incoming papers and information. She needs support and structure and to find ways to spend more times in areas of strength.

Question – Nov 2001

A woman writes that she was diagnosed a few months ago and put on medication but her family, parents, relatives urge her to keep it a secret and are ashamed of it. She is looking for guidelines to deal with relatives.

Sari's response

Shame is a big part of growing up undiagnosed with ADD and unfortunately your parents are feeding into this. You need to be with other people with ADD so you feel supported and break this feeling of shame. Hopefully, you can attend a conference at some point or connect with people on line.

You must have information and support from people who are familiar with the medications that can help you. At first it's not always possible to receive understanding from your family at a time when you need it. This is another important reason to connect up with other women or men who have had similar experiences. Your family will probably come around later once you feel more sure of yourself and are no longer feeling bad about your difficulties. When you are less vulnerable you can explain without apologizing or defending.

You cannot do this alone. You must first come to see yourself in a non-defective way. Then join support groups, online groups, attend conferences or read about others like you. Go to counseling if available and if very isolated you must focus on this first before spending all your energy trying to convince others. Good luck. Let me know if you have trouble finding resources for connection.

Dear Sari – September 2001

Are there any suggestions as to what to look for in a couple's counselor when one partner (me) has ADD?

Dear Reader,

This is a good question. Suggest what to look for in a couple's counselor where one person has ADD. In this case it was a woman.

1. The counselor should not focus all the attention on your problems as the ADD partner.

2. The counselor should remain balanced and appear to both of you to be on both your sides, i.e. the side of the couple not one or the other.

3. By the same token the counselor shouldn't expect the non-ADD partner's feelings to all disappear with the explanation that the partner has ADD. This will just breed resentment. The partner has a lot of feelings built up. They must learn to deal with them in a constructive way, of course, but will continue to feel frustration even after the explanation.

4. The counselor might do well to explore the meaning the ADD behaviors have to each partner, what kind of emotions are generated, and what triggers them. Examples: being ignored may trigger someone to feel abandoned; to be interrupted may trigger someone to feel invisible or discounted as they were in their family of origin. Each person brings a history to the ADD mix.

5. Is the ADD focus covering up for any other problems in the partner or in the marriage? Are we focusing on who left the dirty dishes when there are other bigger problems not being dealt with?

Are the ADD problems causing the couple problems or are the couples individual problems or issues making it much harder to work together to restructure the ADD part of their lives together. These are all fruitful to explore. Communication skills are very important. As my colleague, therapist Ellie Payson, ACSW, describes at workshops, "Imago therapy, when working with an Imago therapist who understands ADD, combines the best of both worlds as it addresses the neurological, psychological, and behavioral issues in the relationship's dynamics."

6. The therapeutic goals must be reinforced and modeled not to get cured, get over it, get responsible, or grow up, but to find a way for each partner to lead satisfying lives together and separately. They do this by focusing on strengths and getting help and needed support, and understanding what is and isn't a luxury. Sometimes it's the non-ADD partner who resists this but often it is the person with ADD who has more difficulty getting needed help because it makes them feels too vulnerable.

7. In couples counseling the goal is often to get to a point where the power dynamics are not skewed by the ADD difficulties, where each is treated with respect and views themselves that way as well, even with the ADD difficulties.

8. Another goal is to come to acceptance that the family is a different kind of one with an ADD member, and to change deeply internalized messages that lead to blame and shame.

9. To understand that medication can often bring changes to a relationship when a partner is not so overwhelmed anymore and can see and articulate problems. Medication may cause couples issues to arise and often the partner is uncomfortable with these changes. A counselor can help stabilize this period of change while the couple finds a new healthy balance. A counselor can predict, prevent, mediate, and educate in order to guide the couple into a safe environment.

Question – May 2001

A woman writes to inquire how she can tell the difference between ADD and depression.

Dear Reader,

This is a very good question and one that is very often difficult to distinguish without careful analysis, even for professionals.

First, I would recommend that you go to a doctor or psychologist who is experienced in telling these apart or understanding the relationship between them because indeed you could have both ADD and depression. What you want to sort out is whether the depression is a reaction to the ADD that will improve when the ADD is properly diagnosed and treated or is it a separate condition that needs treatment along with the ADD. Often when you have ADD, you become depressed because you are so overwhelmed and depleted and your choices are leading you nowhere. You may feel stuck and trapped.

What complicates making this distinction is that when you have AD/HD inattentive type or depression, both can manifest difficulties with activation. Making an effort requires too much energy. Being disorganized in your behavior is also often a manifestation of both.

What you want to understand and sort out is the chronic nature and severity of the symptoms. Often a person becomes disorganized after a major life change like a death or a divorce. At these times of depression or normal grieving, even symptoms like ADD can appear and they can be severe but they CAN STILL BE TRACED to an event rather than ongoing ADD. Or a person can have low levels of depression or chronic attention problems that don't interfere with their lives enough for the ADD diagnosis and requirement of severity.

As you see these need to be sorted out by an open minded and experienced mental health professional with whom you feel like a partner in sorting through these issues. Good luck.

Dear Sari – January 2001

From everything I read, I strongly believe that I have ADD. I talked to my doctor about it and he doesn't seem to put much stock in the idea of ADD in adults. What should I do now? How do I know I have it and where do I find the help I need?

Sari's response

First of all, I would follow your instincts. That doesn't mean you definitely have ADD since you can have the same severe and chronic symptoms from a different cause. But you have something going on that is impacting you, for which you need diagnosis and treatment, so I wouldn't be deterred by your doctor's skepticism. ADD in adults is very real!

At this point I would ask around in your area for a therapist, psychologist or doctor who has experience with ADD in adults. It doesn't matter which kind of professional you start with just find someone experienced and knowledgeable and they will be able to steer you to other professionals you may need to round out diagnostic and treatment services. Keep reading, attend conferences, seminars, and join online groups or local **CHADD** (Children and Adults with ADD) group meetings. You can contact **CHADD** National at **www.chadd.org** or **ADDA** (Attention Deficit Disorder Association) (**www.add.org**). You can email me or ask the discussion forum on this web site for recommendations in your area. A good source is also **ADDconsults.com** who can help you find resources in your area. Just put that inquisitive ADD mind that loves to search to work for you and keep going. Good luck!

Dear Sari

I am sure that I have ADD, from everything that I've read. I've tried to talk to my husband about it, but he's just not interested. He thinks that ADD is just a fad and I've gotten caught up in it. He won't read about it and won't really listen to me and why I think I have it. How can I get him to take this seriously? I think that ADD has really impacted me and explains why I am so disorganized and have trouble keeping up with things. My husband just thinks I'm looking for excuses. What should I do?

Sari's response

First of all it is not unusual at all to have a spouse or family who does not believe ADD is real at first or thinks it is just another fad. Often adults with ADD have been searching for a long time to discover what is going on with them, and may have previously looked into a number of other labels or self-help measures. This tends to put their partners in a mind set that views ADD as just another quick fix. Don't wait for your husband to believe in ADD. That will come later. Just find other support, help and validation now and don't be too hard on him. The best thing you can do is to keep lines of communication open with him. If you change your expectations at this early part of the journey, you won't build up so much resentment and will be more effective later after you are more sure yourself.

If you think you have the symptoms of ADD you need to get support from other sources at this point. Don't wait for and don't expect your husband to come around first. He will be more apt to "take it seriously" when you do. It will take a while for you to get to the point where you have enough inner sureness to convey this to your husband. In the meantime get diagnosed and treated, and get connected with other women who have the same difficulties. This will help you feel less isolated. Continue to become more educated, find help through the same sources listed on page 316.

Dear Sari

I have been diagnosed with ADD several years ago, and have also struggled with depression. Things were going fine for a while. I left a big city, where things were very stressful, and returned home to the small community where I grew up. I met and married my husband about three years ago. Now, we have a 15-month old son and it feels as if my life is coming apart and I can't stand the mess and confusion everyday. It doesn't seem to bother my husband. Also, I've gone back to work, only two short days a week - but even that is overwhelming. When I get home from work I just feel like crying when I face the cereal spilled on the kitchen floor and the dishes I didn't have time to do before I left for work. What's wrong with me? I can't even manage this very part time job, and I feel overwhelmed all the time, trying to keep up the house and keep up with my daughter.

Sari's response

You are discovering the overwhelming situation that so many women with ADD find themselves in at some point. You need to come to terms with the fact that you have a more delicate kind of balance point than many others do which requires more careful planning. Unfortunately, that's another problem for people with ADD! Especially when overloaded, your ability to strategize and plan in these circumstances is severely challenged.

In addition, you are back in the small community where you grew up. This might be putting more domestic expectations on you than you had in the city where things may have been over stimulating but maybe more anonymous. Often our gender role expectations of ourselves increase and our estimation of ourselves grows more negative after we have children. Women with ADD put themselves down at this point because household and domestic work is often the most difficult for them and the stimulation of all the mess and the baby's demands often leaves them feeling no control. This often leads to depression.

I don't know where you are located now but you have to find help. You are drowning and overloaded and so you just need to find one professional or support place to help guide you through this ADD world - to help get you to start to breath again and to help you think through some of following questions and make a plan.

It doesn't sound as if you have anyone helping out at home. What kind of support do you need? Examine your feelings about asking for support from friends or family, or trading if you can't afford to hire help. You may need to renegotiate with your husband for which jobs are better suited to each of you at home rather than splitting directly along gender lines. If you have difficulty with this you may need some counseling to communicate about this.

You also need to look at the kind of job you have and see if that's where the stress is coming from as well. Is your job a good fit? You may find it was too early to take on something new like a job after the move, marriage, baby and ADD diagnosis. Don't quit your job if it is providing the right kind of stimulation and makes you feel good. If that is the case I would up the support at home rather than quit the job. If it's the job that is putting you over the top, and it is not a good fit, I would maybe consider a different one or take a class that might lead you to a more interesting and fulfilling career later.

Are you on medication? It sounds as if the right medication might help block out some of the stimulation and stress. It sounds as if you are already approaching that point when resulting depression takes over and causes a double whammy for you that you have trouble getting out of. Call the same resources that I have listed on pages 316 and 333-335 or at least get help for the depression from referrals your doctor can make.

A good book that to start reading is *"Moms with ADD"*, by Chris Adamec, Taylor Trade Publisher Dallas, TX (2000). Don't try and tackle everything at once. Just remember to start a new positive cycle you may need medication and support. You need to start doing just one thing, taking one step, making one call.

Question

ADD and spirituality. A woman wonders why she doesn't hear more about ADD and affiliations with religious organizations. She recognizes that adults with ADD often don't feel connected to other people and don't take the time for this. She wonders if anyone has addressed this possible important spiritual affiliation in the lives of those with ADD.

Sari's response

The person who addresses the need for "connectedness" in most depth is Dr. Edward Hallowell, known in the ADD field for *"Driven to Distraction"*. Now, the noted psychiatrist has addressed this issue for everyone in his book *"Connect"* (Pantheon Books, NY 1999) in which he certainly includes the need for spiritual connectedness.

In my experience, adults with ADD have a great deal of trouble keeping up their important connections. Time just passes by, they are overwhelmed with other commitments. Many adults with ADD have told me how badly they feel when people mistake this for not caring, when really the opposite is in their hearts. They feel so ashamed usually when they miss an important occasion to connect, that they withdraw more. An accepting supportive place as the writer of this question suggests, where they could gather and re-group, sounds like a wonderful way to try and put more balance into their lives as well as find that much sought after connection that could give them something to hold on to in the middle of chaos.

Question – January 2000

Someone wrote that she is very overwhelmed after being diagnosed. She says she has my tape and sees a therapist but finds it a real struggle to discuss what she is experiencing. She wants to know where to go from here.

Sari's response

It may take a while before you find someone with whom you can share your feelings and difficulties about ADD, whom you feel can understand you and act as a partner. This person doesn't have to be a specially trained ADD therapist even though that would be great. A therapist who is willing to learn the additional issues around ADD and is open to reading what you bring her and is open to what you tell her, who takes it seriously, may be able to help you a great deal. I would supplement that therapy by going to support groups, going online for chat groups for women with ADD and attending conferences like the one I discussed above. You need to connect with other women! Start a thread on this website for others to communicate with you.

Question

This was a question about social skills in adults with ADD. She wondered what kinds of problems adults often have, how it affects relationships, and what suggestions I had for them.

Sari's response

Some of the social skill difficulties leave adults with ADD sometimes hesitant to participate in important situations at work and in their social life. These often lead to anxiety and withdrawal since you don't know if today will be a good or bad brain day. You may not be able to think of a single thing to say during small talk or be able to answer a direct question. You may simply go blank, unable to retrieve information you know. You may not be able to tell a story in a linear way and people may start to stare at you several minutes into the story and you know they aren't following you.

You may find yourself interrupting, wanting to get to the bottom line, and finishing people's sentences for them (because you know what they are going to say!). You may mentally wander off in conversations, not following what is being said, which is especially difficult in groups.

Because of an impressionistic understanding of some of the current topics in the news you may not feel confident in these kinds of discussions.

Because of your slow processing, by the time you figure out what you want to say the conversation has moved on and you just say it anyway even if it doesn't make sense any more. Or you may be afraid you will forget what you want to say and so you blurt it out prematurely. All sorts of things like this can lead to insecurities that affect relationships.

Some suggestions—Write down what you want to say in a group discussion if possible, especially in a work situation. Make little notes to yourself until the right time to add them.

Create situations that work better for you with one on one conversation without distractions.

Often volunteering to be in charge of a group keeps you in control of the agenda.

Talk from your heart rather than your head. This often is easier than trying to recall facts.

On the other hand, try and be with people as much as possible with whom you feel comfortable, with whom you can be yourself. These would be people with the same interests, who value the kind of person you are. Be in situations where you can display your strengths. Spend time in places where other fascinating "eccentrics" may more likely be. Then, even though you will have to sometimes be in these other more awkward situations. You will be developing confidence.Kate Kelly and Peggy Ramundo, pioneers in the field of adult ADD talk about social skills in their book *"You Mean I'm not Crazy, Stupid or Lazy?"*

They say that when selective attention gets in the way in social situations, a person with ADD's perceptions may be flawed by incomplete or inaccurate information.

They say that we watch people in social situations for clues as to how to act and we gauge their reactions to our behaviors. Because we may have an inability to process information efficiently, we can fail to assimilate the new rules quickly enough. This, combined with impulsivity, can lead to numerous social mistakes

They also say that we may have difficulties taking the time to making deep connections, even if we talk to a lot of people in a social setting.

They advise—just concentrate on making a few close friends instead of worrying about creating a large social network.

They also encourage us by saying that many of these quirks that seemed weird as children now often work for adults who are seen as interesting or special. They point out that adults with ADD often have creativity, special talent, humor, or zest for life that can be a social magnet!

Question – December 1999

This is from a woman who was just recently diagnosed with inattentive type of ADD. She says her husband also has AD/HD.

Sari's response

My experience is that this kind of partnership has plusses as well as special challenges. On one hand, the partners might be more accepting and understanding of each other and agree on non-traditional modes of living one's life. On the other hand, they may not always have the ability to compensate for each other as in a "mixed marriage" so there may be more disorder with which to cope.

In addition, sometimes your ADD may be so different that your partner's more hyperactive style that he might completely overwhelm you. Again, on the other hand, it is possible your partner may help activate you while you slow him down a bit.

Because you may have very different styles, you may need some professional facilitation to help you both learn to communicate and to protect, accept and respect your differences.

Question – November 1999

Can you talk about subtle put-downs from the non-ADD partner and the power shifts that occur in relationships with the growth of the ADD partner.

Sari's response

Before treatment, many individuals with ADD put themselves in a one down position with their partner because they feel they have already caused too many problems and so don't feel as if they have the right to assert their desires or wishes. They agree on some level with the negative view held by their partners of them and their ADD. In treatment, hopefully, they grow to a point where they are able to separate these core feelings about themselves from their ADD. This internal shift allows them not to accept these negative attributions from their partners. When they change internally there is often a shift in the power dynamics in a relationship. Also, when an individual takes medication they are less overwhelmed, more clear and able to know and to express what isn't working for them as well and to make their wishes known. All this can lead to an upheaval in the family system even though the changes are healthy. It's important to know these are expected changes and that if you stay with it you and your partner may reorganize at a healthier level of functioning. You may need professional support to handle the anxiety that these kinds of changes sometimes bring.

These and more are archived at www.sarisolden.com

Recommended Resources

What follows is a list of resources and recommendations. It is by no means complete. For up to date resources on the subject always check ADD Warehouse www.addwarehouse.com for newest information. I have not included many fine books and resources exclusively for children and teens with the exception of books on girls. Some of the resources listed in this section will also appear in the Bibliography section since I used them as resources for the book as well. There are resources in the Bibliography you may want to consult as well. They are not all listed in this section.

I have divided these resources into books by topic helpful for adults with AD/HD, women with AD/HD, and professionals. Then there are also recommendations for books that are helpful to women in dealing with their AD/HD but are not written specifically about AD/HD.

Next I have a few audiovisual materials for women followed by magazines and catalogs. Publications that come with membership in an organization are listed with that organization instead of here. After this comes a list of resources for organizational help followed by information on groups that put on conferences and tele-classes on a national level. These are also sites at which you may be able to locate support groups.

Also, included are other online resources that offer either discussion forums or other ways to connect and learn such as online support groups. Websites of some AD/HD experts are also listed here. I have tried to not repeat resources so a source you may expect in one place may be in a different category.

In the coaching section, I only included some places for training and some places to find a coach rather than a listing of all the wonderful coaches. At the end of this resource list there are a few places to read more on the subject of the brain, women's physical issues, women and the brain, and medications. Books are listed as well as good places to start online searches. This is especially important since information is changing so rapidly.

BOOKS

AD/HD In Adults

ADD and Creativity: Taping Your Inner Muse, Lynn Weiss, Ph.D., Taylor Publishing, Dallas, TX 1996

ADD & Romance: Finding Fulfillment in Love, Sex, & Relationships, Jonathan Scott Halverstadt, M.S., Taylor Trade Publishing, Dallas, TX 1999

AD/HD Secrets of Success: Coaching Yourself to Fulfillment in the Business World, Thom Hartmann Select Books, New York, NY 2002

Adult AD/HD (2nd Ed), Michelle Novotni, Ph.D., Navpress Colorado Springs, CO 2003

Adventures in Fast Forward: Life, Love and Work for the ADD Adult, Kathleen G. Nadeau, Brunner/ Mazel Trade, New York, NY 1996

Answers to Distraction, Edward Hallowell, M.D. and John Ratey M.D., Pantheon Books, New York, NY 1994

Attention Deficit Disorder In Adults, 3rd Revised Edition: Practical Help and Understanding, Lynn Weiss, Taylor Trade Publishing; 3rd edition Lanham, M.D. 1997

Attention Deficit Disorder: A Different Perception, Thom Hartmann, Underwood Books, Grass Valley, CA 1993; revised 1997

Attention Deficit Disorder: The Unfocused Mind In Children And Adults, Thomas E. Brown, Ph.D., Yale University Press, Expected publication August 2005

A Comprehensive Guide To Attention Deficit Disorder In Adults, edited by Kathleen Nadeau, Brunner/Mazel, New York, NY 1995

Delivered from Distraction, Edward Hallowell, M.D. and John Ratey M.D., Ballantine Books, New York, NY 2005 — Special note: Alternative treatment Lifestyles (Chapter 25)

Driven to Distraction, Edward Hallowell, M.D. and John Ratey M.D., Pantheon Books, New York, NY1994

Healing ADD: The Breakthrough Program That Allows You to See and Heal the Six Types of ADD, Daniel G. Amen, Berkley Publishing Group; (1st edition), New York, NY 2002

Journeys Through ADDulthood, Sari Solden, MS Walker & Company, New York, NY 2002

Out of the Fog: Treatment Options and Coping Strategies for Adult Attention Deficit Disorder, Kevin R. Murphy, Ph.D. and Suzanne Levert, Hyperion/Skylight Press, New York, NY 1995

The ADDed Dimension: Everyday Advice for Adults with ADD, Kate Kelly & Peggy Ramundo, Scribner, New York, NY 1997

The Link Between ADD and Addiction: Getting the Help You Deserve, Wendy Richardson, MA., Pinon Press, Colorado Springs, CO 1997

View from the Cliff: A Course in Achieving Daily Focus, Lynn Weiss, Taylor Trade Publishing, Lanham, MD 2001

What Does Everybody Else Know That I Don't?, Michele Novotni Ph.D. with Randy Petersen, Specialty Press Inc., Plantation, FL 1999

When Too Much Isn't Enough: Ending the Destructive Cycle of AD/HD and Addictive Behavior, Wendy Richardson, Pinon Press, Colorado Springs, CO 2005

You Mean I'm Not Lazy, Stupid, or Crazy?!, Kate Kelly & Peggy Ramundo, Scribner, New York, NY 1995 — 2nd edition due out in publication 2006

MORE ARTICLES ON ALL SUBJECTS

www.add.org/articles/index.html

www.addconsults.com/articles

CAREER-WORK

ADD in the Workplace: Choices, Changes, & Challenges, Kathleen G. Nadeau, Ph.D., Brunner/Mazel, New York, NY 1996

ADD on the Job, Lynn Weiss, Ph.D., Taylor Publishing, Dallas, TX 1996

Finding a Career That Works for You, Wilma R. Fellman, M.Ed., Specialty Press Inc., Plantation, FL 2000

COLLEGE

Coaching College Students with AD/HD: Issues and Answers, Patricia O. Quinn, Nancy A. Ratey, Theresa Maitland, Advantage Books, Silver Springs, M.D. 2000

Succeeding in College with Attention Deficit Disorders, Jennifer Bramer, Specialty Press, Plantation, FL 1996

Survival Guide for College Students with ADD or LD, Kathleen G. Nadeau, Ph.D., Magination Press, New York, NY 1994

WOMEN, GIRLS AND MOMS

Gender Issues and AD/HD: Research, Diagnosis, and Treatment, Kathleen G. Nadeau (Editor), Patricia O. Quinn (Editor), Advantage Books, Silver Springs, M.D. 2002. **Chapter Four** *The Socio-Cultural Forces,* Ellen Littman Ph.D.; **Chapter Five** *Role Expectations,* Hope Langner, CPCC, MCC

Moms with ADD: A Self-Help Manual, Christine A. Adamec, Taylor Trade Publishing, Dallas, TX 2000

Survival Tips for Women with AD/HD, Terry Matlen, MSW, ACSW, Specialty Press, Plantation, FL 2005

Understanding Girls with AD/HD, Kathleen Nadeau, Ellen Littman, Patricia Quinn, Advantage Books, Silver Springs, MD 1999

Understanding Women with AD/HD, edited by Kathleen Nadeau, Ph.D. and Patricia Quinn, M.D., Advantage Books, Silver Springs, MD 2002

When Moms and Kids Have ADD (ADD-Friendly Living) Patricia O. Quinn, M.D., Advantage Books, Silver Springs, MD 2005

ORGANIZING/STRATEGIES

ADD-Friendly Ways to Organize Your Life, Judith Kolberg, Kathleen Nadeau, Ph.D., Brunner-Routledge, New York, NY 2002

Conquering Chronic Disorganization, Judith Kolberg, Squall Press, Inc., DeCatur, GA 1999

Fidget to Focus, Roland Rotz, Ph.D. and Sarah D. Wright, M.S., A.C.T., iUniverse, Inc., New York, NY 2005

Finding Your Focus: Practical Strategies For Adults with ADD To Get On The Right Track, Judith Greenbaum, Ph.D. and Geraldine Markel, Ph.D., McGrawHill, 2005

Making Peace with the Things in Your Life, Cindy Glovinsky, Griffin Trade Paperback; 1st edition, New York, NY 2002

One Thing At a Time, Cindy Glovinsky, St. Martin's Griffin, New York, NY 2004

Organizing for the Creative Person, Dorothy Lehmkuhl and Dolores Catter Lamping, CSW, Crown Trade Paperbacks, New York, NY 1993

OTHER BOOKS OF INTEREST

Attention Deficit Disorder and the Law: A Guide for Advocates, P. Latham & P. Latham, JKL Communications, Washington, DC1992

Connect, Edward M. Hallowell, M.D., Pantheon Books, New York, NY 1999

The Dance of Connection, Harriet Goldhor Lerner, Quill; 2002

The Dance of Anger, Harriet Goldhor Lerner, Harper & Row, New York, NY 1985, 1989

The Dance of Intimacy, Harriet Goldhor Lerner, Harper & Row, New York, NY 1985, 1989

Dare to Forgive, Edward Hallowell, M.D., HCI, Deerfield Beach, FL 2004

Difficult Conversations: How to Discuss What Matters Most, Douglas Stone, Bruce Patton, Sheila Heen, Viking Penguin, New York, NY 1999

Getting the Love You Want: A Guide for Couples, Harville Hendrix, Owl Books, New York, NY (Reprint edition) 2001

In the Mind's Eye: Visual Thinkers, Gifted People with Dyslexia and Other Learning Difficulties, Thomas West, Prometheus Books, New York, NY 1991, 1997

A Mind at a Time, Mel Levine, Simon & Schuster, New York, NY 2003

On Playing a Poor Hand Well; Insights from the Lives of Those Who Have Overcome Childhood Risks and Adversities, Mark Katz, Norton, New York, NY 1997

The Myth of Laziness, Mel Levine, Simon & Schuster, New York, NY 2003

Reviving Ophelia: Saving the Selves of Adolescent Girls, Mary Pipher, Ph.D., Ballantine Books, New York, NY 1994

Shadow Syndromes, John J. Ratey, M.D. and Catherine Johnson, Ph.D., Pantheon Books, New York, NY 1997

Stop Negotiating With Your Teen: Strategies for Parenting Your Angry, Manipulative, Moody, or Depressed Adolescent, Janet Sasson Edgette, Perigee Books, New York, NY (1st edition) 2002

Too Loud, Too Bright, Too Fast, Too Tight: What to Do If You Are Sensory Defensive in an Overstimulating World, Sharon Heller, Quill, New York, NY 2003

Where to Draw the Line: How to Set Healthy Boundaries Every Day, Anne Katherine, M.S., Simon & Schuster, New York, NY 2000

The Wizard of Oz and Other Narcissists: Coping with the One-Way Relationship in Work, Love, and Family, Eleanor D. Payson, Julian Day Publications, New York, NY 2002

FOR MENTAL HEALTH PROFESSIONALS WORKING WITH ADULTS WITH ADD

Journeys Through ADDulthood, Sari Solden, M.S., Walker & Company, New York, NY 2002—Appendix pages 259-278 *(For information on individual and group consultation based on this model visit www.sarisolden.com)*

ADD and Psychotherapy: A View From Inside, Sari Solden, M.S., Voices: The Art and Science of Psychotherapy, Spring/Summer 2003—pages 71-80

Gender Issues and AD/HD: Research, Diagnosis, and Treatment, Kathleen G. Nadeau (Editor), Patricia O. Quinn M.D. (Editor) Advantage Books Silver Springs, M.D. **Chapter 12** *Neurocognitive Psychotherapy for Women with AD/HD,* Kathleen Nadeau, Ph.D.

A Comprehensive Guide To Attention Deficit Disorder In Adults, Kathleen Nadeau, ed. **Chapter 9** *Psychotherapy of Adult Attention Deficit Disorder,* Edward M. Hallowell, M.D., Brunner/Mazel, New York, NY 1995

A Comprehensive Guide To Attention Deficit Disorder In Adults, Kathleen Nadeau, ed. **Chapter 14** *Special Diagnostic and Treatment Considerations in Women with Attention Deficit Disorders* by John J. Ratey, M.D. and Andrea C. Miller and Kathleen G. Nadeau, Ph.D., Brunner/Mazel, New York, NY 1995

AUDIOVISUAL MATERIALS

Dismissed and Undiagnosed Dreamer, Paula Stanford Human Resources Network, Oklahoma City, OK 1997 (Videocassette) To order, call 405-943-5073

Outside In: A Look at Adults with Attention Deficit Disorder, Family Today Glencoe, IL 1999. (Videocassette)

Women with Attention Deficit Disorder, Sari Solden, M.S., Frontier Publishing, Ann Arbor, MI 1995 – Revised 2005 (2.5 hour CD)— Order through website www.sarisolden.com

ORGANIZATIONAL HELP

National Association for Professional Organizers (NAPO)
4700 W. Lake Avenue
Glenview, IL 60025 USA
Phone: (847) 375-4746 • Fax: (877) 734-8668
International & Canada Fax: (732) 578-2636
e-mail: hq@napo.net
website: www.napo.net

National Study Group on the Chronically Disorganized (NSGCD)
Judith Kolberg, Director
P.O. Box 1990
Elk Grove, CA 95759 USA
(404) 231-6172
www.nsgcd.org

ORGANIZATIONAL PRODUCTS

www.flylady.net

www.myaddstore.com

CATALOGS/MAGAZINES

ADD WareHouse Catalog
300 Northwest 70th Ave., Suite 102
Plantation, FL 33317
954-792-8944
www.addwarehouse.com

ADDitude
ADDitude Foundation, Inc.
PO Box 421
2476 Bolsover
Houston, TX 77005-2518
800-856-2032
www.additudemag.com

FOR CONNECTION

Organizations – Conferences – Teleclasses - Support group locators

ADDA – National Attention Deficit Disorder Association

Focus magazine comes with membership

ADDA
P.O. Box 543
Pottstown, PA 19464
Phone: 484-945-2101
Fax: 610-970-7520
www.add.org

CHADD – Children and Adults with Attention Deficit Disorder

Attention magazine comes with membership

8181 Professional Place, Suite 201
Landover, MD 20785
800-233-4050 or 301-306-7070
FAX: 301-306-7090
www.chadd.org - support group locator on website

Attention Deficit Disorder Resources
223 Tacoma Ave. S. #100
Tacoma, WA 98402
Phone: 253.759.5085
Fax: 253.572.2470
E-Mail: office@addresources.org
www.addresources.org

SUPPORT/INFORMATION/CONNECTION

www.sarisolden.com (Discussion Forum)

www.ADDconsults.com

www.add.about.com

www.addcenters.com

www.AD/HDnews.com

www.admirablewomen.com

www.addvance.com

www.livingwithadd.com

www.managingyourmind.com

www.ncgiadd.org (National Center for Gender Issues for ADD)

Center of Attention (Adults) Miami, FL 305-661-0373

OTHER EXPERTS WEBSITES

www.brainplace.com

www.DrThomasEBrown.com

www.drhallowell.com

www.johnratey.com

www.thomhartmann.co

OTHER GROUPS FOR SUPPORT USING MY MODEL

(E-mail sarisolden@aol.com for information on availability)
RENEWAL - Getaway Workshops for Women
JOURNEYS - Support and Education for men and women
MHP'S with ADD - Sari's Groups for mental health professional with ADD

COACH –TRAINING AND PLACES TO FIND THEM

www.addcoachacademy.com

www.addcoach.com

www.addcoaching.com

www.americoach.org

www.nancyratey.com

ADD COACH DIRECTORIES

www.addconsults.com

www.add.org

THE BRAIN

A Comprehensive Guide To Attention Deficit Disorder In Adults, Kathleen Nadeau ed., Brunner/Mazel, New York, NY 1995 **Chapter 2**

Driven to Distraction, Edward Hallowell, M.D. and John Ratey M.D., Pantheon Books, New York, NY 1994 **Chapter 9**

Gender Issues and AD/HD: Research, Diagnosis, and Treatment Kathleen G. Nadeau (Editor), Patricia O. Quinn (Editor), Advantage Books, Silver Springs, MD **Chapter 3** *Gender Difference in AD/HD: Neurobiological Factors,* Jay Giedd, M.D., Elizabeth Molloy, Kayla Pope, MA., JD

User's Guide to the Brain: Personality, Behavior, and the Four Theaters of the Brain, John Ratey, M.D., Pantheon Books, New York, NY 2001

You Mean I'm Not Lazy, Stupid, or Crazy?!, Kate Kelly & Peggy Ramundo, Scribner, New York, NY 1995 *Basics of Neurology*— pages 17-20

FOR CONCERNS OF WOMEN WITH AD/HD

www.ncpaMD.com/Menopause.htm

www.ncpaMD.com/Girls_Women_and_ADHD.htm

Gender Issues and AD/HD: Research, Diagnosis, and Treatment, Kathleen G. Nadeau (Editor), Patricia O. Quinn, M.D., (Editor), Advantage Books, Silver Springs, MD **Chapter 10** *Hormonal Fluctuations and the Influence of Estrogen,* Patricia O. Quinn, M.D. **Chapter 16** *Fibromyalgia/Chronic Fatigue and Women with AD/HD,* Jerry Littman, M.D. and Gail Rodin, M.D.

MEDICATIONS

www.help4AD/HD.org

An umbrella organization of CHADD (Children and Adults with ADD) this web site provides articles on medications, fact sheets for information describing how stimulants are used, the various types available, and how to choose, monitor, etc.

www.additudemag.com subsection, "Medical Center"

www.nlm.nih.gov/medlineplus/druginformation.html

www.Rxlist.com

Stimulants

www.baltimorepsych.com/Stimulants.htm-information

SSRIs

www.biopsychiatry.com/ssripharm
SPECIFIC MEDICATIONS

Concerta

www.Concerta.net

Modafinil

http://www.rxlist.com/cgi/generic2/modafinil_cp.htm

http://www.sci-con.org/articles/20040701.html

Folcalin

http://amphetamines.com/methylphenidate/focalin.html

BIBLIOGRAPHY

Note: Some of the references first used in this book are out of print or circulation. Many of the quotes still in this edition were from the very beginnings of discussion on this subject. They were from seminars or tapes, which are no longer available to be referenced. When I am able to I will let the reader know this in the reference section and also where to look for up to date work of that particular author.

Amen, D. (1993) *Windows into The ADD Mind* (Video)
Out of circulation. – Look at Mindworks Press for up to date information www.mindworkspress.com

Brown, T.E. (Fall 1999) "New Understandings of Attention Deficit Disorders in Children, Adolescents and Adults: Assessment and Treatment" Focus, *The Official Newsletter of the National Attention Deficit Disorder Association*. pages 3 and 12.

Brown, T.E. (1998) Brown Attention Deficit Disorder Scales, *The Psychological Corporation*, San Antonio, TX

Brown, T.E. (1995) ADD Without and Beyond Hyperactivity, Presented at the *National Attention Deficit Disorder Association* (ADDA) Conference, Merrillville, IN

Brown, T.E. (Spring/Summer1993) Attention Deficit Disorder Without Hyperactivity reprinted *CHADDer* (the magazine at the time of CHADD) Vol. 7, Number 1, pages 7-10. Out of print. Visit www.DrThomasEBrown.com for current information.

Carver, J.M. Article titled *Attention Deficit Hyperactivity Disorder* found on www.drjoecarver.com

Copeland, E.D., & Copps, S.C. (June 1, 1995) Revised ed., *Medications for Attention Deficit Disorders (ADHD/ADD) and Related Medical Problems (Tourette's Syndrome, Sleep Apnea, Seizure Disorders): A Comprehensive Handbook,* FL: Specialty Press

Copps, S.C. (Fall, 2000) "Attention Deficit Disorder: Not Exactly the Midas Touch", Focus, *The Official Newsletter of the National Attention Deficit Disorder Association*

Dickson, T. (Fall, 2004) "Back To Basics: Neurobiology Of AD/HD", *Focus, The Official Newsletter of the National Attention Deficit Disorder Association,* pages 8-9.

Fellman, W.R. (2000) *Finding a Career That Works for You.* Plantation, FL: Specialty Press

Hallowell, E.M. & Ratey, J.J. (2005) *Delivered from Distraction.* New York, NY: Ballantine Books

Hallowell, E.M. & Ratey, J.J. (1994) *Answers to Distraction.* New York, NY: Pantheon Books

Hallowell, E.M. & Ratey, J.J. (1994) *Driven to Distraction.* New York, NY: Pantheon Books

Hartmann, T. (1993) *Attention Deficit Disorder: A Different Perception.* Grass Valley, CA: Underwood Books.

Jordan, D.R. (1992) *Attention Deficit Disorder: AD/HD and ADD Syndromes.* Austin, TX: Pro-Ed.

Jordan, D.R. (1991) "What ever happened to ADD without Hyperactivity?" reprinted, *CHADDer* (the magazine at the time of CHADD) May Edition

Kelly, K. & Ramundo, P. (1995) *You Mean I'm Not Lazy, Stupid, or Crazy?!* New York, NY: Scribner

Langner, H. (Jul/Aug 2000) "ADD: An Invisible Disability". *ADDvance A Magazine for Women with Attention Deficit Disorder.* pages 4-8

Littman, E. (2002) Gender Differences in AD/HD: The Socio-Cultural Forces. (Chapter 4) *Gender Issues and AD/HD: Research, Diagnosis and Treatment.* Nadeau K. & Quinn, P. (Editors), Silver Springs, MD: Advantage Books

Matlen, T. (2005) *Survival Tips For Women With AD/HD.* Plantation, FL: Specialty Press

Nadeau, K.G. ed. & Quinn, P.O., ed. (2002) *Gender Issues and AD/HD.* Silver Springs, MD: Advantage Books

Nadeau, K.G., ed. & Quinn, P.O., ed. (2002) *Understanding Women with AD/HD.* Silver Springs, MD: Advantage Books

Nadeau, K. (Fall 2000) "Healing Wounds, Opening Doors", GRADDA *(The Greater Rochester Attention Deficit Disorder Association) Newsletter.* Rochester, NY

Nadeau, K., ed. (1995) *A Comprehensive Guide To Attention Deficit Disorder In Adults.* New York, NY: Brunner/Mazel

Nadeau, K. (1995) ADD and Women's Issues *Presented at the National Attention Deficit Disorder Association (ADDA) Conference* Merrillville, IN

Nadeau, K. (*for ADDvance*) "Is Your Daughter a Daydreamer, Tomboy or "Chatty Kathy"? She May Have Undiagnosed Attention Deficit Disorder" http://www.addvance.com/help/women/daydreamer.html

Pennington, B.F. (1991) *Diagnosing Learning Disorders: A Neuropsychological Framework*. New York, NY: The Guilford Press

Quinn, P. (2002) "Hormonal Fluctuations and the Influence of Estrogen in the Treatment of Women with AD/HD" (Chapter 10) *Gender Issues and AD/HD: Research, Diagnosis, and Treatment*. Nadeau K. & Quinn, P. (Editors), Silver Springs, MD: Advantage Books

Ratey, N., (2002) Private Interview

Ratey, N., (1995) "ADD in the Workplace". Presented at the National Attention Deficit Disorder Association (ADDA) Conference. Merrillville, IN

Ratey, J.J. & Miller, (Jan/Feb 1992) "Foibles, Frailties and Frustrations Seen Through the Lens of Attention". Reprinted in *Challenge*. Out of print.

Richardson, W. (2005) *When Too Much Isn't Enough: Ending the Destructive Cycle of AD/HD and Addictive Behavior*. Colorado Springs, CO: Pinon Press.

Richardson, W. (2002) Addictions (Chapter 19) *Gender Issues and AD/HD: Research, Diagnosis and Treatment*. Nadeau K. & Quinn, P. (Editors) SilverSprings, MD: Advantage Books

Silver, L., (1992) *The Misunderstood Child*. Blue Ridge Summit, PA: Tab Books, a division of McGraw Hill

Smith, S. (1991) *Succeeding Against The Odds*. Los Angeles, CA: Jeremy Tarcher, Inc.

Solden, S. (2002) *Journeys Through ADDulthood*, New York, NY: Walker & Company

Sussman, S. (2002) Private Interview

Sussman, S., (1995) *ADD in the Workplace*. Presented at the National Attention Deficit Disorder Association (ADDA) Conference. Merrillville, IN

Weiss, L., (1992) *ADD In Adults*. Dallas, TX: Taylor Trade Publishing

Zametkin, A.J. & Nordahl, T.E. & Gross, M. et. al., (1990) *Cerebral Glucose Metabolism In Adults With Hyperactivity Of Childhood Onset, New England Journal of Medicine*, 323(20), pages 1361-1366

ACKNOWLEDGMENTS
TO THE REVISED EDITION

I once read that the best part about writing a book is that it *"brings your tribe to you."* As I reflect on the people I have met, heard from, and come to know since this book was first published in 1995, I know this is true. Some of these amazing individuals have become my clients with whom I have had the privilege to work and others have become my friends, mentors, and colleagues. Becoming a member of this worldwide community that I have come to treasure and feel at home in has been one the most rewarding and satisfying experiences of my professional and personal life.

I will forever be indebted to my publisher, Tim Underwood, for originally encouraging me to write this book and for giving me the opportunity to create this new edition.

In addition to the acknowledgments that remain as originally written, I wanted to also thank the following individuals and groups. I feel very grateful to Ned Hallowell, John Ratey, Kate Kelly, and Peg Ramudo who have come through for me whenever I have asked for their help. The work of these pioneers has given immeasurable help to countless adults over the years and it has meant a great deal to me to have them recognize my efforts.

For this new edition, I want to give great thanks to Jeannie Ballew for her incredible editing and expert guidance through this process. She actually made it enjoyable! Special thanks also goes to Susan Stuart for all her great research for this book. In addition, I am grateful to my local personal and professional support team, Denise Brogdon, Mary Morgan, and Nancy Vaccaro for their patience and their professional, high quality, dedicated work.

Professionally, at the local level in metro Detroit, I want to acknowledge the work of, and thank everyone who is a part of the Michigan Adolescent and Adult AD/HD Network for Professionals (MAAAN), especially Wilma Fellman who founded this organization so that professionals in these areas can work together and support each other. Thanks also to Terry Dickson, Ellie Payson, Terry Matlen, Sally Palaian, Geri Markel, and Judy Greenbaum for their work, friendship, and support. I want to make special mention of Art Robin, Ph.D., who I met when this book first came out after he wrote me a beautiful note. He has given me great encouragement and professional support since then. Thanks also to Roger Lauer, Ph.D., of Ann Arbor, for his fine work with adults with AD/HD and for his professional and personal support.

On a national level, I want to thank the National Attention Deficit Disorder Association (ADDA) and its past and current presidents and board members for all the opportunities they have given me to grow professionally over the years. I also thank Children and Adults with ADD (CHADD), both in Michigan and at the national level, for their support over the years.

I want to thank those in the AD/HD community (too many to mention individually) who have invited me to speak to women all across this country. I especially thank those in the international community for the wonderful and tireless work they do and for inviting me to visit and get to know women in these areas. I want to mention and thank by name Kimiko Sakurai, Yuki Takeshima and Noriyuki Fujii in Japan, Diane Zaccheo and Andréa Bilbow in England, and Michaela Nyffenegger, Verena Schenk-Leu, and Doris Ryffel-Rawak in Switzerland.

To other leaders in this field like Thomas Brown, Edna Copeland, and Stephen Copps, who I now proudly count as friends, I say thank you for your work in the field, your inspiration, and your warm, generous, consistent support. I would like to make special mention of Kathleen Nadeau, and Pat Quinn, for their amazing body of work, influence, and contribution to the field of women and girls with AD/HD.

There are many male and female professionals in the field who, in addition to being experts and leading contributors to the field of women *and men* with AD/HD, have enriched my life personally and brought fun, laughter, friendship, and connection into my life again like I haven't known in years. So I want to give special appreciation to Ellen Littman, Nancy Ratey, Sue Sussman, Jerry Mills, Wendy Richardson, Thom Hartmann, Hope Langner, Sydney Sauber, and Reggie Carey.

I want to especially acknowledge and thank the women who attend all the conferences and give me such an incredible outpouring of love and support year after year. You have no idea how healing it has been. Some I depend on seeing every year, like Jeri Goldstein and Peggy Clover, and then there are people like Cindy Giardina and Malka Engel who I met in recent years who are so amazingly warm. I just want you to know how much your kindness has meant to me.

A special word of thanks to the women and men I have worked with over the years who have shared their stories, struggles, and triumphs with me. I am grateful for the trust you have placed in me, and I am continually inspired by your courage and strength.

And, of course, thanks and love to my friends and family, especially my grown son, Evan. My mother and father, David and Marion Shubow, are no longer alive, but they were tremendously proud of this book when it first came out. I thank my husband's family, the Solden's and the Schildhorn's, for their love and acceptance.

Since I first published this book, I now have a daughter, Dasha, for whom I am eternally grateful. I am continually amazed at her innate understanding and acceptance of AD/HD. To Dasha and to my husband, Dean, to whom this book is still dedicated for his continuing devotion and love . . . *this* woman with AD/HD says *thank you.*

ACKNOWLEDGMENTS FROM ORIGINAL EDITION
(1993)

I want to acknowledge a long list of people who have supported me through the years, both personally and professionally.

First, I want to thank the group of people who specifically helped give shape to my ideas in order to see this project through. It was in large part the encouragement of my publisher, Tim Underwood that gave me the impetus to undertake this project. He recognized that what I had been observing and discussing with him was important and worth writing about. I am extremely grateful to have such a wonderful executive assistant, Susan Berneis. She has been incredibly patient during the course of this project, and extremely skillful at being able to sort out my "over-creations" to turn them into understandable form. Great appreciation goes to Carol LaRusso, for her skillful and sensitive editing, through which she brought calm and order to my manuscript. It was a wonderful experience to work collaboratively with someone whose abilities and judgment I value so much. I want to acknowledge and thank Howard Morris of Frontier Productions for many of the beautiful graphics in the book. And special gratitude to Kris Vaneck, whose organization skills I admire, and whose friendship I value. As part of the "team," I am incredibly grateful to my husband, Dean, who worked many long hours on this project and did a tremendous amount of editing and synthesizing, patiently helping to sort out and pull together my ideas. He has made an enormous contribution to this book.

I want to express deep appreciation to Dr. John Ratey, Kate Kelly, and Peggy Ramundo for their support, not just in this project, but also for their warmth and encouragement in the course of our personal and professional association. Kate Kelly and Peggy Ramundo's book *You Mean I'm Not Lazy, Stupid or Crazy?!* was an important

346

turning point for me both personally and professionally because it was the first time I read in so much depth about real life experiences of women with ADD. Dr. John Ratey's contribution to the understanding of adult ADD is immense. His two books on ADD, written with Dr. Edward Hallowell, *Driven to Distraction and Answers to Distraction*, have opened up worlds of understanding to countless adults who had been struggling to understand their confusing life experiences. It was a few years before I ever met Dr. Ratey that I discovered a phrase he coined that I have frequently quoted ever since when emphasizing the importance of viewing adults through . . . "The Lens of Attention."

In addition to those people I just mentioned who helped me with this current project, this book owes its culmination to experiences that started several years ago. I am well aware that I wouldn't be at this point without the support, encouragement and belief of many people along the way. I take this opportunity to express to them my sincere gratitude.

I will always appreciate the opportunity Caroline Summer gave me to enter and explore this world of invisible disorders. I thank the entire staff at Family Service Agency in San Rafael, California, for creating such a supportive and accepting environment, which allowed me to grow and develop my ideas. Eternal gratitude and love to Darlene Klaif who is always with me, guiding all my work; she gave me enough room and respect to develop who I am as a therapist. Dr. Beatrice Pressley encouraged me in a quiet but powerful way to develop the creativity she saw and appreciated in me. Dr. Geraldine Alpert supported and guided me as I tried to understand my confusing set of life experiences. It was her openness to new possibilities and explanations that ultimately led me to discover the answers I needed.

When I relocated to Ann Arbor, Michigan, from California, I was given a chance early on to become part of the national ADD community by presenting my ideas at the annual adult ADD Conference held in Ann Arbor. I want to thank Jim Reisinger for giving me this opportunity.

During the last few years at conferences across the country I've had the chance to get to know many individuals in the ADD professional community. These are incredibly warm, accepting, and fun people with whom I quickly felt at home. I want to give special thanks to Dr. Kathleen Nadeau for graciously supporting and encouraging my ideas on Women and ADD.

On a personal level, I want to acknowledge Lisa Csaklos, who made my beginning work in this field so much fun, and who, by being a model of *organization*, allowed me to more clearly understand *disorganization*. Words cannot adequately express my feelings for my friend, Adriane Lonzarich, who has been there all along, with constant support and understanding. Her special gift of treasuring small moments of beauty and valuing differences has been a continual inspiration for me. I want to mention a few long-time friends with love: Annie, who could fold clothes in perfect rows at an early age; Chi-Chi, with whom I had to flee our dorm room at midnight to escape the mess; and De-De, who got up at five A.M. to watch the moon and the stars with me. I want to express my love and appreciation to all my many other friends through the years, for their support and encouragement.

I was fortunate to grow up in a family that valued differences and creativity. I express my love and gratitude to them for the chance they gave me to develop and grow in my own way. My mother, Marion Shubow, gave me a unique combination of support, structure, and freedom that allowed me to be able to develop my strengths without having to struggle to conform to more traditional cultural expectations. My father, David Shubow, taught me the underlying principle of the creative process that in order to create, one must first be able to destroy. This concept of thinking about the ability to disorganize as a way to create new structures influenced my ideas about living successfully with ADD. My brother, Michael, taught me that even brilliant people, if they hate to wear wool pants, need to go on a less traditional route through life. And finally, Marie gave me tremendous understanding and acceptance that has stayed with me even though she's been gone for many years.

I want to also thank Lucille Solden and the rest of my husband's family. Their encouragement and constant support has made a tremendous difference to me. I especially want to thank Jodi, who each day I know her, teaches me to respect the mysteries of the brain and the power of the human spirit.

I want to express great love and respect for my son, Evan, who has taught me every day of his life about the complexity and resiliency of human beings. His determination has filled me with wonder and has made me vigilant in both my work and personal life about noticing small successes and recognizing quiet strengths.

My husband and best friend, Dean, has given of himself in this project more than I even could imagine someone would give to another person. More important than the wonderful partner he has been in this project though, is the partnership we have in our life together. So much of what I know about living successfully with ADD has come as a result of our success together. It is with deep appreciation that I thank Dean for his unwavering support and love.

To all the women who struggle with disorganization and who have shared their stories with me so openly — I want to give special thanks. You inspire me each day to continue to break out of traditional molds, and spur me on to continue to find ways to compensate for my difficulties so that I can continue to pursue my strengths. Most importantly, I want to thank all the clients with "invisible disorders" with whom I've worked. In the face of confusion and pain, you have given me the privilege of witnessing remarkable portraits of perseverance, strength, and courage.

ABOUT THE AUTHOR

Sari Solden, MS, LMFT is a psychotherapist in private practice in Ann Arbor, MI who has worked with men and women with AD/HD for the past 15 years.

A graduate of the University of Michigan, Sari moved to the San Francisco area where she obtained a Master's Degree in Clinical Counseling at California State University. She holds a Marriage and Family Therapy license in California. After 20 years in the bay area she returned to her native Michigan where she is licensed as a professional counselor.

The author of *Women with Attention Deficit Disorder* and *Journeys Through ADDulthood*, which is for both men and women as well as mental health professionals, Solden trains mental health professionals on counseling adults with AD/HD and is a prominent speaker at both at national and international AD/HD conferences, as well as a frequent contributor to publications on this subject. She serves on the professional advisory board of ADDA and has served on the program conference committee for national CHADD. Her areas of specialization include inattentive AD/HD, women's issues as well as long term counseling issues for men and women not diagnosed until adulthood.

Sari was the 1996 recipient of ADDA's award for outstanding service by a helping professional.

Sari currently lives in the Ann Arbor, Michigan area with her husband Dean, daughter Dasha, two dogs, one cat, and nine sheep. She also has a grown son, Evan.

July 2005

INDEX